D0940990

Toward a Theater of the Oppressed

THEATER: Theory/Text/Performance

Enoch Brater, Series Editor

Around the Absurd: Essays on Modern and Postmodern Drama edited by Enoch Brater and Ruby Cohn

Tom Stoppard and the Craft of Comedy: Medium and Genre at Play by Katherine E. Kelly

Performing Drama/Dramatizing Performance: Alternative Theater and the Dramatic Text by Michael Vanden Heuvel

The Plot of the Future: Utopia and Dystopia in Modern Drama by Dragan Klaić

Shaw's Daughters: Dramatic and Narrative Constructions of Gender by J. Ellen Gainor

How Dramas End: Essays on the German Sturm und Drang, *Büchner, Hauptmann, and Fleisser* by Henry J. Schmidt

Critical Theory and Performance edited by Janelle G. Reinelt and Joseph R. Roach

The Actor's Instrument: Body, Theory, Stage by Hollis Huston

Acting as Reading: The Place of the Reading Process in the Actor's Work by David Cole

Presence and Resistance: Postmodernism and Cultural Politics in Contemporary American Performance by Philip Auslander

Ionesco's Imperatives: The Politics of Culture by Rosette C. Lamont

The Theater of Michael Vinaver by David Bradby

Rereading Molière: Mise en Scène from Antoine to Vitez by Jim Carmody

O'Neill's Shakespeare by Normand Berlin

Postmodern Theatric(k)s: Monologue in Contemporary American Drama by Deborah R. Geis

The Player's Passion: Studies in the Science of Acting by Joseph R. Roach

Theater at the Margins: Text and the Post-Structured Stage by Erik MacDonald

To Act, To Do, To Perform: Drama and the Phenomenology of Action by Alice Rayner

Tom Stoppard in Conversation edited by Paul Delaney

After Brecht: British Epic Theater by Janelle Reinelt

Directing Beckett by Lois Oppenheim

Susan Glaspell: Essays on Her Theater and Fiction edited by Linda Ben-Zvi

The Theatrical Gamut: Notes for a Post-Beckettian Stage edited by Enoch Brater

Staging Place: The Geography of Modern Drama by Una Chaudhuri

The Aesthetics of Disturbance: Anti-Art in Avant-Garde Drama by David Graver

Toward a Theater of the Oppressed: The Dramaturgy of John Arden by Javed Malick

Toward a Theater of
the Oppressed

The Dramaturgy of John Arden

Javed Malick

Ann Arbor

THE UNIVERSITY OF MICHIGAN PRESS

Copyright © by the University of Michigan 1995
All rights reserved
Published in the United States of America by
The University of Michigan Press
Manufactured in the United States of America
⊗ Printed on acid-free paper

1998 1997 1996 1995   4 3 2 1

A CIP catalogue record for this book is available from the British Library.

Library of Congress Cataloging-in-Publication Data

Malick, Javed , 1944–
    Toward a theater of the oppressed : the dramaturgy of John Arden /
Javed Malick.
        p.   cm. — (Theater—theory/text/performance)
    Includes bibliographical references and index.
    ISBN 0-472-10587-6 (hardcover : alk. paper)
    1. Arden, John—Political and social views.   2. Theater and society—
England—History—20th century.   3. Arden, John. Island of the
mighty.   4. Arthurian romances—Adaptations—History and
criticism.   5. Social problems in literature.   6. Arden, John—
Technique.   7. Drama—Technique.   I. Title.   II. Series.
PR6051.R3Z79   1995
822'.914—dc20   95-17397
                                                                        CIP

Dedication

John Arden once wrote that he recognizes as the enemy the fed man, the clothed man, the sheltered man, whose food, clothing, and house are obtained at the expense of the hunger, the nakedness, and the exposure of so many millions of others: and who will allow anything to be said, in books, or on the stage, as long as the food, clothing, and house remain undiminished in his possession.

An obvious corollary of this is that the moment an artist seeks to transgress that *as long as* limit, the moment she/he stamps really hard on the politico-economic toes of the established system, she/he is likely to be prevented from continuing to work in peace and security.

In January 1989, while I was working on an early draft of this book, my friend, Safdar Hashmi, was brutally murdered in broad daylight by a bunch of goons loyal to a local leader of India's ruling party. Safdar, who was thirty-five then, was a highly talented and politically committed theater artist. He was killed while (and because) he and his group, Jana Natya Manch, were performing a street play of radical political import. He, too, had recognized as the enemy the fed man, the clothed man, the sheltered man, and had dedicated his entire life to fighting against that man's traditional privileges.

This book is dedicated to his memory.

Acknowledgments

This book derives from my doctoral work at McGill University. The interest in my work of Darko Suvin, my mentor and now a dear friend, went well beyond the normal duties of a thesis adviser. He not only taught me how to read drama and helped me with his insightful comments and guidance, but he also crucially helped the progress of my work with his generous support and affection. Darko is also responsible for encouraging me to turn the dissertation into this book. Many of the insights this book possesses were directly or indirectly inspired by him and his writings. My debt of gratitude to him is incalculable.

The award of a Commonwealth Research Fellowship by the Association of Universities and Colleges of Canada enabled me to return to McGill to prepare the early draft of this book. I am grateful to the association for this award and to McGill University for its hospitality.

John Arden is known to be wary of academics and critics. Yet he promptly answered every letter of mine and put personal warmth into his responses. I am also grateful to him and Margaretta D'Arcy for their hospitality when I visited them in Ireland. I will always cherish the memory of that day. I am also obliged to them and to their publishers, Methuen London Ltd., for permission to quote from their various works.

Abha Sur, Mriganko Sur, and Rajiv Jain helped in various ways in preparing the physical manuscript of this book.

Finally, and on a more personal level, I wish to acknowledge the love and support that I received from Neeraj throughout the long period of my work on this book. Although she did not entirely exempt me from my share of the household responsibilities, she did make generous allowance from time to time. As a fellow academic, she also read my work and offered helpful comments.

Contents

Introduction

The *poetics of the oppressed* is essentially the poetics of liberation.
—Augusto Boal

This book is partly an attempt to correct the critical neglect of John Arden's work. Even after four decades of an active writing career, the corpus of criticism on this major contemporary playwright has remained largely inadequate, in both volume and quality, to the historical significance of his work. Arden's pioneering contribution in reintroducing on the British stage a style of writing that later came to be recognized as Brechtian itself should have received more attention.

What is more, in recent years this neglect seems to have been reinforced by an ideological prejudice (even hostility) against the openly partisan politics of his and Margaretta D'Arcy's later, Irish plays. In 1972, Arden abandoned a promising career in London's metropolitan theater in favor of an openly political form of theater committed to the cause of socialism and anti-imperialism. In opting out of the regular theater circuit, he also seems to have dropped out of the restricted field of vision of the mainstream critics and scholars of modern drama. As a result, although he and D'Arcy are still writing excellent dramas—as evidenced in their recent radio series, "Whose is the Kingdom" (which traces the growth of Christianity from a loose collection of persecuted underground cults to an institutionalized and homogenized patriarchal creed of the Roman Empire)—they are no longer written about except in the occasional newspaper review. Arden, who at one time was considered a promising playwright of the postwar generation, is now regarded as a kind of cultural persona non grata who, presumably under the corrupting influence of his Irish/Catholic/female/radical wife and artistic collaborator, Margaretta D'Arcy, has renounced art for the sake of propaganda (Hayman 1980).

This dichotomous viewpoint, a fundamental feature of bourgeois aesthetics, which regards artistic value and political commitment as mutually incompatible, is precisely the kind of approach that Arden has consistently opposed in his dramatic and nondramatic writings. He firmly believes that all art is propaganda: it propagates either the hegemonic ideas and values or the ideas and values that run counter to (or subvert) the interests of the hegemonic order. By making his work in the theater subservient to the interests of the society's dispossessed and by articulating the demand for an egalitarian reordering of the world, he has consciously chosen to link himself with the latter.

It is not that there has been no change in Arden's position. He has changed, in his own words, from a "loosely left-wing" writer who wrote about "the social and historical hinterlands" of Britain to a committed revolutionist affirming "from his own hard experience the need for revolution and a Socialistic society: and moreover convinced that his artistic independence and integrity is strengthened rather than compromised by so *doctrinaire* a stance" (Arden and D'Arcy 1988, 13; Arden 1977, 158). However, as I have tried to make clear in the following chapters, this transformation was neither as sudden nor as illogical as Ronald Hayman's theory of "conversion" seems to imply. Nor was his early association with the "legitimate" British stage as smooth and tranquil. For, even during the first fifteen years of his career, when he wrote more or less within the terms of that theater, he grew increasingly more conscious of (and dissatisfied with) its artistic and social limitations. In other words, the final parting of the ways, usually regarded as the outcome of Arden and D'Arcy's quarrel with the Royal Shakespeare Company over its production of *The Island of the Mighty,* was in fact long in the making.

This book is concerned with the compositional principles of Arden's work rather than the more usual textual or thematic readings of individual plays. It treats the entire body of Arden's work as one dramaturgically coherent opus and endeavors to identify and examine the main artistic and cognitive emphases immanent in it. This approach, I may add, is based on the assumption that it is only within the overall dramaturgic framework that the full significance of Arden's work and its place in the history of modern drama and theater can be recognized. The more common practice of offering textual analyses of individual plays, one by one and in chronological order, implies that the plays are monadic atoms of which the playwright's universe is composed—that the "naked" or isolated particular is both genetically prior and analytically more economic than its interaction with the general. An unavoidable consequence of my approach is that I have had to assume a basic familiarity with the individual texts on the part of the reader. Nonetheless, both brief and quite detailed textual analyses of specific exemplary segments of plays (and of one whole play) are included wherever such an analysis is found to be necessary or helpful in substantiating or developing my argument.

The corpus of Arden's writings is fairly wide and varied. Since 1957, he has written—alone or in collaboration with D'Arcy—at least twenty stage plays, several radio and television plays, works of fiction, poems, and a large number of essays, reviews, and newspaper articles on a variety of subjects ranging from current political affairs to the nature and function of art. In addition to these, over the years he and D'Arcy have been responsible for numerous theatrical happenings and experiments (such as a three-day "public entertainment" at Kirbymoorside, Yorkshire, in 1965, and a day-long "war carnival" at New York University in 1967) for which no published texts or even scenarios exist.

In this study I have confined myself to the stage plays written by Arden (alone or jointly with D'Arcy) mainly during his career in the professional theater. In other words, the book covers all of his/their work for the stage from *The Waters of Babylon* (1957) up to and including *The Island of the Mighty* (1972). This does not mean that their work in other forms (namely, radio and television dramas, community theater, agit-prop, and so on) and their work outside the professional theater since 1972 are altogether absent from the horizons of my discourse. What it does mean is that, in offering detailed textual discussions to illustrate my points, I have tended to confine myself mainly to the plays written for the professional theater.

This restriction of scope is prompted by prudence as well as analytical necessity. Since Arden and D'Arcy are living producing writers, it was necessary to find some significant cutoff point for delimiting the scope of this study. *The Island of the Mighty* was selected as the cutoff point not only because this trilogy of remarkable complexity and magnitude was D'Arcy and Arden's last work for the professional theater but because it marked a radical turning point in the artistic and political careers of its authors. Moreover, interesting and significant as their recent work outside the "legitimate" theater is, this continuing phase in D'Arcy and Arden's careers is still incomplete, and it is beset with all the practical and historical problems that a homeless, dissident drama faces in today's highly organized and institutionalized western society.

Arden and D'Arcy's experience outside the regular stage—particularly their experiments in the immediate and relatively more ephemeral forms of the community theater—was of great importance to their work even during the early years of their professional careers. It provided them with the opportunity to experiment under radically different social and artistic conditions. It enabled them to verify in practice many of their early orientations and notions about the nature and function of the theater as both an art form and a social institution. These experiments profoundly influenced the development of Arden's dramaturgy and caused his work to move steadily toward an openly improvisational and revolutionist form of political drama, a form that was incompatible with the conventions and assumptions of even the most liberal kind of regular theater. The influences and implications of these experiments will be noted and discussed in this study. However, since such experiments are generically different from what the term *stage play* commonly denotes, and therefore require different (or at least basically modified) methods of analysis, they do not enter the purview of our study directly.

Many of Arden's plays have been written jointly with Margaretta D'Arcy, an Irish actress and playwright whom he married in 1957. With her he has also collaborated on a number of community and agitational theater projects. By his own acknowledgment, the collaboration with D'Arcy has had a profound influence on Arden. From the beginning, he had "a strong attraction toward the celtic elements of the British tradition" and there was "a decided injection of Irish vitality into practically everything [he] wrote" (Arden and D'Arcy 1988, 13). But the strong commitment to the cause of Irish nationalism, so preponderant in his post-*Island* work, is in large measure a result of his association with D'Arcy.

It should be possible—and, in another context, even interesting—to attempt a distinction between Arden's solo work and his work with D'Arcy and to examine them separately or comparatively. This study, however, shall not attempt any such distinction. It will treat the differences between the two groups of plays as part of the implicit author's artistic and political development. It shall try to demonstrate that (and how) Arden's approach in his dramaturgic opus evolved, following its own internal logic as well as in response to external influences, to a clearer and more precise understanding of the craft of playwriting and its social function. This will indicate, I hope, that a number of more or less open speculations (and insinuations) from politically unsympathetic critics about how the association with a radical D'Arcy contaminated an innocent, neutral, and genuine Arden are irrelevant and prima facie illogical.

The central hypothesis explored in this study is that there are two fundamental and related constitutive features of Arden's dramaturgy: diachronically, its adherence to the forms, conventions, and techniques of popular or traditional theaters, and, synchronically, its radical political emphasis as expressed in a categorically plebeian and communitarian bias. I hope to demonstrate that Arden's decision to link his art to the neglected and scorned forms of popular tradition was a political choice, whether he himself was initially conscious of it as such or not. Conversely, his political development flows out of the central logic of his dramaturgic orientation, of his craft choice.

This double choice, even at an early stage, implies a rejection of the established theater with its illusionist aesthetics and middle-class, individualist ideology. In its place, Arden's work was oriented toward developing an emblematic form that permitted (and even promoted) a historical and collectivist standpoint. It is essential, therefore, to distinguish his work from the works of his contemporaries (such as John Osborne, Harold Pinter, and Arnold Wesker) who, their initial angry or nonconformist moral stances notwithstanding, ultimately failed to break away from the mainstream cultural and ideological tradition. On the other hand, Arden's work can be related to that radical alternative tradition in modern drama and theater that is associated with early Soviet playwrights such as Mayakovsky, with Bertolt Brecht, and with numerous radical groups and artists who emerged during the 1960s all over Western Europe and North America. Like the other exponents of this tradition, Arden employs techniques and conventions of popular theater to arrive at a form that is distinguished by (1) its "epic" or episodic structure, (2) its ludic or nonillusionist style, and (3) its focus on shared social relationships and conflicts from an expressly historical and plebeian standpoint. The result is a kind of dramaturgy that, with increasing consciousness and emphasis, communicates a dialectical vision of the world—a vision in which critical and celebratory impulses operate simultaneously. Such a vision reveals in a given sociopolitical order and system of human relationships both corruptions and potentials for change and renewal.

The five chapters that follow deal with five different aspects of Arden's dramaturgy. These aspects are not mutually exclusive. Rather, they are differing but overlapping perspectives, or analytical categories, which seem most illuminating and useful in approaching my subject. Besides offering a brief overview of the historical moment in which Arden emerged as a playwright, a discussion of new trends in the British theater of his time, and an overview of the critical responses to his work, chapter 1 is concerned mainly with determining the place of Arden's work within the context of dramaturgic history. Chapter 2 focuses on Arden's characteristic dramaturgical practice of formulating an action episodically and thus giving it what Brecht at times called an "epic" structure. Chapter 3 attempts an examination of the collectivistic or supraindividual emphasis of his plays on the level of dramaturgic agents, implying a privileging of the social over the individual and the psychological. Chapter 4 deals with the nonillusionist nature of Arden's dramaturgy and its performance possibilities. Chapter 5 is concerned with that crucial phase of Arden and D'Arcy's political and artistic development that eventually led to their last and most ambitious play for the professional theater.

Thus, while chapter 1 opens the argument by establishing certain fundamental emphases of Arden's dramaturgy and suggests some appropriate approaches, chapter 5 attempts to integrate the argument on a more significant (because more comprehensive) level of cognition. By concentrating on a detailed dramaturgical analysis of D'Arcy and Arden's last work for the regular theater and by elucidating the political and artistic horizons that the play embodies, chapter 5 points both backward, to the history and development of the work of these playwrights in the professional theater, and forward to the new, and in many ways radically different, kind of work that they have been involved in since their angry withdrawal from that theater.

Certain aspects and terms recur throughout this study. They are not necessarily absolute or universal categories but analytical tools. Their validity is to be proved by their usefulness in illuminating Arden's art and our discussion of it. Most of these terms are of local significance, that is, they are used to illuminate some particular point or element at some particular stage of my discourse. Such terms and notions are defined wherever they are used. However, two key concepts, *dialectical* and *popular,* are used throughout and are of crucial and overall significance in our discussion here.

The term *dialectical* derives from *dialectics,* which basically means "a progressive unification through the contradiction of opposites" (Williams 1976b, 107). In Marxist theory it is closely aligned with *materialism* and is used to designate a method and approach that analyzes and views the world historically, seeing history in terms of the modes and relations of production and the material contradictions immanent in them. In his later years, Brecht used the term *dialectical* (preferring it to his earlier *epic*) to describe a theater (or a world view) that does not merely reveal things and states of affairs but also shows them as impermanent and therefore alterable (see Mayer 1971). It is in this Marxian-cum-Brechtian sense that the term *dialectical* is used throughout this study to signify an approach that sees social orders, institutions, interests, concepts, morals, and relationships as historically produced and determined by people and therefore alterable by them. When dealing with politics, it is an approach or vision that not only criticizes and rejects a given imperfect social order but also recognizes its potential for change and renewal. When dealing with human relationships and situations, it does not use absolute moral standards of good and evil but examines their social and historical basis. In art, such a vision usually expresses itself as a combination of critical and celebratory impulses; it does not merely present an image of the existing order of things but, by treating it as impermanent, also implies the possibility (hope or fear) of an alternative, more or less happy, order.

The terms *popular* and *plebeian* relate to a concept of "people." They are used to designate "of," "for," or "in relation to" the broad masses of unprivileged or underprivileged groups, in conscious distinction to their economically and politically powerful masters or rulers. As such they are essentially class terms and embody a politically subversive horizon related to what Brecht calls "a fighting conception" of people and popularity (Brecht 1964, 108). When used to designate a culture or tradition, it points to the cultural forms created or cherished by the common people or lower classes. These forms have usually constituted a culture that distinguishes itself sharply from the official or ruling-class culture both artistically and ideologically (cf. Bakhtin 1968). The two distinctive features of popular cultures are their emphasis on the communal or shared experience and their playfulness, which allow them to combine robust fun and pleasure with cognitive seriousness of purpose.

Chapter One

Situating Arden

If, however, the aesthetic of the theatre ceases to remain in the background, if its forum is the audience and its criterion is no longer the effect
registered by the nervous system of single individuals but the degree to
which the mass of spectators becomes a coherent whole, then the critic as
he is constituted today is no longer ahead of that mass but actually finds
himself far behind it.

—Walter Benjamin

John Arden began his artistic career in the difficult and contradictory
world of a war-ravaged Europe. It was a world precariously perched on a
political see-saw of hope and despair, a world in which the painful memories of a long and brutal war and the economic devastation that it had
caused were kept alive by the twin menaces of the Cold War and the
H-bomb. The British found themselves in a particularly unenviable situation. Britain was up to its ears in debt, its overseas investments had been
severely depleted during the Second World War and a heavy burden of
overseas military commitments had been acquired. All this had created a
virtually hopeless economic mess, which was causing a slow but steady
undermining of the welfare state. The economic and psychological un-
certainties that followed the war (and the dismantling of the British
Empire that followed in its wake) had increasingly revealed the existing
political situation to be a corrupt and unreliable one in which theory and
practice, promise and achievement, were in sharp, and often incompre-
hensible, contradiction. The euphoria and the hope of a socialist future,
unleashed by Labour's spectacular electoral victory following the war,
was short-lived. Within a few years, the generation of English youth that
had welcomed the Labour victory in 1945 as the beginning of a new era
was already feeling deeply frustrated and betrayed by the irresolute nature of Labour politics, its inability to break with the established social
order. They felt equally let down by new disclosures of Stalinist atroci-

ties and Soviet despotism, clearly demonstrated a few years later by the Hungarian uprising and its brutal suppression.

This feeling of disillusionment and betrayal in the sociopolitical realm was matched in the cultural field by a climate that was socially and artistically too conservative to encourage and support anything new, innovative, or genuinely contemporary (see Hewison 1981, 6–11). The British theater of the period, too, was completely class-bound and thoroughly devitalized. The context and experience of human relationships were changing constantly, but the theater in England seemed to possess a disturbing insularity to contemporary life and its problems. It was dominated, on the one hand, by the polite, morally complacent conventions of middle-class drawing-room comedy, merrily producing plays of little aesthetic value and almost no cognitive significance, and, on the other, by what seemed like an obsession with revivals, which had the effect of keeping "the new playwrights out" (Hewison 1981, 8). Noting that there was no reflection of postwar life in the contemporary English theater, Richard Findlater wrote in 1952:

> In 1951 playmakers are still timidly exploring the problems of maintaining country houses, and discussing the etiquette of the Guards. Middle-class families are commonly depicted with a full crew of butlers and housemaids, and the working class are not depicted at all—except as comic relief. . . . England, behind the footlights, is still a right little, tight little island, where family virtues are secure and there is no trouble with servants or foreigners. To make this pattern of life more credible, plays are frequently set back in the pre-1914 age, which is, it seems, the land of heart's desire for the nostalgic English. (pp. 112–13)

A few years later, Kenneth Tynan, who was then the young drama critic of the *Observer,* found the theater scene equally dismal and uninspiring. His position, forcefully asserted in the angry style characteristic of both him and the period, was that "apart from revivals and imports, there is nothing in the London theatre that one dares discuss with an intelligent man for more than five minutes" and that the situation has remained the same for "the last thirty years" (1976, 148).

It was in this context that the new, "angry young" dramatists emerged, and their work was immediately hailed as revolutionary. The most vocal partisan of this new movement was, predictably, Kenneth Tynan himself. He wrote:

> After the launching of the English Stage Company at the Royal Court in 1956, and the revelation of John Osborne, a semblance of serious thought and a flood of non-refined feeling invaded the theatre. . . . Moreover, one found . . . that one's social and political beliefs were being engaged and challenged in a way that English drama since Shaw's heyday had rarely attempted. (1976, 11)

What the new dramatists, with their loud and spirited concern for what were purported to be the problems and aspirations of the lower classes, endeavored to achieve—and, within certain limits, did achieve—was a revitalization of a largely debased, stagnant, and class-bound theater. Forcing English drama out of its polite, comfortable, and complacent middle-class situations, they refocused it on the "real" (albeit mainly emotional) problems of lower-class youth—represented, for example, in Osborne's Jimmy, Wesker's Ronnie, and Delaney's Jo in *Look Back in Anger,* the *Wesker Trilogy,* and *A Taste of Honey,* respectively—and their rude, dingy, and claustrophobic rooms and kitchens.

Thus, this putative revolution in the English theater was no more than what John Arden later described as merely "a revolution of content" (1977, 49). Its main concern lay not in presenting or developing a new and different style of theater but in updating, with recognizably contemporary and local subject matter and idiom, the old form of naturalism. One reason for this was that in the English theater of the 1950s naturalism was virtually the only immediately available tradition. In dramaturgy as well as in performance, the naturalist-illusionist conventions were predominant. Important attempts elsewhere in Europe (mainly in the Soviet Union and Weimar Germany) to break out of this nineteenth-century liberal form and forge a truly political and contemporary theater were buried under the double blanket of conservative disapproval and both Hitlerian and Stalinist destruction, right up to the Berliner Ensemble's London visit in 1956, and even after that.[1] Nearer home, the important example of Sean O'Casey's drama was sadly neglected or undervalued; the popular forms of entertainment, such as the music hall and the pantomime, had become devitalized and were in the last stages of their decline; and a historically important tradition of sporadic attempts toward radical theater—represented mainly by the Workers Theatre Movement and the Unity Theatre during the thirties and by Joan Littlewood's Theatre Workshop in the forties and fifties—were successfully marginalized and therefore failed to make any significant impact on the course of the British theater in general.[2] A crucial consequence of this severely restricted perspective was that a whole radically alternative current in modern dramaturgy and theater, culminating in Brecht's theater, remained unavailable to the new playwrights of the 1950s.

Apart from the mainstream theater, which remained stolidly wedded to a cognitively lesser (because commercialized) form of realism, the only locally available nonnaturalist kind of drama was verse drama in its twentieth-century revival. Of all the major examples of this drama— from W. B. Yeats to Christopher Fry—the joint efforts of W. H. Auden and Christopher Isherwood and the works of T. S. Eliot were of relatively great significance, but they failed to provide a viable alternative to naturalism. While Eliot's endeavor to create "a new form of verse which shall be as satisfactory a vehicle for us as blank verse was for the Elizabethans" (1960, 44) achieved a remarkable success with his consciously antihistoricist religious play *Murder in the Cathedral,* it broke down in his later plays when he tried to tackle contemporary and secular situations and themes, which compelled him to make compromises with the conventions of naturalism.[3] Similarly, the consciously left-wing dramas of Auden and Isherwood, although interesting for their use of robustly nonnaturalist forms and conventions of popular entertainment, failed ultimately, in Raymond Williams's words, in "the achievement of any dramatic integrity" (1976a, 195) and lost their appeal and interest when the radical political atmosphere of the thirties, which had provided their immediate context, petered out.

On the other hand, Ibsenian drama had come to be widely regarded as a form particularly suited to expressing political and social concerns in emotionally intense and subjective terms. A great majority of the better-known "social" dramas were in this tradition. The real source the new English playwrights were drawing upon in their plays was not so much an integral view of society or history as their own subjective perceptions. Their plays were largely inspired by an autobiographical impulse. Rather than investigating the material conditions of collective existence, they were concerned mainly with expressing their own inner selves, their intensely felt responses to the world as they experienced it. So, while seeking to reinvigorate and revitalize a static theater and to make it capable of dealing with their own unique experience of society, elders, morality, and so on, Osborne and the other "angry young men" might have felt that, its recent stagnation and trivialization notwithstanding, naturalism was the only effective form with which to work. For, as Simon Trussler has observed, naturalism

> seemed to provide the most direct means of transmuting personal experience into art for dramatists who were more concerned with what they said than how they said it. . . . [When] the mannered accretions of the Rattigans and Hunters had been scoured away, its formal directness seemed as new as its subject matter. (1968, 130)

The feelings of frustration, pain, anger, and discontent came across in the writings of the new dramatists loud and clear, but also in predominantly emotional and subjective terms, because the key to a lasting and deep reorientation of insight—the dramaturgic form, the very structure and style in which this experience was formulated—remained firmly rooted in the naturalist tradition and structure of feeling.

Thus, the new drama's rejection of the established theater meant, mainly, a rejection of its outdated dialogue and subject matter. It replaced the complacent politeness, the gay and comfortable drawing-room atmosphere, and the preoccupation with inanities, which had characterized the existing middle-class drama, with an emotionally charged style, passionate articulation of moral concern, congested bed-sitters, and lower-class characters and situations. Historically significant as the achievements of the new drama might have been, there was no conscious attempt on the part of the playwrights to transcend the essentially illusionist and individualist (i.e., bourgeois) horizons of English drama and theater.

Arden's Approach to Theater

The only exception to this preoccupation with the naturalist form was John Arden's work. Even at the beginning of his career, and despite the usual critical practice at that time of clubbing Arden, Osborne, Wesker, and Pinter together, he bore little resemblance to any of the other new playwrights. After his debut, he wrote four full-length plays in quick succession—*The Waters of Babylon* (1957), *Live Like Pigs* (1958), *Serjeant Musgrave's Dance* (1959), and *The Happy Haven* (1960). Like the early plays of Osborne and others, these were all produced by the Royal Court Theatre in London, which, under George Devine's dynamic leadership, had become the center of the new drama. But they were radically different from anything written by the "new-wave" dramatists. Instead of a passionate and emotionally intense style, Arden wrote in a predominantly comic style that must have seemed nonserious or too lighthearted to many. For it was a style that reflected no overt social or moral passion, no burning sense of anger, outrage, or grievance. This situation was compounded by the fact that, whereas other playwrights of his generation tended to work within the established conventions of modern drama, Arden was trying to reach back to older, almost forgotten traditions, forms, and conditions of popular performance.

Arden's effort to recuperate the lost or neglected traditions of popular drama and entertainment was a profoundly significant artistic preference rather than a chauvinistic, antiquarian, or nostalgic revivalism. It grew out of his endeavor to restore to theater its lost popularity and its ability to entertain and enlighten at the same time. It is not that he lacked cognitive seriousness or sociopolitical concern. But, radically reorganizing the dramaturgic structure of feeling, his focus was on the indissoluble union of the issues presented and *how* they were presented. This was also an ideological choice—and Arden was to become increasingly conscious of it as such during the sixties. Basically, it meant two things: first, a recognition (in strict congruence with modern criticism) that form is the key to meaning in culture; and, second, a rejection of the individualist implications and emphases of the dominant forms of modern drama in favor of a more communal or collectivist focus reworked from the older traditions. In a brief essay, published in 1960, which has the quality and significance of a manifesto, Arden explained his artistic preference and its implications, distinguishing them from the choices made by some of his contemporaries.

> To use the material of the contemporary world and present it on the public stage is the commonly accepted purpose of playwrights, and there are several ways in which this can be done. Autobiography treated in the documentary style (Wesker). Individual strains and collisions seen from a strongly personal standpoint and inflamed like a savage boil (Osborne). The slantindiculor observation of unconsidered speech and casual action used to illuminate loneliness and lack of communication (Pinter). . . . What I am deeply concerned

with is the problem of translating the concrete life of today into terms of poetry that shall at the one time both illustrate that life and set it within the historical and legendary tradition of our culture. (Arden 1965c, 125)

Declaring that the "bedrock of English poetry is the ballad," he pointed out that the writers who have built close to this tradition (he named Chaucer, Shakespeare, Jonson, and Brecht) "have known, almost as an unnoticed background to their lives, the enormous stock of traditional poetry, some of it oral, some of it printed and hawked at street-corners, some of it sung from the stages of the music-halls" (p. 126). A theater built on or around this popular tradition, he argued, was likely to have greater appeal and effectiveness because "this tradition is the one that will always in the end reach to the heart of the people" (p. 120). As for the cognitive potential of these traditional poetic forms, or their capacity to comprehend and illuminate life and its problems, he felt confident that they

> can carry any strength of content from tragedy through satire to straightforward comedy, and neither be drowned in it nor seem too portentous. Social criticism, for example, tends in the theater to be dangerously ephemeral and therefore disappointing after the fall of the curtain. But if it is expressed within the framework of the traditional poetic truths it can have a weight and an impact derived from something more than contemporary documentary facility. (p. 128)

This essay is an early example of Arden's theoretical writings on the nature and sources of his work. His artistic as well as political commitments were to undergo several significant changes during subsequent years, culminating in his and D'Arcy's angry withdrawal in 1972 from the professional metropolitan theater. Nonetheless, the essay is not only seminal but it has a crucial significance for an adequate understanding of Arden's dramaturgy and its implications. It envisions a poetic theater, which is popular in appeal and artistically as well as socially vital. Such a theater, as exemplified in Arden's own plays, has—as shall be seen later—certain basic similarities with Brecht's epic (or, better, dialectical) theater. These similarities go beyond the similarity of the sources from which the two playwrights derive their conventions and techniques, and they signify a fundamental ideological affinity. As stated, Arden's initial preference for building on or around a lost tradition was (as in the case of Brecht) in itself an ideological choice, and, as time went by and Arden grew in experience, he became increasingly conscious of this. It was inspired by a recognition of the greater artistic as well as cognitive potential of the traditional forms in dealing with social problems. Clearly, the kind of poetic theater that Arden postulates allows the playwright to critically examine, and even denounce, the imperfections of an existing social order while affirming and celebrating the ingenuity, resourcefulness, and collective strength of the people. It was precisely through such a combination of critical and celebratory impulses that the traditional theaters had in the past been able to communicate an exciting experience in which robust entertainment and social meaning were not divorced but inextricably linked. Such a theater, as Arden remarked in another essay, "has had and will always have a more basic appeal than any other, because it is founded upon a more inclusive view of life" (1960, 15).

Arden and His Critics

Radically different from anything with which the twentieth-century English theater in its dominant forms was familiar, Arden's early plays ran for fewer performances and attracted smaller audiences than did those of his contemporaries. Reviews in the press ranged from openly hostile, through ambivalent, to frankly puzzled. Arden himself has recorded this with his characteristic humor in the rhymes that constitute his preface to *The Workhouse Donkey*.

> Some critics said:
> This Arden baffles us and makes us mad;
> His play's uncouth, confused, muddled, bad.
>
> Said Arden:
> Why do you accuse me and abuse me
> And your polite society refuse me,
> Merely because I wear no belt nor braces?
> There would be reason for the wry mouth in your faces
> And reason for your uncommitted halting speeches
> If you would but admit I wore no bloody breeches.

In comparison to all that has been written on other playwrights of his generation—for example, Osborne, Wesker, Pinter—the existing body of critical material on Arden is slight not only in volume but in substance. It is largely rooted in the controversy and confusion that Arden's dramaturgy provoked with its determined refusal to conform to the critically and conventionally accepted forms and norms of bourgeois theater. Most of this critical material consists of isolated responses to individual plays (the favorite being *Serjeant Musgrave's Dance*) or to some specific aspect of his drama. There is previous little by way of a systematic, comprehensive, and sustained discussion of his work and its significance as a whole.

There are certain stock issues around which much of the critical discussion of Arden's drama has been conducted in the past. One such issue, particularly in relation to his early plays, is his supposed moral ambivalence, a capital crime in an age in which *commitment* was the catchword. In one way or another, this question of commitment has remained at the center of much Arden criticism from the beginning. When his first plays were produced, in an atmosphere of revival of the socially committed form of naturalism on the English stage, it was felt that, contrary to the current fashion, they revealed no clear bias in favor of one or the other side of a dramatic argument. For an audience accustomed to illusionist dramaturgy and its moral spoon-feeding—an audience that, for example, had identified readily with Jimmy Porter's historically impotent but emotionally and rhetorically powerful "anger" against the Establishment—it was bewildering, if not altogether outrageous, that a dramatist should write plays about what seemed to be recognizable problems of contemporary social and political life— municipal corruption, prostitution, colonial wars, pacifism, and so on— without taking sides. There was little effort to explore whether Arden's failure to live up to the expectations of middle-class theatergoers might have been a conscious choice on his part rather than a symptom of artistic deficiency. What this requirement of a debased "commitment" actually meant was that these audiences and critics expected playwrights to valorize a particular character or point of view so as to make it easy for them to identify with it. Arden did not oblige them because his view about how a play ought to dramatize an argument was radically different. He believed that the practice of providing spectators with what he called a "cosy point of reference" tends to produce "awful sentimentality, particularly if the play handles any sort of social or personal problem" (1966, 43). In 1963, in an interview with Albert Hunt, he said:

> I don't understand this assumption that some people have that you have to present the audience with a character they can identify with.

I think you can identify with any character at any given moment of the play. I never write a scene so that the audience can identify with any particular character. I try and write the scene truthfully from the point of view of each individual character. (Arden 1965a, 15)

Arden's refusal to isolate and valorize a particular character or point of view within a play was thus a fundamental aspect of his conscious dramaturgic design: it had little to do with moral/political commitment or its absence. Yet this is precisely what most of his audiences and critics, accustomed as they were to a different (that is, Ibsenian) kind of dramaturgy and theater, were unable to grasp. Many of them continued to apply to his plays the standards derived from the naturalist tradition. More often than not, this led them to mystify the expressly ethical and political implications of the plays. For example, one critic, discussing *Serjeant Musgrave's Dance* and its performance possibilities on the assumption that Arden's "method is to have us identify with Musgrave," finds in the play "the story of *one man's* quest for an identity he can live with and an order he can live by" (Skloot 1975, 209). Such a reading, needless to say, amounts to a gross distortion and mystification of both the form and the ideological implications of Arden's dramaturgy. Here it turns a clearly political play into something it (or any play by Arden) certainly is not: a discourse in which the key conceptual category is the self.

To a certain extent, this early confusion and bewilderment subsided in the late fifties when, in the context of an increased (and steadily increasing) interest in Brecht's work, the critics began to have an inkling that Arden's dramaturgy was similar to that of his German counterpart. The preoccupation with the theme of commitment was not quite abandoned. It continued to provide a common focus for a good deal of writing on his work. But there was what may be described as a reversal of emphasis: the same aspect that was previously regarded as his unpardonable weakness now came to be seen as Arden's peculiar strength. In other words, ambiguity or impartiality came to be regarded as the main value of his dramaturgy. John Russell Taylor was the first to argue that Arden "permits himself, in his treatment of the characters and situation, to be less influenced by moral preconception than any other writer in the British theatre today," and that his "attitude to his creation is quite uncommitted" (1963, 84). Since then, this liberal or humanist view of Arden's dramaturgy, which presents at best a half-truth, has continued to inform a great many critical readings of his work. It is true that Arden's dramaturgy in the early plays evinces no overt, declamatory morals and no illusionist empathy with good protagonists versus black villains. But its upshot is, in fact, simultaneously more deeply ethical and more political (because collective) than that of any other English contemporary of his. Interestingly, and quite logically, such a liberal criticism may turn quite illiberal when faced with Arden's later activism and more direct involvement in political and communal forms of "alternative" theater. For example, in 1969, Simon Trussler lamented Arden's increasing entanglement in the more radical, openly political forms of theater, and he praised, by contrast, the greater vitality and "insidiousness of Arden's approach" in his earlier plays, which "defined not dogmas but dilemmas" (1969, 181). Similarly, in 1980, Ronald Hayman accused Arden of renouncing "art and art values" in favor of "community," declaring that "Arden hasn't given up writing plays, he's just given up writing good ones" (1980).

The problem with this preoccupation with the question of commitment or bias is that it focuses on only one important feature of Arden's dramaturgy, his refusal to conceive characters and situations moralistically (that is, illusionistically). In doing so, it isolates this aspect from its implications and function within the totality of his dramaturgy and reduces it to a matter of individual style and/or idiosyncrasy, if not of eccentricity, within a more or less naturalist framework.

Another widely held view of Arden's work is that his plays deal with the conflict between freedom and order. This conflict, often described in essentialist terms, as one between *the* individual and *the* society, is perceived by some critics as the fundamental ideological tension and principle of Arden's dramaturgy. Many doctoral dissertations and most of the early Arden criticism offers readings of individual plays in these or similar terms. I have mentioned one such (if decisively skewed) example in Robert Skloot's approach to *Serjeant Musgrave's Dance* (1975). An earlier example of a basically similar approach can be found in Richard Gilman's essay, "Arden's Unsteady Ground" (1966). Gilman, who advocates a psycho-sociological approach based on Freud's *Civilization and Its Discontents,* sees such a conflict as the "controlling impulse" of Arden's work.

This conflict of the self, or its spontaneous element, with the organizing, abstract, equally self-interested and therefore inherently repressive action of politics is complemented and enlarged by another encounter which runs through most of Arden's work. This is the confrontation of a deadly impulse toward purity (which may be fanatic attempts to do away with it) and the impure, flawed, capricious, and uncodifiable nature or reality beneath our schemes for organizing it. (p. 56)

The psychological—indeed, archetypal—emphasis of this approach has the effect of dehistoricizing Arden's approach to life and its problems, which, as we shall see in the subsequent parts of this study, is an expressly and emphatically historical one. This reduction of the dramatic conflict in Arden's drama to a single and simple ahistorical conflict on an archetypal or existentialist pattern leads to a seriously distorted view of his work. In other words, the principal weakness of such an approach is related to the severe restriction of its focus. Concentrating almost exclusively on a single thematic aspect and then generalizing from it, it produces a misplaced emphasis that ignores the complex nature of Arden's dramaturgy as a whole.

Rich and uninhibited variation of style and verbal forms is yet another aspect of Arden's dramaturgy that has drawn critical attention. It is, for example, the subject of Andrew Kennedy's essay (1975), which examines the playwright's frequent and abundant use of the traditional and "archaic" languages and concludes that

Arden's "tradition," by leaning too much on the archaic or regional languages, risks insulating itself. With all its liveliness, it is a language not "open" to the way language is being lived and remade under the pressure of new modes of thought and being. (p. 214)

Again, what is important here is the fact that this conclusion is reached by the critic through an analysis of only one level, the verbal level, of language in isolation from both the dramatic situation and from the other forms of expression (suggested attitudes, gestures, movements, and so on) that drama employs and that collectively constitute the theater's composite language. This composite language is particularly vital in the traditional and popular forms of drama on which Arden has always built. It can be understood only when we approach drama as potential theater, when our reading of a play is informed by a constant alertness to its performance horizons. Handicapped by his specialized, and therefore limited, focus, Kennedy fails to pay adequate attention to this character of theater language. He also fails to take into account the expressly and fundamentally playful and artful nature of Arden's dramaturgy, which, like the popular dramaturgists of the medieval and Elizabethan traditions, as well as Brecht, achieves its effect through estrangement rather than recognition, identification, and the illusion of reality.

The composite language of theater is the subject of John Russell Brown's *Theatre Language* (1972), a study of Arden, Osborne, Pinter, and Wesker. The comprehensiveness of Brown's critical focus—he is not interested "in words alone" but in "every means of expression that the theatre possesses and that can be controlled" (p. 14)—makes his book one of the few relatively important attempts to come to grips with Arden's dramaturgy as a whole. The twin emphases of his essay are: Arden's conscious and explicit artificiality; and his exploratory attitude toward problems. He describes Arden's theater as "artificial theatre" in which not only the language but the style of presentation and dramaturgic design emphasize a play's artificiality. "The fascination of his plays," Brown argues,

> lies chiefly in what is going on, not in careful debate and sustained argument, not in a progressive revelation of inward tensions, purposes or despair, not in verisimilitude of setting or behavior, not in a display of temperament or sensitivity.

This artificiality of his theater makes him "a primitive among dramatists" but not a "true primitive" because he chooses this style, self-consciously, for "intellectually perceived reasons" (p. 193).

The central concern of an early Arden play, Brown argues, is to "illustrate attitudes and explore a problem" (p. 194). His commitment or didacticism is not an obvious, simple commitment to any ready-made or preconceived moral and social values or viewpoints. Unlike Aristophanes and Jonson, or even Brecht, with all of whom he shares many significant characteristics, Arden's plays do not present a "double view" (p. 220). His is a more flexible position—it is "committed only to an attempt to understand" (p. 209), to the exploration of a problem in its own terms. His dramatic purpose, Brown suspects,

> requires climactic incidents where what is revealed must be exploratory and honest before all else. Arden wishes to use the theatre to

create or release a response that cannot be predicted, to discover
what is involved in certain human activity.

In other words, Arden pursues drama "almost for its own sake, as a
surrogate for conscious, considered intellection, as a means of discovery
in its own terms, not as a stimulus for debate or a platform for verbal
affirmation" (p. 227).

Brown offers some useful insights. But, instead of pursuing them to
their logical conclusion, he falls back on the easier, more orthodox emphases. For example, despite Arden's refusal to take explicit sides or
supply ready-made answers to specific questions that a play may raise, he
does not perceive the world (as Brown suggests he does) as one "that no
one can fully understand" (p. 234). And Arden and D'Arcy certainly do
not see theater as "a surrogate for living," whatever Brown may mean by
this. Theater, for Arden, has been in all of its significant moments, and
again should be, a dynamic social institution as well as an art form vitally
linked to the shared life of the community. The exploratory spirit of his
plays does not exist for its own sake, nor is its complexity confused or
perplexed. It treats history as a process within which the world can be
understood and altered. As Arden himself once declared, "that there is no
hope I do not believe" (1965c, 127).

Thus Brown, in the final analysis, is unable to transcend the critical
position that imputes ambiguity to Arden's work or an aesthetics that
valorizes such ambiguity for its own sake. Moreover, even his critical
approach, like that of so many others, is based largely on the analysis of
individual plays and on rather literal readings of Arden's own nondramatic writings and utterances. He does not seem to realize sufficiently that
for a fuller understanding of Arden's work it is necessary to complement
the examination of individual plays with an overview of his opus as one
significative whole.

In this respect Albert Hunt's work on Arden is of pioneering significance. His book-length study, *Arden: A Study of His Plays* (1974), was the
first important attempt to focus on the fundamental artistic and ideological assumptions of Arden's dramaturgy. It stressed the ideological significance of Arden's rejection of the established forms in modern theater
and his decision, instead, to use styles, techniques, and conventions of
various popular traditions. The dominant feature of the modern professional theater, Hunt argued, is illusionism, which makes it a theater of
"acceptance," that is, a theater "that can only work by persuading you to
leave your critical, questioning faculties outside, and allow yourself to be

carried along by a tide of emotion" (p. 24). He contrasted this to the popular tradition in theater, which stretches from the modern music halls and pantomimes back through Shakespeare to the Middle Ages and has "precisely the opposite aim: to question appearances" (p. 28). Stressing that Arden rejected the theater of illusion not because it could not convey his response to life and society, Hunt observed: "In contrast to the theatre of illusion's simplified view of life, Arden's response is built on an intense awareness of contradictions, of the existence of opposites in any given situation. It's a dialectical view" (p. 31). The reason he uses popular forms of theater is because they allow him to express this dialectical view "not in terms of abstract, theoretical arguments—but of a concrete form of theatre" (p. 31).

The main significance of Hunt's book, as I have mentioned, lies in this marrying of ideological significance with Arden's choice of form and conventions. This overview of Arden's dramaturgy informs his reading of the individual plays, which is, therefore, particularly interesting and helpful. It illustrates with concrete examples the playwright's use of conventions and techniques from the popular tradition and shows how they alter the meaning of a dramatic event and, therefore, of the play as a whole. Although Hunt's relatively brief book tends to be too involved in offering a polemic defense of Arden to provide a fully sustained examination of his dramaturgy, its significance in the corpus of Arden criticism is seminal. It contains important hints about the kind of approach Arden's plays require and has inspired some of the best texts of Arden criticism—such as Helena Forsas-Scott's excellent essay on *Serjeant Musgrave's Dance* (1983).

Two things emerge from this brief review of Arden criticism. First, the existing body of critical material, although marked sporadically by useful insights, largely fails to fully appreciate the significance of Arden's work. Second, there is by now a general recognition that Arden's theater is consciously different from the dominant forms of modern drama and therefore requires different critical standards of judgment. Yet nowhere is there a full, sufficiently systematic discussion of what seems to be the central question for an understanding of Arden's dramaturgy, namely, its place in the context of the main European (and global) dramaturgic and philosophical traditions. Such a discussion would involve a detailed study of the main artistic and ideological emphases of his dramaturgy in a historical perspective.

In his book *To Brecht and Beyond* (1984), Darko Suvin writes: "From the very large number of modelling possibilities, one or (at exceptional periods of strife) a few become dominant in a given sociohistorical constellation or age" (p. 4). Taking our cue from these observations, we can identify in twentieth-century western drama two distinct and rival dramaturgic traditions or modeling possibilities. These two traditions have been contending for supremacy almost throughout the century, each major change in the sociopolitical climate tilting the balance in favor of one or the other. We may identify these traditions as: the dominant bourgeois tradition, the axiomatic basis of which is in the ideology of individualism; and an alternative tradition based on some form of collectivism. In a further (and finer) distinction, the latter should be subdivided into revivalist (usually religious) collectivism (cf. Yeats and Eliot) and a historical and ideologically postbourgeois collectivism found in the works of, say, Mayakovsky, Meyerhold, Piscator, Brecht, the San Francisco Mime Troupe, Bread and Puppet, McGrath, and Dario Fo. In what follows we shall discuss these rival currents in modern drama at some length with a view toward determining Arden's place in relation to them. Our purpose here, however, is not to offer exhaustive descriptions of all the significant developments *within* these two traditions but to identify and describe only the general forms or paradigms of these two dramaturgic types for the strictly functional purpose of historical perspective.

Dominant Bourgeois Tradition

"Modern drama," wrote Lukács, "is the drama of the bourgeoisie; modern drama is bourgeois drama" (1968, 425). Although this assertion was made three quarters of a century ago, it remains an essentially correct description of the dominant traditions of western drama even today. To say this is not to deny that modern drama, particularly in its critical phase (since Ibsen), has often taken a conscious and explicit antibourgeois moral stance, that it has had a rich and variegated history of formal experiments and innovations, and that it has produced a number of exceptions in periods of antibourgeois revolutionary fervor. Yet in the ideological implications and orientations of dramaturgic and theatrical forms, as also in the composition of its audiences, it has continued to be solidly middle-class. It distinguishes itself, on the one hand, from the prebourgeois (particularly medieval and Elizabethan) traditions, and, on the other, from the twentieth-century attempt at a radical break and renewal, mainly by its axiological basis in the ideology of individualism and illusionism.

Both these axioms are best illustrated in what is commonly described as the drama of naturalism. Individualism, which forms the epistemological basis of the dominant European and American culture, particularly since the eighteenth century, is integrally allied to the materialist and atomist emphases of bourgeois theory and practice. It defines the horizons of the bourgeois world view, revealing both its strengths (in comparison with the earlier metaphysical modes and forms of thought) and its limitations (in comparison with what may be called postindividualist, particularly Marxist, theory and practice). Illusionism, on the other hand, is a common artistic manifestation of this epistemology or deep form. It endeavors to produce "mirror images" of observed life and setting, which, on the one hand, blur the reader or spectator's awareness of the essential fictionality of an artistic text with a view to maximizing and intensifying the emotional impact, and, on the other, restrict that text's artistic and cognitive range.

As already noted, both individualism and illusionism are closely linked to naturalism. Although naturalism developed as a conscious emphasis and stylistic term in drama only in the nineteenth century, it has had a long and varied history, which has been usefully traced by Raymond Williams. He notes two main senses in which the term was used prior to its full-scale development in drama. First, it was used in the late sixteenth century in "a form of conscious opposition, or at least distinction, between revealed (divine) and observed (human) knowledge" and as such signified "a philosophical position allied to science, natural history and materialism" (Williams 1977, 203). The early and general manifestations of naturalism in this sense can be seen in the tendency toward consciously secular and social emphasis that goes back, in drama and fiction, to the seventeenth century (prose comedy, domestic drama) but becomes particularly pronounced in the eighteenth-century "bourgeois tragedy" of which Lillo's *The London Merchant* is a good example. It is reflected, in particular, in the reliance upon observed (and, as Williams has pointed out elsewhere, contemporary and indigenous)[4] social life as the source of dramatic action.

The term *naturalism* was also used, in the mid-nineteenth century, particularly in painting, to indicate a "method of 'accurate' or 'lifelike' reproduction" (Williams 1977, 203). This second meaning of *naturalism,* obviously related to what we have here identified as illusionism, continues to be the sense in which the term is popularly understood and used in relation to drama and fiction. However, according to Williams, naturalism in drama in its fully developed form combines both these senses; that is, it designates not only a method but also an ideological position. It indicates, in Williams's words, "a movement in which the method of accurate production and the specific philosophical position are organically and usually consciously fused" (p. 203). This twofold emphasis of naturalism is explicitly present in Zola's well-known defense of naturalist drama.

> In effect, the great naturalistic evolution, which comes down directly from the fifteenth century to ours has everything to do with the gradual substitution of physiological man for metaphysical man. In tragedy, metaphysical man, man according to dogma and logic, reigned absolutely. The body did not count; the soul was regarded as the only interesting piece of human machinery; drama took place in the air, in pure mind. Consequently, what use was the tangible world? Why worry about the place where the action was located? Why be surprised at a baroque costume or false declaiming? Why notice that queen Dido was a boy whose budding beard forced him to wear a mask? None of that mattered; these trifles were not worth stooping to; the play was heard out as if it were a school essay or a law case; it was on a higher plane than man, in the world of ideas, so far away from real man that any intrusion of reality would have spoiled the show. (1968, 367)

Naturalism in this nineteenth-century conception, then, meant a conscious secular and materialist emphasis in direct opposition to the metaphysical and religious world view of earlier times. But it also meant a style of surface realism, a lifelike and nonemblematic reproduction of the "tangible world." In this early form of naturalism the exclusion of any supernatural dimension or intervention in human reality was a conscious emphasis.[5]

This naturalism, however, underwent a significant modification when it was combined with a new emphasis that developed in the theories of social and natural history in the course of the nineteenth century: the emphasis of material determinism. Although as early as the eighteenth century Montesquieu had, in *The Spirit of the Laws,* regarded environment not only as background but also as a condition of human activity, and Denis Diderot had stressed the role of the milieu, it was only in the nineteenth century that social and natural environment came to be seen as a decisive, deterministic factor in human destiny. A leading proponent of determinism was Robert Owen, who wrote:

> The character of man is, without a single exception, always formed for him; . . . it may be, and is chiefly, created by his prede- cessors; . . . they give him, his ideas and habits, which are the powers that govern and direct his conduct. Man, therefore, never did, nor is it possible he ever can, form his own character. (1817, 91–92)

This determinist emphasis, a central feature of what is usually de- scribed as social Darwinism, which grew out of a general materialist orientation of bourgeois thought, was mechanical and naive in compari- son with the more complex, dialectical notion of determinism developed by Marx. The specific terms in which it developed in liberal thought during the nineteenth century carried with it a sense of inexorability that made it a modern version of fate or destiny.

Naturalism with this determinist emphasis influenced the major dra- maturgic forms and styles of the period so profoundly that the physical environment, the setting, and the biographical past no longer functioned as mere realistic backdrops lending authenticity to the dramatized action but actually became crucial factors in that action. For example, the en- closed space of the room, within which the action was usually located, often assumed a formal and cognitive significance far beyond its simple illusionist function as an accurate reproduction of recognizable and seem- ingly authentic setting. It represented, in other words, the physical and social environment within which the inhabitants were forced to live out their destinies and which determined the range of their consciousness, choices, and possibilities. In Williams's words, the major naturalist dra- matists

> put on these rooms, prescribed in detail in a new form of writing which was much more than mere "stage direction," because such immediate physical environments were, in their view, necessary elements of the dramatic action. They were, in the fullest sense, *living* rooms: places made to live in certain ways: environments which both reflected and influenced their possibilities of life. (1981a, 169)

Thus, in Strindberg's *Miss Julie,* the kitchen, the Count's boots, and, above all, the bell acquire a significance far beyond their functional value. They actually intervene in the action, directly or indirectly, as a representation of the external (or social) forces that control and define Jean's consciousness. Miss Julie is similarly conceived as a

> victim of the discord which mother's "crime" has produced in a family, a victim, too, of the day's complaisance, of circumstances, of her own defective constitution, all of which are equivalent to the Fate or Universal Law of former days. (Strindberg 1965, 79)

The main problem with this kind of materialism was that it took a simplistic view of the relationship between the human consciousness and the material and social environment. Positing an irreversible and unilateral process of natural and material cause and human effect, it failed to recognize, or sufficiently emphasize, that within certain limits men are also able to alter the circumstances of their existence and thus are capable of shaping their own collective destiny.

The reason for this failure can be found in the ideology of individualism, in the practice of conceiving the world from the standpoint of the individual, which becomes, from the nineteenth century on, the predominant feature of bourgeois thought and practice. It was during this period, as Williams points out, that the concept of *the* individual as "the fundamental order of being" came to replace the earlier notion of *an* individual denoting a "single example of a group," and a new term, *individualism,* was coined to mean "a theory not only of abstract individuals but of the primacy of individual states and interests" (Williams 1976b, 135–36). While naturalism, as a philosophical position, enabled the human gaze to shift from a mysterious and distant god and supernatural forces to the human and secular world of knowable natural and social phenomena, the ideology of individualism imposed a new restriction and confined that gaze, in social, economic, as well as cultural theory and practice, to the individual and its subjective standpoint. "Slowly, in the development of liberal consciousness, the point of reference became not a general order but the individual, who as such embodied all ultimate values" (Williams 1966, 68).

Individualism lies at the base of the dominant forms of drama since Ibsen and determines the choice of subject matter as well as dramaturgic design. It is reflected, first and foremost, in the predominantly psychological and subjective definition of character, relationships, and conflicts. It is reflected also in the privatized or personalized mode—the restriction of dramatic action to personal and familial situations as well as the separation of this private and personal world from the larger, social world outside. But, above all, it is revealed (particularly in the more serious examples of mainstream drama) in a pervasive tragic awareness that the gap that divides these two worlds—the internal world of the individual and the external world of the society at large, with the latter wielding a hostile and overwhelming power over the former—is unbridgeable. Concerned as this drama usually is with exploring the relation between the individual and its environment, the very privatization of its dramatic action (the enclosed space of the nuclear family, the enclosed rectangle of the room) enhances the impression of this separation and expresses, in Williams's words,

> a precise contradiction in bourgeois social relationships: that the centre of values was the individual and the family, but that the mode of production which sustained them—the world they went out into and returned from—was in a quite different social range, much wider, more complex and more arbitrary. (1981a, 171)

Moreover, since the conventional limitations of naturalist method forbade an emblematic mode of representation or rapid change of scenes, this complex social world could not be dramatized directly ("as in the older and simper actions of kings") and forever remained an outside, mysterious force that intervened in the dramatic action only through reports, messages, or visitors.

The tragic consciousness that has persisted in this drama, despite all its technical innovations and immense critical energy, from Ibsen to Beckett, is a direct result of this individualist approach to problems of human existence, for it is only when the world is experienced from the standpoint of the consciously separate individual—that is, the individual thinking and/or acting against a common condition of compromise— that it appears as a force that is external (because made and controlled by others), hostile (because threatening to individuality and its full and authentic development and expression), and overwhelming (because more complex and larger). It becomes at once an unacceptable and an insurmountable fate.

This restriction in the scope of the dramatic action and the consequent lack of diversity in dramatizable relationships and events are accompanied in this kind of drama by an enlargement of the status of the dramatis personae (or agents) who are conceived and presented as fully developed individuals with seemingly complete psychological and biographical backgrounds. They become, for the first time in drama, *characters* in a strict sense of the term. As we saw in the example of Strindberg's *Miss Julie,* the individuality of these characters is consciously emphasized by setting them in a specific social and physical environment and giving them specific prehistories. As the protagonists are usually conceived as unique individuals, the dramatic conflicts in such plays usually underscore the value of individual authenticity and freedom. The uniqueness of personality and its inner tensions and conflicts become the main focus of dramatic interest, making a play, as we shall see in the following chapter, not the dramatization of a fable but the exposition of a psychological state. This subjective standpoint, which, in its final implication, internalizes and desocializes relations between people, leads directly to what Williams has called the drama of "subjective expressionism," which expresses "the action of a single mind at a level at which other persons have reality only in that mind's terms" (1961, 270).

Just as the communal and well-defined, although often metaphysical, world view of the medieval and Elizabethan dramaturgies is replaced in certain dominant forms of modern drama by a narrower, although expressly secular and rational, metaphysics of individualism, the earlier concept of the theater as game and play is replaced by a correspondingly reduced notion of it as illusion. "In England in the Middle Ages," writes V. A. Kolve,

> one could say "We will play a game of the Passion" and mean what we mean when we say "We will stage the Passion." The transition from one to the other is more than a semantic change; it is a change in the history of theatre. (1966, 14)

This changed conception of drama takes the form of artistic illusionism, which, in dramaturgic and theatrical practice, means a detailed reproduction of observed life in such a way that all traces of artistic construction (of a text's status as art) are carefully concealed. Such practice signifies a restriction of the artistic and cognitive potential of the theater, which directly corresponds to the process of individualization and internalization of experience noted above. Moreover, in its internalization of experience and its suppression of the essentially ludic and collective aspects of the theater and theatrical experience, it is related to that process of individualization and psychologization of the carnivalesque that Mikhail Bakhtin traces back to the emergence of bourgeois cultural forms.

Although illusionism reached its full formal development and became a dominant aesthetic principle only in the nineteenth century, the tendency toward it can be traced back to the Restoration. As early as 1672, Dryden, in his *Of Heroic Plays,* argued that various sound effects are essential in the theater

> to raise the imagination of the audience, and to persuade them, for the time, that what they behold in theatre is really performed. The poet is then to endeavor for an absolute dominion over the minds of the spectators. (1912, 91)[6]

The affinity of attitude between Dryden's desire to "persuade" the spectators by exercising "an absolute dominion" over their minds and Zola's ridicule, in the passage quoted above, of boy actors playing female roles is obvious.

It is this absolute dominion over the audience's thought and feeling that illusionist drama and theater strives toward through various means that involve not only the physical conditions of performance (kind of stage, lighting, seating, and so on) and style of acting (Stanislavsky's method, for instance) but also the dramaturgic aspects of the text itself. Here also it is just as evident in a text's dependence upon the detailed reproduction of a specific physical environment—which transforms into a highly particularized and fixed location what in earlier traditions was always treated as a neutral and communal playing area that could be made to designate any place with ease—as it is in that text's absolute reliance upon uniformly natural movements and everyday, colloquial speech.[7] Above all, it manifests itself in a restrictive formulation of dramatic action, which requires that events be selected and arranged in a causal order so that the action should flow smoothly and, as much as is possible, without interruption from one event to the next, weaving a unilinear pattern of mounting intensity leading gradually but inevitably to the conclusion or impasse. Obviously such a dramaturgic formulation is meant to intensify rather than diversify the experience and cannot permit much variation in the range of dramaturgic agents (who usually belong to a narrow range of socioeconomic classes or milieus), the range of activities (which also remain uniformly "natural" and largely verbal), or the range of experiences and relationships (which remain largely emotional and familial, and either exclusively comic or exclusively tragic). The point is to so overwhelm the spectator with the emotional intensity of the dramatized experience that he will lose his ability to either view that experience critically or think of alternative possibilities within a given situation.

A crucial consequence of illusionism is that the process of production and communication of meaning becomes a mechanical, one-dimensional process, a one-way, univocal traffic from the stage to the auditorium. It thus loses the dialogic richness that the constant interjection of the spectator's own thinking can lend to the dramatized experience. Banished from the world of the action and reduced to eavesdropping through the proverbial "fourth wall," the spectators become passive recipients of the given experience and are so restricted in their optical and intellectual vision, and so involved in the emotional and subjective intensity of the presented action, as to have no perspective save the one the play chooses to dramatize. In both of these effects, the illusionist theater assigns to the spectator an intellectually passive role and renders him incapable of intervening, critically or imaginatively, in the dramatized experience.

Dramaturgic and theatrical illusionism, then, consists in the practice of consciously trying to conceal, or deemphasize, the essentially artful and playful nature of drama. Affecting both scripts and their staging, it results, for all the technical enrichment and intensity of feeling, in an impoverishment of the drama's cognitive and artistic resources. In seeking to be as unobtrusive and consistent as possible, it precludes all those forms, conventions, and devices—episodic structure, different forms of direct speech, poetry and songs, music and dance—which could allow drama and theater, as in the Elizabethan age, to communicate the great variety and complexity of human experience. Its plots are so formulated that they seem to flow out of and into the empirical time and space of the performance, and this smooth, unilinear, and causal flow carries with it a sense of inevitability. Similarly, restricting the dramatizable activity to verbal and empirically verisimilar, rather than allowing it to range freely through a variety of colloquial and formal, verbal and physical, it not only reduces the theater's ability to delight and entertain but curtails its semiotic possibilities as well.

The dominant tradition in western drama, then, has continued to combine, in varying forms and proportions, individualism and illusionism. In the more serious and critical examples of modern drama—that is, the examples that reflect a greater degree of cognitive and moral seriousness, that often actively and critically explore the relations between people and their environments, and that, moreover, usually involve conscious attempts to break from the limitations of the official or orthodox forms of thought and art[8]—these limitations may not be as clearly obvious as they are in lesser examples of commercial drama. The limitations are there, nonetheless, and they can be witnessed in the predominantly subjective and psychological preoccupations and the privatized and universalized (that is, absolutized, dehistoricized) modes that have allowed the dramatic focus and the center of values to be shifted from the collective and variegated world of social relationships to the interior, private worlds of the family and the individual and thence, as in the development from subjective expressionism to the absurd, to a seemingly shared, but abstract, universalized, and subjectively perceived, category of "*the* human condition." The result is that, despite a rich proliferation of innovative forms and techniques, developed often in conscious opposition to the orthodox forms of social and artistic practice, no alternative mode of experience, no radically different response to the world, and therefore no explicit or implicit awareness of the possibility of a different and happier condition of human existence could be conceived.

The Radical Alternative Tradition:
Brecht and Arden

The ideological limitation of the bourgeois tradition can be transcended only when, as in Marxism, man is seen not only in terms of his isolated and subjective self but also in terms of his relationship to his fellow beings, and, furthermore, when these relationships and situations are perceived in historical terms, that is, as subject to change and development. In such an approach, the particular and the general, the personal and the social experience and destinies, are seen in their dialectical relationships. Any particular situation comes to be perceived not as an eternally and externally given universal condition but as a humanly and historically produced, and therefore similarly alterable, set of material and social circumstances.

Such a complex world view requires an equally complex and dynamic form and style. One way in which a playwright may approach such a form is by consciously recognizing the communal and playful nature and potential of his art and by conceiving the function of the theater not as creating and maintaining illusions, nor as offering faithful reproductions or "slices of life" in all their emotional intensities, but as constructing, deliberately and emblematically, heuristic models of social life so that spectators are encouraged to undertake an intellectual and critical investigation of "the way people live together" (Brecht 1965, 12).

Such a transcendence of the bourgeois world view became possible at times—such as in the twenties in the aftermath of the First World War and the world's first successful socialist revolution, and in the radical activist climate of the sixties and seventies—when widespread and vigorous attempts were made to redefine the nature and function of the theater, as both an art form and a social institution, in the light of its essential artificiality as well as in relation to contemporary sociopolitical concerns and aspirations, and to develop genuinely popular (or plebeian) forms of dramaturgy and performance. These efforts—spanning several decades and many countries, and comprising the works of many writers, directors and theater groups, from Mayakovsky to Dario Fo, from Piscator to Julian Beck, from Volksbühne in Germany in the twenties to the San Francisco Mime Troupe in the sixties and the 7:84 Company in England and Scotland in the seventies—caused symptoms of a radically new and alternative current to emerge in European drama. Although each example of this richly variegated corpus of artistic theory and practice has its own distinctive features, its own mark, which sets it apart from the others, and although such differences could be of great significance in another context, each example also shares with the others certain basic features of ideological and artistic approach. It is precisely because of this identity of ideological and artistic orientation that it is possible to speak of all these playwrights, directors, and groups as constituting a coherent tradition.

Ideologically, this tradition reflects the epistemological shift that took place with the emergence of Marxist theory and practice in the nineteenth century—a shift that, while it retained the rational and materialist emphases of bourgeois philosophy, replaced the latter's mechanical and individualist form with a dialectical and collectivist one. An important consequence was that the sociohistorical group or polity once again became the source and the center of values, and the relationship between human consciousness and physical environment came to be conceived in complex (rather than simply harmonious or simply antagonistic) terms capable of influencing and changing each other. This relocation of the epistemological focus is evident in radical alternative drama, which does not simply seek to dramatize issues and situations of communal and contemporary concern but also tries to do so within a historical and dynamic perspective. Above all, it focuses on social classes and their collective material interests rather than on individual heroes and their abstract ideals. The dramatic conflict in this kind of drama usually arises out of the conflicts of interest between such sociohistorical groups or classes.

Thus, the plays in this tradition are united by a twofold affinity: negatively by their shared opposition to the "legitimate" forms of drama and theater, but also positively by their common quest for a form that can be cognitively open-ended, more inclusive and diversified, as well as more entertaining. In practice, this has often meant a form able to integrate the pleasures of storytelling, and of vigorous and richly variegated presentation, with those of intellectual contemplation and examination. In their attempts to achieve such a dramatic form, the radical playwrights also demonstrate a common preference for the styles and conventions of the popular forms of theater. Notable among these features are episodic construction, social rather than psychological emphasis, and a playful (deliberately anti-illusionist) style that can combine with ease a whole range of emotions and experiences (tragic and comic, stylized and naturalistic) and often delights in playing with levels of (artistic) illusion and reality. All this has the effect of widening the scope of drama in terms of the magnitude of dramatizable situations and relationships as well as in terms of the richness and variety of the theater's artistic resources.

The radical alternative tradition is also characterized by its relentless search for new and truly popular audiences and by its desire to restore to the theater its communal, public character and bring back to it those larger plebeian sections of society that the bourgeois theater systematically banished. This has usually resulted in either some radical reconstruction of the naturalist stage or an outright abandonment of the fixed and enclosed locations of the conventional theater (with its fixed and individually marked seats, polite atmosphere, financially and socially restricted admission, and so on). Performance may now be carried out in open-air parks, noisy restaurants, crowded marketplaces, and busy shop floors, restoring to the theater its public character and recarnivalizing the theatrical experience so that the relationship between the performers and the spectators can be more pointed, active, and truly dialogic.

The best and most highly developed expression of this radical alternative dramaturgy is found in the work of Bertolt Brecht, described by

Peter Brook as "the key figure of our time, . . . all theatre work today at some point starts or returns to his statements and achievements" (1977, 80). Brecht's work is rooted, on the one hand, in his awareness of the severe artistic and ideological limitations of the dominant tradition, and, on the other, in his equally conscious recognition of the immense potential of the "epic" style and techniques of popular forms of theater and performance. He recognized that the established theater, in its commercial and less serious form, not only represented the world in an "inexact" way but also hypnotized spectators into accepting it as the only correct representation. "The one important point for the spectators in these houses," he observed, "is that they should be able to swap a contradictory world for a consistent one, one that they scarcely know for one of which they can dream" (1964, 188). As for the serious form of middle-class drama, he noted, "The field of human relationships came within our view, but not within our grasp" (p. 188). This drama, Brecht argued, reduces social and historical conditions to mere setting, or backdrop, to an action that itself remains predominantly subjective and private. "The feelings, insights and impulses of the chief characters are forced on us, and so we learn nothing more about society than we can get from the 'setting'" (p. 190).

Brecht was also aware of the tremendous potential of culture as a social institution. "It is precisely theatre, art and literature," he observed, which must provide the means "for a solid, practical rearrangement of our age's way of life" (p. 123). Therefore, working from an increasingly conscious Marxist standpoint, he set out to formulate the idea of a truly postindividualist theater—a genuinely political and collectivist theater that would be more concerned with social relationships and contradictions and would base itself on the principle

> that people's consciousness depends on their social existence, taking it for granted at the same time that this social existence is continually developing and that their consciousness is accordingly changing all the time. (Brecht 1965, 35)

In other words, Brecht wanted a theater that would not only reproduce the surfaces of reality but show it as a historical process in all its dialectical contradictions. It was to achieve this goal that he developed his theory of the epic theater.[9] In one of his many descriptions of this new kind of theater, he defined it thus.

The epic theatre is chiefly interested in the attitudes which people adopt toward one another, wherever they are socio-historically significant (typical). It works out scenes where people adopt attitudes of such a sort that the social laws under which they are acting spring into sight. . . . The concern of the epic theatre is thus eminently practical. Human behaviour is shown as alterable; man himself as dependent on certain political and economic factors and at the same time as capable of altering them. . . . In short the spectator is given the chance to criticize human behaviour from a social point of view, and the scene is played as a piece of history. The idea is that the spectator should be put in a position where he can make comparisons about everything that influences the way in which human beings behave. (1964, 86)

In developing the style and techniques of his dramaturgy, Brecht drew freely upon the conventions of popular theater, both western and oriental. He studied and learned from Elizabethan traditions and Far Eastern dramaturgy, from vaudeville shows and the cabaret, from pantomimes and ballads. In all cases he drew upon their playful and deliberate style, their varied structure, and their immense gestural energy. He derived from them the principles of loose, episodic construction, communal and economico-political (rather than individualist) focus, and humor, combining in a rich and uninhibited mixture direct and topical social comments, discussions, storytelling, jokes, songs, and music. Brecht was firmly of the opinion that there was "a need for naive but not primitive, poetic but not romantic, realistic but not ephemerally political theatre." He believed that the "contrast of art and nature can be made a fruitful one if the work of art brings it to a head, but without smoothing it out." Therefore, he saw in these features a great potential for revitalizing the theater. This could be done by making it simultaneously popular and realistic. By popular Brecht meant "intelligible to the broad masses, taking over their own forms of expression and enriching them / adopting and consolidating their standpoint / representing the most progressive section of the people in such a way that it can take over the leadership" (1964, 154–55). And by realistic he meant

laying bare society's causal network / showing up the viewpoint as the viewpoint of the dominators / writing from the standpoint of the class which has prepared the broadest solutions for the most

pressing problems afflicting human society / emphasizing the dynamics of development / concrete and so as to encourage abstrac-
tion. (p. 108–9)

Popular forms of drama and theater also often produce what Brecht
called the Verfremdung effect (variously translated into English as the
effect, technique, or stance of alienation, estrangement or distancing),
which, in the epic composition of a play as well as in its performance,
"allows us to recognize its subject, but at the same time makes it seem
unfamiliar"; in other words, it "frees socially-conditioned phenomena
from that stamp of familiarity which protects them against our grasp
today" (p. 192).[10] Achieved through a variety of means—episodic or
situational focusing, diversified and paratactic style, and deliberate and
continuous interruptions in the flow of action making representation and
formulation alternate with and complement each other—it emphasizes
the artfulness and theatricality of the presented action while encouraging
a complex and critical response on the part of the spectators. This approach is clearly opposed to illusionist drama, which blurs the distinction
between the fictional world of the play and the empirical world of the
spectators and draws the spectators, through encouragement of passive
and emotional involvement, into the experience embodied in the stage
action, thereby destroying their capacity to criticize it. On the contrary,
the estrangement technique allows epic theater to partly distance the
spectator. The stage action is presented explicitly as an artificially and
playfully arranged and mounted representation that must be viewed with
a combination of sympathy and critical detachment.
    This theory of a new kind of drama, which Brecht developed over
long years of involvement in theater both as a playwright and a director,
and which was to have a profound influence on the development of theater
both in the West and in many areas of the Third World, is best illustrated
by his own dramaturgic practice. It is evident in his nonmoralistic and
expressly sociohistorical treatment of dramaturgic agents and situations, a
treatment that emphasizes not identity and consistency but contradiction
and inconsistency. His plays usually embody a complex interplay of
perspectives, responses, and choices within determinate sociohistorical
situations. His agents are not heroes and villains, not absolutely good or
absolutely bad paragons of virtue or vice. On the contrary, they are
imaginatively constructed figures of complex social relationships, agents
oscillating between the usually incompatible but necessarily internalized
alternatives of a desired happy life versus cruel social alienation arising out

of powerful and explicitly presented social forces (as a rule, other agents). Such agents are often forced to choose from several alternative courses, with some of them making a correct choice (as Grusha does in relation to the abandoned baby in *The Caucasian Chalk Circle*) and some making an incorrect one (like Mother Courage who loses everything she had hoped to save by treating war as a matter of business as usual). "The laws of motion of a society," Brecht believed,

> are not to be demonstrated by "perfect examples," for "imperfection" (inconsistency) is an essential part of motion and of the thing moved. It is only necessary—but absolutely necessary—that there should be something approaching experimental conditions, i.e., that a counter-experiment should now and then be conceivable. Altogether this is a way of treating society as if all its actions were performed as experiments. (1964, 195)

His plays fully reflect this belief.

Another important consequence of Brecht's epic dramaturgy was that it allowed him to recover some of the lost richness and resourcefulness of the theater and restore to drama its traditional element of fun or play, an element that bourgeois aesthetics, with its strict neoclassicist separation of high and low, serious and nonserious, in forms, styles, and subject matter, had banished from the domain of significant drama. "Theatre," he believed, "consists in this: in making live representations of reported or invented happenings between human beings and doing so with a view to entertainment" (1964, 180). Therefore, Brecht made his plays as entertaining as they were cognitively enriching and socially meaningful, and he did so in such a way that the two elements went hand in hand, with the dramatized events acquiring, in addition to their entertaining quality, a "gestic" quality as well.[11] Like other members of the radical alternative tradition, Brecht wanted to "capture" and revitalize the theater "for a *different* audience" (1964, 21). We have already noted his emphasis on the popular. It clearly indicates that his quest was for a popular (plebeian or proletarian) audience; whether he succeeded in achieving this is a different matter, one we cannot go into here.

It is to this radical alternative tradition that Arden belongs. He shares with its other exponents basic aesthetic and ideological preferences and orientations. His affinity with Brecht, in particular, was very marked from the beginning. Arden himself came to recognize this. "I

feel I belong in the same tradition as Brecht," he once said in an interview. The tradition to which he was referring is the rich popular and
plebeian culture that goes back to the Middle Ages, and runs vitally
through the medieval and Elizabethan dramaturgies and theaters, and
could still be found, until a few decades ago, in such residual forms as the
music hall and pantomime.[12] In that interview, Arden recognized that,
like himself, Brecht had built upon this tradition, had

> taken all his dramatic styles and devices from a tradition of writing
> that goes into the middle ages . . . and I think that Brecht's main
> contribution is to revive this type of theatre as a style of writing and
> producing and then apply it to modern problems and modern ideol-
> ogies and modern audiences. (1965a, 17)

In terms of dramaturgic practice this similarity of artistic approach and
preference meant, as we shall see in the subsequent chapters, a common
predilection for episodic structure, collectivistic sociopolitical emphasis,
and a gay and consciously anti-illusionist style.

Arden's relationship to the bourgeois theater and to the popular
prebourgeois forms—like Brecht's relationship to them—is complex. It
is based on a conscious recognition of the artistic as well as the ideological limitations and potentialities of both, and therefore it cannot be reduced to a total rejection of one or a wholesale acceptance of the other.
Broadly speaking, he derives from the modern tradition its secular and
materialist concern but rejects its individualist world view, which, as
noted, often leads to a tragic awareness that an unacceptable world exists
but exists inevitably. In place of the individualist world view he puts
across, with increasingly conscious emphasis, a historical and materialist
standpoint. Similarly, from the popular traditions of the prebourgeois
periods, he derives their collectivist bias and communal concerns, and
their freedom from illusionist and individualist restrictions, but he rejects
their static (ahistorical) views of community, human nature, and social
relations. The history of his dramaturgic practice, from the early *The
Waters of Babylon* to his last professionally staged play, *The Island of the
Mighty* (and beyond that to Arden and D'Arcy's more recent work outside the established theater circuits), testifies to a continuous and increasingly conscious endeavor to rework these two elements into a form that,
in its ultimate implications, transcends them both and links itself to what
we have here described as the radical alternative tradition in contemporary European and North American theaters.

Chapter Two

Drama as Storytelling: Arden's Epic Construction

A play that was all atmosphere with no plot at all would be my preference.
—John Van Druten

Everything hangs on the story; it is the heart of the theatrical performance.
—Bertolt Brecht

In "An Introduction to the Structural Analysis of Narrative," Roland Barthes identifies functions and indices as the two main structural components of any narrative. Function, he says (following Vladimir Propp), is "an act of a character, defined from the point of view of its significance for the course of the action"—in other words, it is what is conventionally called an "event." The term *indices,* on the other hand, subsumes "personality traits [and] information with regard to identity"—in other words, the elements that constitute the psycho-biographical aspect, or the "character," of an agent (Barthes 1975, 247). On the basis of different combinations of these elements, Barthes goes on to distinguish between two kinds of narrative. "Some narratives," he says, "are predominantly functional (such as popular tales), while some others are predominantly indicial (such as psychological novels)" (p. 247).[1]

Dramaturgies, too, can be classified in terms of whether the main structural emphasis or focus of interest is on story, which may be defined as a complete sequence of events, or on character, which is to be understood here as the psycho-biographical dimension of an agent. Such a division already exists, although not in a fully developed form, in the works of a number of scholars since the time of Aristotle. It is implicit, for example, in Marvin Rosenberg's notions of linear versus contextual (or vertical) forms of drama and in Bernard Beckerman's distinction between intensive and extensive dramaturgic modes (Rosenberg 1958,

41

passim; Beckerman 1970, 186). It also corresponds to Georg Lukacs's distinction between narration and description (1971, passim). All these approaches, though having at times quite different horizons, suggest a typological distinction between what I will here call character-based and story-based dramaturgies. Such a distinction can be particularly useful as a periodizing category, providing "discursive models for historical understanding" (Postlewait 1988, 300) and illuminating significant developments in European dramaturgy since the Middle Ages. As such, it helps describe two transitions of profound political, artistic, and ideological significance: the first from the medieval (and Elizabethan) dramaturgies to the modern (Ibsenian) one, and the second from the latter to what I described in chapter 1 as the radical-alternative current in twentieth-century drama and theater.

My hypothesis is that, while the predominantly functional or story-based form usually signifies an ideological orientation toward, and valorization of, some form of collectivism, the other, predominantly indicial or character-based mode indicates an individualist world view. The second transition, involving a return to the story-based form, I suggest, is connected with the historical, usually Marxist, world view. This view, as we saw, seeks to recuperate the collectivist emphasis of the earlier periods from a specifically modern—that is, rational, materialist, and historical—standpoint, which is arrived at in conscious and systematic opposition to the atomist emphasis in bourgeois thought and practice, yet without sacrificing the liberating effects of the early bourgeois attack on the primitive and static forms of collectivism. Thus, it can be shown that in the specific case of European social history, the transition from the first dramaturgic type to the second coincided with the transition from predominantly feudal social relations, with their religiously sanctioned collectivist world view, to a predominantly bourgeois social order and its ideology of individualism. On the other hand, in modern radical dramaturgies the storytelling interest reemerges and preoccupation with the psychological complexities of the character shifts to a dialectical emphasis. This emphasis focuses, simultaneously, on the contradictions in dramaturgic situation and the alternative possibilities available to situation-bound and relationally defined characters, and it will be seen to be closely bound up with the rejection of the hegemonic individualist ideology in favor of the utopian horizons of a state of collective social (often socialist) happiness.

Thus, the typological distinction between character-based and story-based dramaturgies, if used historically, can be of immense critical value. To repeat, in such a usage *character-based dramaturgy* refers to a preoccupation with individualized agents (which as a rule become contradictory "characters"), their inner emotions and individual psychology, suggesting, in Barthes's words, a structural preponderance of indices or indicial emphasis. Since the term *character* denotes an emphasis on inner life and psychology, a dramaturgy based on it would tend to stress privatized, synchronic (in-depth), and therefore monologic space-time. This kind of dramaturgy, we have seen, is of relatively recent vintage and is significantly contemporaneous with the emergence of the bourgeois world view whose ideology of individualism it embodies.

Story-based dramaturgy, on the other hand, refers to dramaturgic constructions that focus on events rather than separate agents as characters. Since events are generated by consequential interaction among agents, as well as between agents and objects, a dramaturgic construction structurally focused on events emphasizes supraindividual relationships in a dialogic or shared social context. Such a story-based construction usually embodies a multilinear (episodic) and polyvalent (that is, diversified, multivocal, even polarized) space-time. Historically this kind of dramaturgy reflects a nonindividualist (or collectivist) world view such as was dominant in prebourgeois societies and became available again in our own time, albeit in a radically altered form, in Marxist theory and practice.[2]

Two Dramaturgic Types in Historical Perspective

The story is perhaps the earliest form and the basis of all imaginative expression. It is certainly the basic structural element of oral tradition as well as of those literary traditions that developed in close contact with the culture of the lower classes. Even today, it continues to be one of the dominant aspects of popular entertainment, as is indicated by the immense popularity of crime thrillers and science fiction, comics and melodramas, war movies and westerns—all forms that share a strong interest in vigorous narrative action. The focus on story is also the central aspect in all popular dramaturgies. Traditional theaters all over the world—the Indian and the Balinese, the Chinese and the Japanese, the ancient Greek, the medieval European, and the Elizabethan—are characterized by their strong storytelling interest. Indeed, they can be described as story based in the sense that each of them invariably *told* a story and said whatever

else it wanted to say *through* that story. Greek tragedy, as Richmond
Lattimore says, "is a kind of story-telling, whatever else it may be"
(1964, 2). The same holds true in the English tradition, from the Middle-
English fragments of *Interludium de Clerico et Puella* and the Robin Hood
play fragments, and from the earliest known liturgical drama of the
Three Maries, through a variety of religious and secular dramatic forms,
to Marlowe, Shakespeare, and Ben Jonson, or from the quasi-dramatic
texts of Lydgate's Mummings in the early fifteenth century to the recently recorded texts of the Mummers' Play.[3]

The words *story* and *history* are etymologically connected. This connection can be witnessed in the fact that traditional folk cultural practice
made no distinction between the two. Myths, legends, tales, sagas, romances, and myriad other narrative forms of the folk tradition embody a
kind of folkloric history of different peoples. Traditional theaters usually
derive their stories from the stock of myths, scriptures, legends, folklore,
and popular history. The traditional Indian and Balinese theaters, for
example, are based on stories from Hindu mythology, while the material
of Greek tragedy was drawn "almost exclusively from the legends and
myths which in Homer, Hesiod, and their successors, or in oral tradition, constituted a sort of loose history of the Greek world from the
beginnings to the Dorian conquest" (Lattimore 1964, 2–3).[4] Similarly, in
the Middle Ages, the Corpus Christi cycles depicted what was supposed
to be the entire cosmic history from the Creation to the Last Judgment
using biblical stories for an outline. Dramatic adaptations of traditional
narrative material continued to be a common practice during the Tudor
period and culminated in Shakespeare.[5]

This use of familiar material from popular history and folklore
served as an extremely important link between the plays and their audiences and made the theater a truly popular, vital, and dynamic social
institution. As Beckerman observes, "The selection of stories and the
sources from which they stem establish a preliminary and significant
relation of audience to action" (1970, 172). By relying on popular and
folkloric as well as religious narratives, plots in the medieval and Elizabethan dramaturgies embodied and communicated a shared communal
experience, an aspect that was further enhanced by performance style and
the conditions of staging, both of which favored a direct, collaborative
relationship between the performers and their spectators.

According to Wellek and Warren, "To tell a story one has to be
concerned about the happening, not merely the outcome." In other

words, story is concerned with "external action—or action in time," rather than with "contemplative stasis" (Wellek and Warren 1977, 215). As such, it is inimical to any excessively psychological interest in the individual character(s). Emphasizing external action foregrounds inter-agential relationships and their development in time. This emphasis on time as a process also forms the basis of Chatman's distinction between a resolved plot and a revealed plot. The former, he argues, is characterized by "a strong sense of problem solving, of things being worked out in some way," a significantly "strong sense of temporal order," and devel-opment that is a process of unraveling. In a revealed plot, on the con-trary, we feel from the beginning "that things will stay pretty much the same. It is not that events are resolved (happily or tragically), but that a state of affairs is revealed." As a result, in a revealed plot, the sense of time as a process of change is undermined and "events are reduced to a relatively minor, illustrative role" (Chatman 1978, 48).

The structural predominance of storytelling interest, therefore, has crucial consequences for the dramaturgic form. Just as the basic unit of story is the episode, which, by definition, is a discrete subsequence of events, the basic structural segment of story-based dramaturgy tends to be the scene, which also is a short, crisp, and relatively discrete subse-quence.

The story-based popular dramaturgy is characterized by a predilec-tion for episodic, or scenic, construction, although the scenic division is not always formally identified. The Mummers' Play, for example, pre-sents a series of narratively autonomous stock episodes, involving vig-orous physical action, linked by the traditional folk motif of death and renewal. A similar delight in events and vigorous action is found in medieval and Elizabethan dramas. *Mankind,* the earliest known play of the popular repertory, presents a series of encounters between Mankind and his tempters. The interest in the play is so centered upon the rapid succession of events that at one point, when Mercy has to make a long speech expressing its *inner* anguish at Mankind's inconstancy, that char-acter finds it necessary to apologize to the spectators with the words "My inward affliction yieldeth me tedious unto your presence" (Wickham 1974, 29).

What may be called the evental emphasis of medieval drama is fur-ther reinforced by the traditional nature of its agents, which are largely drawn from the repertory of popular and traditional figures—prophets and saints, stock and allegorical figures, moral and social types. As such, they are typical rather than individual (see Suvin 1988). Active and action generating, they possess a greater degree of narrativity and theatrical vitality than do the fully individualized characters who tend to become, as in the individualist drama since Ibsen, excessively introspective, thus generating a feeling of contemplative stasis. The absence of a subjective dimension allows the story-based agents to function as fully exteriorized (textualized) and emphatically relational constructs that do not seek the spectator's complete emotional involvement in their individual destinies. Instead, whatever their immediate or local interest in performance, they direct the spectator's attention toward the larger, shared world of supra-individual relationships which, in any given play, they collectively emblematize.

Like other Elizabethan dramatists, Shakespeare inherited this delight in external action and episodic structure, and he developed this traditional form into one of the world's greatest dramaturgies. He intensified, no doubt, the agential element, giving his main characters a relatively greater degree of individuality and motivation. But he also retained the predominance of the storytelling interest and episodic construction. His plays dramatized stories derived from history, popular romances, and folklore, in a form that is remarkable for the scope and diversity of its evental emphasis. Although the episodic structure of Shakespeare's dramaturgy is somewhat obscured by the neoclassical five-act division that later editors imposed, it is still possible to see that the basic structural unit of his work is the scene.[6] Each scene, while part of an overall complex and poetic design, is like a distinct episode, possessing an immediate interest of its own. His drama is characterized by the variety and multiplicity of such scenes. And, since each scene is short in duration, the action moves with remarkable rapidity from one scene to another, from one spatial-temporal and social situation to another, creating a multidimensional and panoramic experience. As M. C. Bradbrook has observed

> Shakespeare's theater was very near to the cinema in technique: his tricks of showing a series of short separate actions, each one cut off before it is finished . . . which gives a sense of merged and continuous waves of action, is a common habit of Eisenstein and Pudovkin. (1960a, 14)

Such an arrangement of parts plays down the perception of linear and single causality since the relationship of one part to another comes across as loose rather than tightly causal. The result is a diversified emphasis, or what Beckerman calls "the patterns of coemphasis" (1970, 182). Thus, Shakespeare's dramaturgy—like all story-based dramaturgies, in which different events, and often sequences of events, alternate with each other, each creating its own immediate emphasis—diversifies rather than intensifies the dramatic experience and the spectator's response to it.

Such an epic structure implies a view of the action from the outside, from a vantage point affording a more comprehensive overview. S. L. Bethel called this the principle of "multi-consciousness" (1944, 29). Brecht, arguing that the dominant characteristic of popular dramatic tradition is "the audience's ability to respond simultaneously and unconsciously on more than one plane of attention at the same time," referred to it as "complex seeing." Combined with the nonillusionist style and conditions of staging that such dramaturgies imply, it is similar to Brecht's Verfremdung effect insofar as it encourages thinking *above* the flow of the play rather than simply thinking *within* it (Brecht 1964, 44).

These story-based dramaturgies belong to a culture that was still predominantly collectivist. This collectivism was sanctioned by tradition and religion. Individual deviation from the collective norm was considered unacceptable behavior and was severely criticized and punished, in drama as in society. By the time of Shakespeare, this collectivist culture had begun to lose its stability. Tensions and contradictions had developed with the rise of a new mercantile class, which was finding the rigidly conservative social norms and static hierarchies increasingly unacceptable. Shakespeare's plays were written from within the old collectivist framework, although they also (and significantly) reflect some of the tensions and contradictions of his time. Despite their greater individuality, complexity, and depth (compared to the static allegorical types of medieval drama), his major characters were conceived primarily as supraindividual agential forces within, and inseparable from, complex narrative designs focused on shared social relationships.

Loss of Story in Bourgeois Liberal Drama

In contrast to the story-based, diversified structure of the early popular dramaturgies, bourgeois dramaturgy in its most significant examples (since the eighteenth century but most particularly in the critical Ibsenian variant), has a character-based structure and tends toward a devitalization, occultation, and (as in some recent examples of the Absurd drama) even complete elimination of the story.

The transition from a predominantly feudal social order and culture to a fully bourgeois society and culture was long and gradual. It spanned several centuries and several revolutions—political, intellectual, and economic. Equally slow, and in close proximity to this general process of change, was the transition from the story-based to the character-based dramaturgy. By the nineteenth century, the bourgeois hegemony over cultural institutions and practices was fully established. It included the complete transformation of theater into a distinctly middle-class art form and institution consciously separate from the residual forms of the politically vanquished popular/collectivist culture. It is significant that the full development of character-based dramaturgy also occurred during this period, and, ironically, found its best expression in the dramatists whose conscious moral stance was antibourgeois. This corresponded to the transition, in Georg Lukács's terms, from experiencing to observing, and from the predominantly narrative to the predominantly "descriptive" mode of representation, which signified, in Fredric Jameson's paraphrase of Lukács's argument, "a purely static contemplative way of looking at life and experience . . . equivalent in literature to the attitude of bourgeois objectivity in philosophical thought" (1981, 200–201). The emergence of this passively contemplative stance, in both drama and the novel, indicates, as Lukács points out, the collapse of a vital relationship to "action and to the possibility of action" (Jameson 1981, 200–201). Whether one shares the precise horizons of Lukács or not, it is clear that this type of writing results in a paucity of events and therefore comports a significant erosion of the narrative, or storytelling, interest in drama and prose fiction.

This devitalization of the narrative element has been correctly described by one critic as a "fundamental dramaturgical event of Individualism" (Suvin 1984, 45). The preoccupation with the psychological, inner life of the character, privatization of the dramatic action, and the sense of helplessness and impasse—all of which, as we have seen, point to the individualist ideology of the bourgeois drama—also add up to a form that already precludes the possibility of most actions, and therefore of a storytelling interest primarily concerned with time and change. The very enlargement of the status of the main dramatis personae into seemingly "authentic" individuals, whose inner tensions and conflicts then become the main focus of dramaturgic interest, makes a play not the dramatization of a story as much as the revelation of a psychological (often pathological) state. As a result, events become merely peripheral and do not form the mainspring of a play's experience, which is usually one of static, intensely subjective contemplation of reality.

The restriction of the dramatic focus to a small number of isolated individual consciousnesses, often to only one, also profoundly affects the arrangement of parts and the perception of causality in a play. Consequently, instead of a multisegmented scenic structure, character-based plays tend to be divided into a few formal segments of relatively long duration. These segments are arranged in such a way that the play unfolds through a process that itself grows increasingly imperceptible, from the spectators' point of view, as the action tends to remain largely unilinear with few evental and spatial-temporal variations. In other words, the passage of time becomes qualitatively unvaried, less and less perceptible as a possibility of choice and change. This negative perception of time is further reinforced in the Ibsenian kind of dramaturgy in which the dramatized action itself is often conceived as a fatal consequence of an action in the undramatized past. As Beckerman observes,

> Ibsen's structural skill lies in his ability to utilize the past as a scourge of the present, to introduce it as a force at crucial moments, and thus to link the characters with their own past and with that of others. (1970, 186–87)

Consequently, the whole pattern of experience usually becomes self-reflexive, and the few events that do occur are often perceived as tragically inconsequential.

To sum up, the erosion of the storytelling interest in particular, and the aesthetic prejudice against vigorous events in general,[7] correspond to a shift in the focus of interest from the community and communal relationships to the individual and his consciousness. Whereas a play in the prebourgeois traditions presented a communal situation and external action, an individualist play presents "non-narrative felt life" (Rosenberg 1958, 178). As a result, for all its emotional intensity and psychological depth, a play in this tradition usually fails to embody the kind of storytelling interest that was found in, say, the Mysteries, *Mankind, Doctor Faustus,* or *King Lear.*

Radical Alternative Drama

Such an interest returned to drama in a significant and sustained manner only with what I identified above as the radical alternative drama, which, flourishing mainly during periods of political activism and revolutionary upsurge in this century, is characterized by its conscious preference (in both dramaturgy and performance) for the forms and conventions of the popular, plebeian traditions. This predilection, in conjunction with what may be called an expressly ludic (as opposed to illusionist) concept of the theater—a concept in which, as we shall see, the elements of vigorous fun and cognitive enrichment are integrally linked—invariably led to story-based dramaturgic constructions.

In postwar English drama the two dramaturgic paradigms can be seen coexisting and clashing precisely in the juxtaposition or opposition of Arden and the other playwrights of his generation. For example, Osborne's play *Look Back in Anger,* which inaugurated the postwar revival of drama in England and set the model for the new playwrights and directors, stresses an isolated character and his consciousness rather than events. It possesses, therefore, little narrative interest. Throughout that play the narrative situation remains a virtually static permutation of a single plot device: the girl leaves the boy who takes up with another girl until the first girl returns. The dramaturgic means employed—the uniform and enclosed private space and time; the unilinear causal flow of the action (which seems to possess neither a clear beginning nor a categorical conclusion); the severely restricted range of dramatic activity (naturalistically verisimilar verbal dialogue and, largely, monologue); the highly individualized, simultaneously representative, and eccentric central character with a weighty past; and the unvaried plot structure—all undercut whatever narrative interest the play might possess and instead reinforce the feeling of stasis.

The same structural predilection for the character (as opposed to the story) can be seen in the early plays of Wesker and Delaney. As for the extreme case of Pinter, another major contemporary of Arden, the question of story as a significant dramaturgic element does not even arise. In his drama, as in Beckett's, human relationships and communication are experienced not only as problematic but as impossible because every gesture and word addressed by one character to another becomes ambiguous, mysterious, even menacing, and events themselves are neither logical nor consequential.

In contrast to such dramaturgies, Arden's, like Brecht's, has from the beginning sought to restore to the theater its traditional storytelling interest. "When I construct a play," Arden said in a 1961 interview with Tom Milne and Clive Godwin, "I think first in terms of a story." This creative procedure, the emphasis on narrative, is evident in all his plays as the shaping principle behind their structure and style. It allows his work to be distinguished sharply from the character-based dramaturgies of the past.

Conceived and presented as interesting tales or fables, Arden's plays are marked by vigor, vitality, epic magnitude, and highly diversified spatial-temporal as well as agential structures, embodying a large number and variety of evolving events, frequently changing situations, and a wide range of relationships signifying the plurality of social existence and experience. In the early plays, the stories were invented by Arden, while in the later ones they are usually derived from history and legend. However, they all combine a strong storytelling interest with sociohistorical emphasis. The stories, even when they are invented and not derived from folkloric tradition or popular history, invariably possess the flavor, vigor, and eventfulness of a traditional narrative, signifying a predominantly functional rather than indicial emphasis. In fact, Arden's move away from the invented stories of contemporary life of the early plays (*The Waters of Babylon, Live Like Pigs, The Happy Haven, Serjeant Musgrave's Dance,* and *The Workhouse Donkey*) toward the more derived stories of his later historical-legendary plays (*Armstrong's Last Goodnight, Left-Handed Liberty, The Island of the Mighty,* and *The Non-Stop Connolly Show*) may be related to his preference for dealing with cognitively significant concerns and issues within the frame of what, as we saw in the last chapter, he calls poetic truth. It is poetic in the sense of the old ballads, that is, overarching and collectively representative. According to Arden,

The essential element of the theatre is that there the writer speaks through the lips of his actors; it does not necessarily give him an opportunity for direct statement. He has to find a fable that will itself express his image of the world and express it in a way that will make sense to the audience. (1964b, 705)

His early concern with "the problem of translating the concrete life of today into terms of poetry that shall at the one time both illustrate that

life and set it within the historical and legendary tradition of our culture,"
and his desire to give his plays "an impact derived from something more
than contemporary documentary facility" (Arden 1965c, 125, 128) was
lost on both London critics and audiences whose responses were condi-
tioned by the dominant dramaturgical tradition. Furthermore, one may
well speculate that the unclear and unsharp ways in which the social
conflicts of postwar England were negotiated led to great difficulties for a
dramatist striving for a historical perspective on events.

By turning to historical and legendary sources for his stories, Arden
was also reversing the course taken by modern drama centuries ago. This
course is described by Beckerman thus.

> The most revolutionary change in European theatre occurred when
> artists went to observed life for story material . . . it was not until
> the seventeenth century for comedy and the eighteenth century for
> the rest of drama that dramatists consistently utilized contemporary
> life as a story source. Although it is true that until then observed
> experience had always found its way into the drama in some man-
> ner, it had done so within the frame of myth, legend, and romance.
> In the nineteenth century the practice of selecting the story from life
> triumphed and, though frequently challenged, still remains the
> dominant method for the creation of plot. Audiences have come to
> see the stories as documentary cases subject to the test of personal
> credibility. (1970, 172–73)

It was precisely this illusionist "test of personal credibility" on the part of
his audiences that Arden hoped to prevent by setting (and distancing) his
plays in historical and legendary pasts. In dealing with specific histories,
as we shall see later, he interpolated a good deal of legendary and folkloric material and conceived the dramatic actions as parables rather than
as documents or chronicles. This enabled him to retain and emphasize
the storytelling interest of a play while presenting events in a more
inclusive, complex, dynamic, and therefore more profoundly historical
and socially representative—that is, poetic—perspective.

Story and Plot

One way of looking at a play's use of story as the structural basis of
dramatic action is to apply to it Beckerman's notion of a plot-story ratio.

Using plot to signify the "sequence of units of activity" actually dramatized and presented in a play, and story to designate "all incidents and activities that occur before, after, and during [a] play, onstage *and* offstage," Beckerman argues that the kind of proportion that a dramatist establishes between these categories "sets preconditions for his dramatic structure" and reflects "the magnitude of the play as conceived by the artist." Examination of plot-story ratio, therefore, provides "insight into the intended scope of a work, and thereby into the problem of how parts relate to the audience and to each other" (Beckerman 1970, 171–74).

As useful as Beckerman's description of the plot-story ratio is, it is not without limitations. It provides little help, for example, in dealing with a specific kind of dramaturgic practice. Beckerman himself mentions only two possibilities for the plot-story ratio: either it is one-to-one, as in Shakespeare and Brecht, or the plot is smaller than the story, as in Ibsen and the Ibsenians. He fails to take into account a third, cognitively significant and historically verifiable, possibility in which the plot is larger than the story—as in Brecht's *The Caucasian Chalk-Circle* in which the story is framed within a much larger and deeper (though etymologically related) notion of history.

Arden's later historical-legendary plays, as will be seen, are precisely of this third kind. Therefore, in dealing with them I shall use the term *story-telling* instead of *plot-story ratio. Story-telling,* in my use of the term, implies a pragmatic, dialogic activity that is immanent to the *context* (rather than only the *text*) and in which somebody is saying something specific, at a specific moment, for a specific purpose.

In Arden's dramaturgy, as in those of the Elizabethans and Brecht— as, indeed, in all story-based dramaturgies—an initial situation gives us all the basic terms of the action to follow. The action ends after the tension and conflict generated by the precipitating event have been fully resolved, leaving, as it were, no loose ends. This gives to his plays a sharply defined beginning and a strongly marked ending, and it allows the presented action to come across as a self-contained logical whole that requires little or no prehistory or posthistory. *The Waters of Babylon* is remarkable for its loose, Music Hall or variety type of structure. But it also possesses a strong story line. It dramatizes a thrilling tale of great intricacy in an exciting theatrical form. The play's story concerns a Polish émigré in London, Krank, who is at once a pimp, an impostor, the owner of a notorious lodging-cum-brothel establishment, and (under a different name) an architect's assistant. This genial man of several identi-

ties has a shady existence. Anticipating trouble from the local authorities
in connection with his "lodging house," he commissions the services of
one Charlie Butterthwaite, a colorful and ingenious fixer, to bail him out
of his legal and financial difficulties. Meanwhile, another complication
develops in Krank's eventful life. His friend and compatriot Paul, to
whom he owes five hundred pounds, tries to blackmail him into joining
a plot to assassinate Soviet leaders during a London visit. Eager to raise
the money to pay his debt to Paul, and so to escape this blackmail,
Krank, again helped by Butterthwaite, conceives a scheme to defraud a
certain municipal fund. Complications and accidents follow, in rapid and
hilarious succession, as everything goes wrong. The scheme to rig the
lottery becomes a fiasco, Paul's bomb is stolen (perhaps by an IRA-
sympathizer, Cassidy), and Krank is finally exposed and accidentally
shot by Paul.

The "chrono-logical" sequence of this double-plot story is clear.[8] It
begins with the Krank-Butterthwaite collaboration, to which all subsequent events are in one way or another connected, and ends when the
collaboration fails and Krank is accidentally killed. The play is constructed so that the entire story unfolds within the duration of the plot,
thus establishing a one-to-one ratio between the two.

In comparison with the intricate narrative of *The Waters of Babylon,*
Arden's second professionally staged play, *Live Like Pigs,* has a simpler
story to tell. It concerns the conflict that results when a family of gypsies,
the Sawneys, are forced to move into a new, "proper" house by the
welfare authorities. Again, establishing a one-to-one plot-story ratio,
Arden opens the play with the event that precipitates the subsequent
action and forms its initial situation. The first scene shows the Sawneys
moving into their officially allotted house. Their encounters with a government official, with each other, and with a neighbor reveal what kind
of people they are and how they are responding to this virtually forced
"rehabilitation." Paraphrased, the scene roughly reads like this: "Once
upon a time, the welfare authorities in contemporary England moved a
household of unwilling gypsies into a Council Estate house in a middle-
class neighborhood, which was totally incompatible with their free,
boisterous, and amoral life-style. . . ." The central conflict of the play,
developed with logical stringency, is that between the Sawneys and their
outraged neighbors. It eventually explodes into a full-fledged riot, which
leads to the disintegration and evacuation of the undesirable but un-
quenchable gypsy household. Thus, the play's ending is equally emphatic in its conclusiveness.

The central conflict in *Live Like Pigs* is the direct result of the introduction of a new, alien, and incompatible element into an existing situation. It is resolved when this alien element is removed and the normal—
that is, polite, urban, and middle-class—order is restored. The central
events of Arden's two other plays from this period, *Serjeant Musgrave's
Dance* and *The Workhouse Donkey,* result from a similar cause and constellation. The plot, as well as the story, in each of these plays commences with the arrival of some alien element into a closely knit and
more or less isolated community, threatening the normal state of affairs
and relationships and leading to a good deal of confusion. The sequence
of events that this inaugural event precipitates is concluded and resolved
only when the alien element is expelled from the community.

In the "unhistorical parable" of *Serjeant Musgrave's Dance,* the
action—which is modeled on the traditional pattern of the Mummers'
Play of Plough Monday (cf. O'Connell 1971, and Forsas-Scott 1983)—
takes place in a northern colliery town whose only connection with other
parts of the country is by means of a waterway. For most of the play's
action, the waterway remains frozen, because of winter, and so the town
is cut off from the outside world. The town's economy, too, is paralyzed
by a colliers' strike, which has made for a very tense situation. Into this
explosive situation Musgrave and his men are inserted ostensibly to recruit for Her Majesty's army but actually to bring home to the local
community the horror of colonial wars. This new complication in an
already complicated situation results, among other things, in acts of
violence that leave two men dead. The complication is resolved at the
end when the thaw sets in. Dragoons arrive just in time to crush Musgrave's violent and idiosyncratic antiwar demonstration in the market
square. The conclusiveness of this terminal event and the restoration of
the "normal" order is further reinforced by the Officer's remark: "The
winter's broken up. Let normal life begin again" (III.i). The last phrase,
"begin again," is picked up and repeated in the Bargee's drunken circular
song and dance.

Like *Musgrave, The Workhouse Donkey* is set in an isolated northern
community. The central figure in the story is the colorful, ingenious,
roguish, and benevolent Charlie Butterthwaite (here a Labour alderman)
whom we met in *The Waters of Babylon.* The story is mainly concerned
with his decline and fall from official, or "legitimate," politics. However,
his fall and the events that bring it about are intricately related to the
appointment and the eventual withdrawal of a new police chief, Feng,
who is a stranger to the community and whose disciplinarian, morally

strict, and legalistic attitudes are incompatible with the easygoing morality of the place. We may read the story as one of Feng's comically
pathetic sojourn in this community, or as one of Butterthwaite's spectacular decline and fall, since each is but the flip side of the other. The
story's inaugural event in either reading is the introduction of an alien
element, Feng, into the "normal" condition of this secluded community.
Similarly, the story's terminal event in either reading is the fall of Butterthwaite from official politics and the related removal of Feng from the
community. Arden has cleverly incorporated a double event at both the
beginning and the end of the dramatized action. The opening scene is a
public ceremony, which is also used by the mayor to welcome the new
police chief. This scene shows, among other things, Feng's firm resolve
to root out crime and moral evil from the community as well as Butterthwaite's hostile and distrustful response to him. Similarly, the last
scene involves another public ceremony, which is disrupted by Butterthwaite and his plebeian supporters. During this last sequence of action,
Feng resigns, to the relief of everybody in the play, and decides to return
to London, while the troublemaking Butterthwaite, already expelled
from official Labour politics, is physically removed from the stage by the
police. The conclusiveness of the narrative action is underscored by Arden when he ends the scene with various gestures of political and personal reconciliation and a chorus indicating the resumption of the usual
two-faced relationship of contention and collusion between the two "legitimate" parties—that is, the restoration of the normal order, which
was threatened equally (though from opposite ends) by Butterthwaite
and Feng.

Arden's practice of making his dramatic action a well-defined and
self-contained whole is equally evident in his later plays, which derive
from historical and/or legendary sources. Since the action in these plays
is expressly historical and political, Arden strives to give it completeness
not only in terms of the play's microcosm but in terms of the implicated
social history. He usually begins by setting up the significant background
or the sociohistorical context of the play's main action, thereby ground-
ing the centrally dramatized conflict in history. As a result, the sequence
of events that forms the main body (or the plot) of the play's action often
begins appreciably later than the play itself.

The story of *Armstrong's Last Goodnight* is derived from a sixteenth-
century ballad. In adapting it for the theater Arden retained much of its
storytelling excitement and folkloric color. But he also made free and

imaginative use of various historical sources for significant elaboration and historicization of the popular legend. The play, like the original ballad, concerns the conflict between a border outlaw, Johnny Armstrong, and the king of Scotland. Yet it does not commence with events depicting this conflict. It opens instead with a conference convened between the royal commissioners of Scotland and England to negotiate a peace treaty between the two realms. There's a storytelling directness in Lindsay's prologue.

> There was held, at the Berwick-upon-Tweed, in the fifteenth year of the reign of James the Fifth, by the Grace of God King of Scotland, and in the nineteenth year of Henry the Eight, by the Grace of God King of England, ane grave conference and consultation betwixt Lords Commissioner frae baith the realms, anent the lang peril of warfare that trublit they twa sovereigns and the leige peoples thereunto appertainen. The intent bean, to conclude the said peril and to secure ane certain time of peace, prosperity, and bliss on ilk side of the border. (I.i)

The subsequent action dramatizes the meeting between the two parties of royal commissioners. In the course of this meeting we learn, among other things, that a major cause of tension between the two kingdoms is the menace of the border outlaws. The English, accusing the Scots of encouraging these outlaws, insist on a clear guarantee from the Scottish king that the raids across the border will stop. We also learn that among all the Border outlaws Johnny Armstrong is the "hardest to suppress" and that Scotland has already appointed "ane confidential emmissair to treat furthwith Armstrong, seek some fair means of agreement, and in the end secure baith the lealty and obedience of this dangerous freebooter" (I.i).

This confidential, royal "emmissair" turns out to be Lindsay himself. His vow to wear his official coat "nae further / Till Armstrang be brocht / Intil the King's Peace and order" (I.ii) forms the inaugural event of the play's story and the beginning of the main sequence of its events.

Just as Arden provides the historical context by means of a dramatized general introduction before the commencement of the main story, he also inserts into the play what may be called a general conclusion. This conclusion follows the story's final event—namely, the treacherous execution of Armstrong—and, like the general introduction,

it runs through two scenes. Its function is to underline the story's parabolic significance as well as to remind us that Armstrong's story is but a
small part of a vaster, immeasurably more complex, and by definition
inconcludable narrative of history. Lindsay's words to the king reinforce
the definitiveness of the story's ending, but, by their ironic emphasis on
"this year," they also underline the open-endedness of history and the
temporary nature of political success.

> Naething mair, sire. The man is deid, there will be nae war with
> England: this year. There will be but small turbulence upon the
> Border: this year. And what we hae done is no likely to be forgot-
> ten: this year, the neist year, and mony year after that. Sire, you are
> King of Scotland. (III.xvi)

Similarly, his last comments, which are directly addressed to the spectators and probe into the "moral" of the story, unmistakably embody the
gesture of winding up.

Thus, the introductory and concluding sequences in *Armstrong's Last
Goodnight* function as an explicit political and historical frame that both
encloses the personal story of Armstrong and gives it a cognitive open-
endedness. This dramaturgical practice has the effect of making the plot,
in a seeming paradox, larger than the story.

Left-Handed Liberty, which is about the Magna Carta, dramatizes a
complex period of medieval English history from an ironically modern
point of view. Arden uses a rich mixture of discussion, satirical ballads,
direct commentary, and dramatized sequences of action. But he also uses
well-defined cutoff points for his narrative: the rebellious barons con-
fronting King John as the beginning and John's premature death on the
eve of his march on rebel-occupied London as the ending. This allows
the play's action to acquire a storylike structure.

The revolt of a nobility against its monarch and the rather ludicrous
death of that monarch in the midst of an armed conflict are by themselves
emphatic and significant as the inaugural and the terminal events of a
narrative sequence. In Arden's dramaturgical treatment, however, they
acquire an even greater emphasis because of the narrative directness with
which they are introduced to the spectators. The play opens with a
prologue in which Pandulph, in a manner reminiscent of Music Hall
chatter ("well, you may read your Bibles, it is all there"), introduces the
medieval world-picture in which the Earth-centered Ptolemaic cosmol-

ogy and the Church-dominated medieval world view are presented as analogical and interrelated. Then, after a brief first scene, which dramatizes John's last meeting with his ailing mother, we are given a spatial-temporally unlocated scene, which immediately precedes and introduces the opening event of the main sequence. The scene consists of a direct address, spoken by John himself, who gives us a quick résumé of the developments leading to the baronial revolt of 1215 (I.ii). The scene that immediately follows this direct address dramatizes the revolt, and thus the play's story begins. Similarly, in another unlocated scene preceding the last one, John makes another direct address to the audience and introduces the play's terminal event: his premature and, from his own point of view, untimely death.

An important effect of these speeches, with their directness and apparent insistence on precision (about dates, places, and so on), is that they not only prepare the spectators for the events that follow, but they implicitly involve the audience in framing the play's action. Moreover, such distinctly defined beginnings and endings give the play a quasi-epic or storytelling structure. Framed thus, its action becomes, at least on one level, the story of the last turbulent years of King John's reign—John himself refers to it at one point as the "dramatization of the life and death of me" (III.vi). At the same time, in the interaction of direct-address frame and framed presentation, of story and plot, the logical import of the play's main event—the rebellion leading to an ironically polysemous Magna Carta—becomes analyzable in its main meanings until they are exhausted and the story is completed. For, although Arden gives *Left-Handed Liberty* a strong narrative interest, he does not allow it to obscure the larger historical interest and significance of the play's action. In fact, the play is concerned not simply with the presentation of a specific annalslike or chronological history in a storylike form (although it is concerned with that, too) but also with a critical examination of it. This examination and analysis are facilitated by the use of an epic or storytelling form, which allows Arden to repeatedly interrupt the flow of the action, to depart significantly from the official Magna Carta story (the chronology), and to intersperse presented activity throughout with direct comment and analysis. Major examples of such analysis are found at the beginning and near the end, and they are almost entirely expository and discursive in nature. Through a variety of techniques, involving a sophisticated combination of direct commentary, out-of-character dialogue, and interspersed bits of dramatized activity, we are given a fairly detailed analysis of the general historical context, the genesis, and, above all, the larger implications of the charter.

These examples of largely direct historical discussion do not, however, detract from the play's immediate storytelling interest. On the contrary, placed as most of them are at the beginning and near the end, these segments also function as a general introduction and general conclusion to the play's action, and, enclosing it as it were within a bracket or frame, they give sharper definition to the logical structure of its events. Just as the storytelling interest is not allowed to obscure the more profound historical implications, the historical framework is not allowed to devitalize the play's interest at the level of the story. Arden has here (as he did in *Armstrong's Last Goodnight*) progressed to a dramaturgy that sets the well-defined narrative logic of action within a larger dialectical logic of history. This makes for a remarkably dynamic form, which, through a complex interplay of techniques and conventions, requires of the spectator an alertness and agility of mind as he shifts his imaginative gaze between history and story, between life and art, between a given imaginary sequence of events and their larger historical significance and context, and between the spectator's own time and a historical past.

It is clear, then, that in Arden's drama the plot-story ratio is either one-to-one (as in the early plays) or larger than one (as in the later plays). Moreover, the action in his plays, opening and ending with definitively inaugural and conclusive events, constitutes a logical whole. This sense of narrative wholeness is further enhanced by the fact that Arden's plays usually open with some form of direct address, formal verse, or song, which signals the play's commencement. Also, the opening action in a play by Arden invariably involves either highly peculiar people performing some ordinary function peculiarly (such as Krank eating his breakfast or the gypsies moving into a new place) or people involved in some significant and singular business (a public ceremony, a political summit, and so on). Similarly, his plays always end with some emphatically conclusive event (such as the expulsion or death of the protagonist), which is almost invariably followed by some form of choral or formal comment. This means that Arden never cuts off an action in the middle of an emotionally tense moment but allows the action to subside and the atmosphere to relax, making an objective response possible on the part of the spectator. For example, in *Serjeant Musgrave's Dance,* after the emotionally tense moment of Musgrave's maniacal antiwar demonstration and its failure, Arden proceeds not only with the "begin again" song and dance but adds another scene, which presents a more sober, postmortem analysis of Musgrave's position and role. The play ends on a note of cautious but unmistakable optimism with Attercliffe's words "They're going to hang us up a length higher nor most apple-trees grow, Serjeant. D'you reckon we can start an orchard?" (III.ii). This remark is clearly a piece of *Galgenhumor* "in which a condemned criminal dispels our pity by turning his situation to witty advantage," which prevents us from making any intense "psychical expenditures" and frees us to think about the situation in a more relaxed manner (Eagleton 1981, 157–58).

Needless to say, this dramaturgic practice is in direct contrast to the naturalist tradition in which the dramatic action commences almost imperceptibly, without any formal signal, and with the characters usually involved in some perfectly ordinary, everyday activity or routine domestic chore. Similarly, naturalist plays tend to end—again, without any formal signal—in a moment of high emotional intensity, before that intensity has had time to work itself out and subside. Such imperceptible beginning and ending of the action (as well as its smooth, causal flow) in a "well-made" or Ibsenian play heightens the illusion of spatial-temporal continuity and contiguity between life and play. On the contrary, Arden's drama, by frankly revealing rather than concealing the boundaries that define the scope of its narrative action, by clearly displaying, as it were, the seams that bind the events together into a complete fictive whole, stresses its own status as a hypothetically and artfully constructed topos or semantic space, the relation of which to empirical life and experience is like that of an exemplum to the thing exemplified.[9] Conceived and presented in this fashion, a play becomes not an illusionistic reflection of some given reality but frankly an artificial and heuristic model of that reality.

Another, and related, consequence of this practice of unfolding the whole story within the duration of a plot is that the logic of events becomes obvious to the spectators. We clearly see not only what happens but also how and why it happens. In *The Workhouse Donkey,* Butterthwaite falls because of his recklessness and refusal to conform to the established norms as well as because of the treachery and betrayal by some of his friends and colleagues. We are clearly shown his reckless acts as well as their treachery. Feng, similarly, must go because he, too—albeit in his own, opposite way—refuses to conform to the local establishment. The Tories and Labourites join hands in the end because, their electoral rivalries notwithstanding, they share a vested interest in maintaining and perpetuating the established order. All of these factors and their actual manifestations are shown to us directly in the play's events. The consequences, thus, are evidently related to specific and directly dramatized actions, choices, or responses. They are not universalized as part of a general human fate or condition, or mystified as the results of the malevolent operation of some outside force.

Multlinear Composition

Characteristically, the sharply defined and enclosed form of Arden's drama, based as it is on a preponderance of story over plot, embodies an extensive and diversified internal structure, often all the way from the level of whole sequences to the basic and smallest unit of an event. It is usually what may be called a multilinear structure; in other words, his plots usually contain more than one sequence of events, each sequence being a potential or actual story in itself.[10] For example, the main action in *The Waters of Babylon,* as we saw, comprises two distinct narrative strands, one related to Krank's problems with the municipal authorities and his desperate attempt to overcome them, the other to Paul's bomb plot and his decision to blackmail Krank into permitting the use of a section of his brothel-cum-lodging-house to manufacture the dangerous device. Furthermore, Arden gives the play a form similar to a Music Hall comedy or variety show. This enables him to incorporate a number of other smaller and subsidiary narrative strands or episodes, each of which produces its own little sequence of events with its own particular interest: for example, Krank's sexual involvement with his architect boss, Barbara; Loap's affair with Theresa; her brother's melodramatic reaction to her "immoral" profession; and Barbara's successful seduction of a West Indian but zealously puritanical municipal councillor. Likewise, in *Live Like Pigs,* the central conflict between the Jacksons and the Sawneys is juxtaposed with conflicts representing other narrative strands—the conflict between the Sawneys and the authorities (the government official, the police, the doctor), the one between the Sailor and his wife, the Sawneys's conflict with the Blackmouth, and generational and marital conflicts within the Jackson family. The Old Croaker and her daughter create their own sequence of events. Similarly, in *Serjeant Musgrave's Dance,* the central action of Musgrave's response to the outrage and brutality of colonial war is juxtaposed with another major narrative strand that runs throughout the play—the colliers' strike and the authorities' response to it.

Although Arden's interest in multilinear narrative is evident throughout, it reaches its climax in his later historical-legendary plays. The action of *Serjeant Musgrave's Dance*, or that of *The Workhouse Donkey*, had involved an entire community, from the rulers to the ruled. It had, therefore, embodied a correspondingly large and diversified narrative structure. This diversity was significantly enhanced when the focus of Arden's drama shifted from local communities and municipalities to complex national and international polities. The process reached its peak in *The Island of the Mighty*, which focused on vast and complex constellations of ethnic, class, and ethical situations that acquired epic proportions and demanded a trilogy. D'Arcy and Arden repeated this epic structure in *The Non-Stop Connolly Show*, which was conceived and presented as a day-long theatrical event.

Arden's usual method is to present an initial situation and impulse (the arrival of a new police chief in *The Workhouse Donkey*, the rebellion of the barons in *Left-Handed Liberty*, the invasion of Britain by land-seeking, starving peoples from the continent in *The Island of the Mighty*) and then to dramatize different responses to it. These in their turn create situations that are responded to differently by various individuals or groups, and so forth. For example, *The Island of the Mighty* begins with the English invasion of Britain. In the first scene we see Arthur's militaristic response as the self-appointed protector of Britain. The scene that follows dramatizes the response of Balin and Balan to the same situation but from a genuinely patriotic position: having lost their family and property, they have actually suffered at the hands of the invaders. Their response, in its turn, is responded to by Merlin who asks them to join Arthur's Roman army. The early events of the subsequent scene show the different responses of the two brothers to Merlin's suggestion. And so on. It is this method of progressive diversification and proliferation of the narrative that produces the multilinear quality of Arden's drama. It also allows each sequence to possess its own distinct beginning and end (such as the parting of ways between Balin and Balan and their ultimate reunion in a blind, fatal combat). A play composed thus acquires a complex structure of stories within stories.

The illusionist dramaturgy concentrates on a single sequence of events that appears incomplete. In composing a plot it follows a unilinear pattern of intensity, creating a single, unified emphasis and a severely restricted narrative focus, which must concentrate on that emphasis entirely and exclusively. Even diverse strands that might be inherent in the story are, through manipulation of the plot, strictly subordinated to the main emphasis (for example, the Mrs. Linde–Krogstad strand in *A Doll's House* and the Regina-Engstrand one in *Ghosts*). As a result, the dramaturgic action acquires a rigidly centripetal and revelatory form or design.[11] In Arden's plays, on the contrary, the various narrative strands are only loosely and generally related (the sequence leading to Butterthwaite's burgling of the Town Hall, for example, and other sequences in *The Workhouse Donkey*), so that each creates an immediate and local narrative interest and emphasis. They crisscross the entire action of a play and give it a centrifugal, or epic, form. As we move from one scene to another—or sometimes, even within a single scene, from one event to another—we experience an unmistakable and theatrically exciting shift in narrative focus. The diversified shape that this process imposes on the action (encompassing, as we shall shortly see, a rich variety of times, places, and events) creates the experience of a panoramic view of a dramaturgic constellation that signifies life at large rather than that of a keyhole peek into a private, privatized, and severely limited world, as in the illusionist, character-based dramaturgy.

Spatial-temporal Variation

In drama, spatial and temporal variations usually correspond to the number and length of the formal segments into which a play is divided. In chapter 1, I mentioned that in naturalist dramaturgy, which traditionally uses a unilinear plot encompassing a relatively narrow range of time and place, the number of formal divisions in a play is relatively small, and each of these formal segments tends to be relatively long. As a result, the action unfolds uniformly, evenly, and almost imperceptibly throughout a play, numbing the spectators' awareness of the fictionality of the performed actions. We also saw that, in contrast to this, the diversified structures of medieval and Elizabethan (particularly Shakespearean) drama, which often use multilinear plots, employ more numerous and relatively shorter formal divisions, commonly identified as scenes. Hamlet's preference for a play "well-digested in the scenes" (II.ii.460) is the artistic preference of a whole dramaturgic tradition.

The basic compositional unit of Arden's dramaturgy, like that of Shakespeare or Brecht, is such a scene. His division of a dramatic action into a number of short, discrete scenes corresponds to the breakdown of an epic into episodes. Arden has used episodic structure from the beginning of his artistic career. Although in *The Waters of Babylon* the scenes are not textually identified as such, they are there nevertheless and can be easily distinguished. They are delimited by means of shifts in spatial-temporal location as well as shifts in the narrative focus. For example, Act One can be shown to consist of three distinct scenes. In the first, the action takes place inside Krank's house one early morning. The central event of this scene is the commissioning of Butterthwaite to devise a plan for putting Krank in favor with the local administration. The scene changes when the action moves to a street outside a London Transport public lavatory, and its central event is Krank's change of identity from the owner of a notorious lodging house to a respectable architect's assistant. The third scene takes us to the architect's office where Paul declares his intention to use Krank's house to manufacture a bomb.

Since *The Waters of Babylon* uses a stage convention different from illusionism (that is, from the visual illusion of shifting locations), so that the stage can be verbally and imaginatively reconstructed to represent different places, the change from one scene to another does not require an overt interruption in the performance. The characters merely walk around to arrive at a new "location." Nonetheless, the action is internally interrupted, since each shift in location and narrative focus is indicated to the audience by a direct comment. When Krank arrives at the lavatory (in what I identify as the second scene of Act One), he informs the spectators:

Here is that extremely convenient arrangement, a gentlemen's convenience with a door at either side of it. A most remarkable, and, I think, beautiful phenomenon. I am about to be reborn: in this twentieth-century peculiar ceremonial womb, glazed tiles and electric light beneath the gold pavement stones of London, hygienic underground renascence, for me, is daily routine.

Similarly, after his return from the lavatory (at the beginning of what I identify as the third scene in this act) we are again directly addressed by Krank who informs us about his new identity and destination. The only other example of this in Arden's work occurs in *The Royal Pardon,* a children's play written with D'Arcy. This play is formally divided into two acts of almost equal length (in terms of performance time), a division that designates a shift of location from England to France. However, each act is internally (not explicitly) subdivided into several scenes. There are four such scenes in the first act, depicting the place where the players and Luke encounter the police, the makeshift gaol, somewhere on the

road to London, and the English king's palace. Similarly, the second act
is divided into the boat (crossing the English channel), the French coast,
the office of French customs, and the French king's palace. The scenic
division is not textually identified or marked by the playwrights because
the play is dramaturgically designed to require no scenery, thus permitting a continuous and brisk performance of each act.

Except for these two plays, in all of Arden's major works the internal division of the action into scenes is further reinforced by a formally or
textually explicated division. The scenes in these plays are identified and
numerically marked, or even—as in the case of *The Hero Rises Up, The
Island of the Mighty*, and the Connolly plays—given short descriptive
titles and emblems. These explicit divisions identify and stress variations
in time and space. Thus, in *Armstrong's Last Goodnight* the scenically
divided action moves rapidly to and fro between the king's palace, Armstrong's castle, and the forest that serves as a wild frontier separating the
other two spaces. Similarly, in *Left-Handed Liberty, The Island of the
Mighty*, and *The Non-Stop Connolly Show*, the spatial-temporal continuity is constantly interrupted as the action ranges freely, in an epic sweep
rare outside the medieval and Shakespearean traditions, through different
parts of medieval England, Arthurian Britain, modern Europe, and the
United States.

A scene is a situational unit possessing unity of time and space. In an
epic narrative, however, this unity may be broken down into smaller
situations, signifying a process of increasingly finer variations in time
and place. In Arden's drama, this process is found at its best in *The Island
of the Mighty* and *The Non-Stop Connolly Show*. The location of *The Island*
as a whole is Arthurian Britain in early sixth century. Its action spans an
unidentified period in far-flung parts of the island. This period, however,
is distinctly divided into three major phases, corresponding to the three
parts of the trilogy. The first part begins with reports of an immanent
English invasion of Britain and Arthur's preparations to meet it; it ends
with the news that "an enormous force of English" has been sighted off
the coast. The second part mainly "tells" the story of the decline and fall
of Arthur, who is faced with both the English invasion and a massive
popular revolt, led by Medraut, against him and his Roman principles. It
begins with preparations for the campaign against the British and ends
with a brutal war in which both Medraut and Arthur are destroyed. Part
Three, the coda of the trilogy, is subtitled *A Handful of Watercress: Con-
cerning Merlin—How He Needed to Be Alone and Then How He Needed Not*

to Be Alone. It dramatizes the parable of Merlin's madness and recovery, ending with his death.

Each of these parts not only contains a main story but includes several others. Thus, in the first part, besides the picaresque adventures of Balin and Balan, we have the stories of the Bondwoman and the bandit Garlon, of King Pellam and Arthur's expedition against him, and of the pagan Picts and the disintegration of their tribal culture. In the second part, too, several stories—among them the legend of Branwen, the parable of the two mutually distrustful tribes, and Arthur's marriage with Gwenhwyvar and her ferocious hostility—are presented. The third part, set chronologically after Arthur's death and containing some episodes that are not strictly connected with Merlin's story, not only takes a major strand of the main narrative on to its conclusion (Merlin's death) but winds it up didactically by bringing into a sharp and coherent cognitive focus the diverse motifs and emphases of the trilogy as a whole.

Each of these three major segments is further subdivided into scenes. The first part contains ten such scenes, the second part eleven, and the third part thirteen. Although on the whole these scenes contribute to a chronologically progressive pattern of narrative action, they do not always exist in consecutive relationship to the preceding and following scenes. For example, the actions in the first and the second halves of Part One, Scene Four, are temporally parallel rather than consecutive. After Balan wins the battle with the old Pictish "king" and becomes the new king in Galloway, Merlin, in his role of epic and omnipresent narrator, tells us:

> I was elsewhere when all of this
> Went on—I will tell you the place:
> The land of Wirral, to the south,
> Where Pellam King has tried to bring disgrace
> To my General's face.
>
> (I.iv)

By means of this simple verbal device we are transported to a new locality, across considerable geographical distance and backward in time, as well as to a different sequence of events. This example also shows that, although the explicit division in the play is confined to scenes, a scene itself is often internally subdivided into smaller situational units. To illustrate this further, let us examine another example from the trilogy.

In terms of spatial-temporal situation, Part One, Scene Three, can be subdivided into three situational units. In the first, the time is evening. The action takes place at the gate of the ancient fort in Carlisle, described by Merlin in a rhymed verse as

> Built by the Roman Caesars four centuries past and gone.
> Precise and rectilinear in well-square blocks of stone.

As the events in this situational unit (such as Balin's encounter with the Chief Porter) make clear, the action here takes place outside the gate. It ends with Merlin's entry into the fort. The second situational unit, which begins with the meeting between Taliesin and Merlin, obviously takes place inside the fort. This change in the spatial location, however, is signified simply by the departure of the Chief Porter from the stage. There is no pause in the performance and no other visual indication of the change.

> MERLIN: . . . Will you permit me to enter?
> CHIEF PORTER: With pleasure, Chief Poet. (*He stands aside and then goes out.*)
>
> *Enter Taliesin in his official dress.*

The third situational unit, which takes place the next morning, shows Arthur in council inside the fort. Only a short pause in the performance separates it from the preceding situation. We see Merlin being led to his bed at the end of the second situational unit, and then, after the pause, an officer of Arthur's army enters with the dragon standard and other Companions and supervises the arrangements for the formal meeting.

This brief examination of *The Island of the Mighty* reveals the rapidity and ease with which the narrative unfolds, proliferates, and diversifies from sequence to sequence, episode to episode, and situational unit to situational unit, covering a great range in and of time and space. It also testifies to the fact that Arden shares with the popular dramaturgic traditions their complete disregard for the Aristotelian unity of time and place. As his predilection for the principle of variety-structure (found in the popular and traditional forms of theater) indicates, he also shares their tendency toward an increasing proliferation and diversification of narrative action. Like them, too, he prefers that performances or "shows" not be overly restricted in duration (see his remarks in the preface to *The*

Workhouse Donkey). This early tendency gained new strength after his and D'Arcy's visit to India in 1970 and their experience of the traditional folk theaters there. Enriched by this experience, they wrote the Arthurian trilogy, in which they were able to incorporate, more freely and with greater confidence, a vast amount of diverse narrative material. But it was only after their withdrawal from the established British theater that they were able to realize their desire for less restricted performances with such plays as *The Non-Stop Connolly Show.*

Arden's dramaturgy allows time and space to be perceived as varied and variable phenomena. However, the spatial-temporal variations and variability in his work is perceived mainly in qualitative terms. That is, a situation is defined and delimited socially so that it acquires a gestic quality in the Brechtian sense of the term. Each scene is written in such a way that it foregrounds some socially significant and specific aspect of the dramatized events and relationships. For example, in *The Workhouse Donkey,* the change from I.ii to I.iii signifies a socially significant shift from a private space to a public one, from the formal, constrained atmosphere of a dinner party to the casual and free atmosphere of a pub, from a restricted number of invited guests of predominantly upper-class background to a richly variegated and relatively freer community of lower-class drinkers, from a safe situation in which the main activity is polite conversation to a potentially explosive one in which the activities range from boisterous jokes, laughter, songs, betting, borrowing, and lending money, through illegal and confidential medical consultation, to the mischievously manipulated committee meeting with its mockery of "democratic procedure," and finally to a police raid.

These are clearly two qualitatively distinct social situations, or, more precisely, class chronotopes, which determine what kind of people might be found in them as well as how they might relate to each other. At the party, Wellesley, the illegimate daughter of Blomax (a local doctor of ill repute) is the only socially odd person. She is brought there by the host's son who, ignorant of her background, is romantically attracted to her. She does not find favor with the family not only because she is not "dressed well enough" but because her father is "not a persona grata" (I.iv). Similarly, when Gloria, who has aligned herself with the upper class as the glamorous hostess of a posh nightclub, suddenly shows up in the pub, Blomax welcomes her with the lines:

> Gloria! Good gracious me! We don't expect to find you these days slumming in the midst of the town in this dreary old boozing-

ken! . . . I am surprised, my dear Gloria, that you can tear yourself away from that expensive establishment of yours out there on the bypass.

This variation of situation on the level of the gestic quality of the dramatized actions, situations, and relationships allows time and space to be experienced not merely phenomenologically but with a richness suggesting politically significant texture. As the action in a play moves from scene to scene, it encompasses a wide range not only of physical time and physical space but of human existence and experience, thereby communicating a panoramic and complex view of society and of its fundamental plurality of socioeconomic levels, interests, and possibilities.

Evental Variations

In drama, events, like space and time, can be uniform or diverse. In an illusionist play, the thematic spread of events tends to be narrow. The forms of activity that they involve also tend to be more or less restricted to the empirically verisimilar (excluding the frankly artificial) and verbal (excluding the gestural or bodily) activity of everyday conversation. The order of events and their unilinear, causal arrangement further reinforce their uniformity. Such a restricted range of events and dramaturgic activity embodies and communicates a correspondingly narrow, if emotionally intense, perception of human possibilities. On the other hand, when events are richly varied and numerous, as in the popular and Elizabethan dramaturgies, and when their logical, sequential order is deliberately and repeatedly interrupted to create, as it were, cognitive openings in the formally closed logical structure of the story, the separation of one event from another becomes more pronounced, and their relationship appears to be one of juxtaposition and analogy rather than strict causality. Such epic dramaturgy communicates a correspondingly wider and more richly variegated view of human existence and experience.

The diversification of narrative in Arden's composition and its gestic emphasis go down to the basic level of the events themselves. Multilinear narratives, combining as they do several potential or actual stories within an overall epic framework, imply an abundance of events. Such dramaturgic narratives produce a loose, episodic structure in which action moves from event to event in an abrupt, staccato rhythm. Also, since in such a play each discrete event receives its own independent emphasis, we find a pattern of coemphases. This pattern is evident throughout Arden's drama, which is conceived, as he tells us, in the manner of a ballad, in which the action "goes as in Japanese films—from sitting down everyone suddenly springs into furious running, with no faltering intermediate steps" (Arden 1965c, 127).

Part One, Scene Three, of *The Island of the Mighty,* as we have seen, is remarkable for its diversity of events as well as in terms of the variety and range of the theatrical activity involved. The action ranges from cool deliberation to violent physical action; from solemn courtly to vigorous primitive ritual; from natural language to extraordinary screams, chants, and mime; from conversational prose to rhythmic verse, songs, and dance; and from a mood of serious concern to humorous, and even stock, comic acts (such as Arthur's difficulty in returning a sword to its scabbard). Furthermore, each event possesses a gestic quality that is often explicated or underlined through direct comment or formalized dialogue. For example, in the encounter between Merlin and the brothers Balin and Balan, the attitude of each carries a clear sociohistorical emphasis. Merlin consciously seeks to exploit the brothers' grievance against the English to Arthur's advantage (cf. I.ii), attempting to recruit them for the general's Roman army. Hesitation and argument on the part of the brothers about the wisdom of joining Arthur makes clear the larger sociohistorical implications of the alternatives available to them and the separate choices they make. This gestic emphasis allows the playwrights to signify and foreground elements of historical choice and political manipulation despite the more traditional Arthurian story, which emphasizes the element of fate. Such historicization of folkloric material is, as we shall see, a significant characteristic of Arden's attitude toward his traditional sources.

Arden, thus, constructs his plays epically. His plots incorporate whole stories, which allows them to come across as logically complete, well-defined, self-contained structures, marked or distanced from the empirical time and space of the performance. Scenic composition and, within each scene, a large number and variety of events (which, as formally discrete segments create their own immediate foci and interests), signify so many openings or aporias within a closed macrostructure. Since an event is a consequential unit of action involving a specific spatial-temporal situation, choice, or response—which in Arden, as in Brecht, is conceived gestically in sociohistorical terms—each such event embodies the possibility of a new beginning and therefore of altering the course of the action. These formally discrete events, in other words, function as a series of tableaux. A tableau, as Barthes defines it,

> is a pure cut-out segment with clearly defined edges, irreversible and incorruptible: everything that surrounds it is banished into nothingness, remains unnamed, while everything it admits within its field is promoted into essence, into light, into view. (1973, 70)

Such a clearly demarcated event or episode implies a process of cognitive selection and reconstruction: "it has something to say (something moral, social) but it also says that it knows how this must be done; it is simultaneously significant and propaedeutical, impressive and reflexive, moving and conscious of the channels of emotion: (p. 70). Thus, the diversity and multiplicity of formally discrete episodes in Arden's drama communicate not only a panoramic and complex view of reality but imply the variability and potential alterability of any given human situation. Consequently, a dramatic action, although a formally sealed and closed structure, comes across as cognitively open-ended. In other words, in Arden's drama, as in Brecht's, we are shown not just a given reality but the sociohistorical process through which that reality is produced, maintained, and altered. This cognitive open-endedness is particularly evident at the agential level of his dramaturgy, that is, at the level of the types of relationship and conflict that his plays characteristically dramatize.

This will be the subject of our discussion in the following chapter.

Chapter Three

Supraindividual Emphasis and Dramaturgic Agents

The decisive historical events which today's drama of great issues should be presenting takes place in huge collectives and can no longer be portrayed from the point of view of a single human being.

—Bertolt Brecht

Arden's work has always been categorically political in that it explicitly foregrounds the public and the social, privileging it over the private and the psychological. Focus on shared social life and its tensions constitutes a central cognitive and dramaturgic emphasis in his plays, and, as such, it not only informs his choice of subjects and themes but also operates as a basic compositional principle underlying the very structure of his plays. For an adequate understanding of the nature and significance of Arden's dramaturgy, therefore, it is crucial to grasp the full implications of this emphasis.

It is important to remember that his dramaturgy builds upon popular traditions of the past and that, in this and several other respects, it is similar to what we have described as the radical alternative tradition in contemporary drama. In all of these traditions, the main agents are not conceived individualistically, not in the original robust and monadic form nor in the more recent, and weaker, schizophrenic form. They are conceived, instead, in socially relational terms, signifying a collectivity or some segment thereof. Arden shares this approach. Like other radical alternative playwrights such as Mayakovsky, Brecht, or Dario Fo, he uses what may be called an exteriorizing/collectivizing method of conceiving and presenting agents. This method allows him to deprivatize his agents, so as to preclude any individualist or purely subjective perception of their status and roles, and to invest them instead with an emphatically supraindividual (that is, sociopolitical or socially typical) significance. This also allows the dramaturgic interest in his plays to be focused not on one or a very few isolated individuals and their private lives and consciousnesses but on sociohistorically significant polarities of collective human existence and experience, thus making his work more deeply social than the socially conscious dramas of the Ibsenian tradition.

Such dramaturgic practice is obviously in direct contrast to the character-based tradition, which is marked by an increasing interiorization of the sources of action and conflict. As pointed out earlier, this tradition conceives its main agents psychologically and introspectively—as "closed monads . . . governed by the laws of 'psychology'" (Jameson 1981, 160). Such a character's inward orientation (toward its own inner life and consciousness) becomes more significant than its outward orientation (toward the larger, external world of fellow beings, objects, and social relationships). This process of progressive interiorization, which produces a structural preponderance of the indicial emphasis and causes the narrative interest to atrophy, also leads to the privatization and restriction of both the physical space (the room) and the emotional and experiential space (the nuclear family). This creates and reinforces a split between the psychological, formally monologic, inner space of the individual and the larger, shared, and expressly dialogic outer space of the collective.

An important aspect of this subjective emphasis is that even intimate relationships—such as those between husband and wife, parent and child, or between lovers—are often experienced as ambiguous, problematic, and even oppressive. This souring of personal relationships, suggestive of a weakening of human relationships in general, produces a corresponding devitalization of dramatic speech and behavior. First, the intensely introspective feelings and experiences of a character cause a breakdown in free and direct communication with the spectators, who are in any case treated as the proverbial "fourth wall"—in other words, as conventionally absent. Second, they tend to render that character increasingly inarticulate, thus creating great difficulties in fluent and unambiguous communication even among the characters themselves. Therefore, spoken words and actions communicate their meanings only obliquely or impressionistically, so that the textually manifest aspects of the character, like the visible tip of an iceberg, become significant not for what they actually say or disclose—and thus render evident and verifiable for the spectators—but mainly for what they merely suggest and

cannot fully express.[1] In short, in an interesting paradox, the very preoccupation with the inner life of the character in individualist dramaturgy
precludes the possibility of full and clear realization of that character on
the manifest level of the text. Much of the peculiar richness and intensity
of this kind of drama derives precisely from this nagging sense of uncer-
tainty, inarticulateness, and ambiguity of experience, which is correlative
to interiorization of the character and the loss of overt action.

Arden does not share this subjective and introspective emphasis, this
preoccupation with what Strindberg called the soul-complex. His agents
come across as remarkably straightforward, non-self-indulgent beings
who tend to be so lacking in psychological depth and individualist complexity that, in comparison with illusionist characters, they might appear
superficial. This "superficiality," however, is of a special kind, and it
signifies a deliberate dramaturgic and ideological choice rather than a
conceptual or artistic deficiency. It is related to the fact that in Arden's
plays—as in those of Brecht, Shakespeare, Jonson, and the Mummings—
the site of significant action and conflict, or the ultimate point of reference, is not the individual, not even the nuclear family, but invariably
some larger collective category.

Arden from the beginning rejected the ideologically and artistically
constricting preference for the private, familial, and "psychological"
types of action, putting on the stage actions of a more social and political
kind involving public and semipublic situations and institutions and a
rich, socially differentiated range of agents, relationships, and experiences. His entire opus, from *The Waters of Babylon,* to *The Island of the
Mighty,* and beyond, shows that this expressly sociopolitical emphasis in
his dramaturgy, in consonance with his own political development, has
continued to grow in depth and complexity. It shows, for example, that
the locus of action in his drama has developed significantly from the
relatively restricted civic neighborhoods of *The Waters of Babylon* and
Live Like Pigs, or from an even more strictly localized clinic-cum-old-
people's-home in *The Happy Haven,* through the entire, if small and
isolated, communities of *Serjeant Musgrave's Dance* and *The Workhouse
Donkey,* to the much vaster and more complex national and international
polities of *The Royal Pardon, Armstrong's Last Goodnight, Left-Handed Liberty, The Hero Rises Up, The Island of the Mighty,* and *The Non-stop
Connolly Show.* Arden's thematic concerns have similarly progressed
from microlevel politics (local forms of political corruption in municipal
politics and the problems of specific kinds of social outcasts), through

consideration of such political and moral issues as war and peace, and oppression and freedom, to an examination, in specifically class terms, of contradictions and mutations of political power and revolutionary strategies for social salvation. With this expansion in the scope and complexity of dramatized action, there has also been a corresponding increase in the range and complexity of the agential structure and an intensification of focus on the public and shared aspects of experience and relationships. As a consequence, Arden's dramaturgic universe has come to be populated with figures representing social beings who are actively involved with one another and in whom the personal and the societal are not separated and pitted against each other but are combined in a dynamic, interactive relationship.

Treatment of Individual Agents

Arden's dramaturgic agents are usually so conceived as to suggest social and moral types rather than unique and private personalities, or, properly, characters. They are defined, first and foremost, in terms of their social existence—such as political, economic, and/or professional status, function, or ideological position—rather than in terms of their unique psychological make-up. On the whole, they come across as variations on the basic types of the politician, the ruler, the industrialist, the feudal lord, the worker, the peasant, the soldier, the policeman, the buffoon, the spoilsport, and several specific subcategories of the social outcast (prostitute, gypsy, outlaw, con man, rebel, and so on) For example, the major agents in *The Waters of Babylon* are variations on the outcast type. Although differentiated by the details of their ethnic or geographic backgrounds, they share certain fundamental traits. They are all outsiders to the official social and cultural establishment of the English metropolis. They share a shady existence, eked out through unorthodox and "morally reprehensible" means, outside (or on the fringe of) respectable society and the legal economy. And they all possess the remarkable qualities of sensuality (even amorality), vivacity, roguishness, and ingenuity. In *Left-Handed Liberty,* King John, despite (or rather because of) his unique traits or idiosyncrasies, combines the qualities of a medieval autocrat with those of the clown or the fool.[2]

The actions and interest of such socially defined figures in any play by Arden stem from the compulsions and pressures of their social positions and material circumstances. Moreover, the circumstances or socio-

historical settings that condition their behavior are themselves represented and enacted directly by other agents (the MPs and councillors in
The Waters of Babylon, for example) so that they are not constructed, in
Brecht's words, as "mysterious powers (in the background) . . . , [but
as] created and maintained by men (and [which] will in due course be
altered by them)" (1964, 190).

This emphasis on socially typical aspects does not mean, however,
that a more individual dimension is altogether missing from Arden's
definition and differentiation of the main agents. It emphatically does not
mean that they are perceived entirely as faceless, lifeless, static puppets or
allegorical figures. But it allows individuality in his plays to be perceived
in a way that differs radically from what comes across in bourgeois
individualist culture. There are two main reasons for this difference.

First, Arden foregrounds what critics have increasingly come to
recognize as the perennial fictional and dramaturgic practice of constructing an agent's individuality selectively and rudimentarily from precisely
chosen traits of social biography, behavior, and temperamental disposition, all of them subsumed under a proper name. Akin to what he once
described as the "primary colors" of the ballad, these semantic traits
individuate an agent, allow her or him to be distinguished from others,
and thus add to that agent's imagined reality. They do not suggest an
isolated subjectivity nor do they allow individual subjectivity to become
the dominant focus of dramaturgic interest. On the contrary, they are
usually so conceived as to allow the psychological and the social, the
individual and the typical, to be dialectically linked.

These individuating traits of Arden's agents tend to be mainly of
two kinds: temperamental and biographical. Of these the temperamental
traits are often incorporated as obsessive aspects of individual agents—
for example, Musgrave's morose and disciplinarian disposition; Butterthwaite's indomitable, gay spirit; Armstrong's ruthlessness combined
with his simple-minded vanity, impulsiveness, and, as Arden describes
it, "a certain innocence of spirit"; and King John's (often genial) crafti-
ness. Furthermore, entirely and directly manifest at the level of the
dramatized text, these traits do not suggest fundamentally inarticulate
psychological experiences but usually signify some general or sociohistorically typical attitudes or humors. We do not see them as innately
given and unique aspects of a psyche but rather as distinctive features of a
dramaturgic role and type, which become interesting not in themselves
but only in relation to a play's action. For example, Musgrave's moral

strictness, militaristic rigidity, and religious fanaticism, which clearly set him apart from the others in the play, are concretely manifested in his verbal and physical behavior as well as in his attitude toward others. At the same time, they also suggest, as Arden has hinted in his prefatory text, a typical representative of the puritan, Cromwellian soldier, and therefore a specific ideological legacy of the bourgeoisie.[3] Musgrave cannot, therefore, in any adequate analysis, be separated from his structural function within the totality of the play's agential design. Moreover, because such temperamental traits are externally perceivable, they exteriorize rather than interiorize an agent. They are also theatrically exciting because they are action generating, and by adding color to an agent's stage presence and behavior they accentuate our perception of its theatricality (as opposed to its illusionist "reality").

The biographical traits too are conceived and presented by Arden in general, rather than strictly and uniquely individual, terms. They usually comprise age, sex, vocation, and ethnic and class appurtenance. Occasionally they may also involve certain elements of an agent's past, but these usually relate to shared social experiences rather than to exclusively private ones. For example, in *The Waters of Babylon,* the reference to Krank's experience during the Nazi occupation of Poland is no doubt an element in his personal history, yet it is also part of a collective historical tragedy. His own poetic expression of this experience, in his "Dolorous Song," deindividualizes this element. Butterthwaite's workhouse origin is another example of such biographical traits in which the personal and the shared, the particular and the general levels of significance, are indistinguishable. The interest of such references to an agent's pre-story experience is usually related in Arden's dramaturgy to that experience's ability to contribute to the action. This is done either syntagmatically, by generating new sequences of events (as the revelation of Krank's Nazi past does)—that is, by introducing and/or explicating a complication in the story—or paradigmatically, by helping the audience to better apprehend some particular aspects of an agent's behavior (as Krank's past explains his vehement disapproval of Paul's fanatic and violent patriotism, while Butterthwaite's workhouse background throws significant light upon his staunchly plebeian sympathies and nonconformist behavior). As such, these pre-history elements, too, become functional and cognitive aspects of a dramaturgic agent rather than merely suggesting an empirical individual outside the text.

Thus, the individuating traits of both kinds (the biographical as well as the temperamental) are such that they allow the individual agent's experience or attitude to be related to (rather than isolated from) some general, shared social experience or attitude, and thus they generate what may be called a collectivizing emphasis.

Another important factor that makes a difference in our perception of individuality in Arden is that he emphasizes the relational status of agents by foregrounding their dialogic construction. Dialogue, Peter Szondi writes, is "the common space in which the interiority of the dramatis personae is objectified" (1987, 53). Arden's drama is characterized by an abundance of verbal and gestic energy, which dialogizes his agents. Being among the most communicative fictive beings in modern drama, these agents are, as it were, constantly turning themselves inside out by talking freely, readily, and unambiguously to one another and often directly to the audience. This also allows their inner, subjective aspects to be exhaustively externalized at the manifest level of the text, leaving nothing of that unarticulated and inarticulable reserve of feelings and experience that usually gives the naturalist character its impression of authenticity and depth.

Communicative even in normal circumstances, Arden's characters tend to become particularly eloquent under extraordinary circumstances that would render naturalist characters introspective and incoherent, if not altogether speechless. Most of the songs, verses, and other instances of formal speech in Arden's plays occur precisely at such moments of emotional or situational complexity or tension. They function to crystallize a particular emotion, experience, or response as well as to clarify and exteriorize the contradictions within an agent or a situation so that the articulated experience acquires an exciting immediacy and directness and, at the same time, becomes a part of some larger experience. In Act Three of *The Waters of Babylon,* Krank's "Dolorous Song," a ballad, crystallizes as well as expresses the agent's experience of and response to a situation that is obviously part of a collective tragedy. Another, similar instance occurs in the play when, at the narratively as well as emotionally difficult moment when he is accused by his friend and compatriot, Paul, of being an erstwhile Nazi soldier, Krank explains his position with such remarkable readiness and candidness that it literally disarms Paul. It also explains an important plot complication in such a way that the emphasis is diverted from the character to a historical and collective situation of which the individual is a more or less exemplary part (pars pro toto). Arden's opus affords many examples of such speeches, which deindividualize and exteriorize an experience or response. In *Armstrong's Last Goodnight* (I.iv), Meg, when she finds the body of her treacherously murdered lover, expresses her grief in a combination of prose and poetry, which, as Albert Hunt observes, has a harsh and brutal realism: "A woman weeps over the ugly, snarling body of a distasteful man. But the very harshness communicates strongly and directly the reality of her grief" (1974, 94). Yet it also communicates a critical response to the general political situation that the play as a whole implies. This is also underlined by Lindsay's comment:

> The grief of this woman is the grief of the commonweal of Scotland. Naebody to hear it, and but few to comprehend it, if they did. And of those few, how many could comprehend the means of consolation? (I.v)

In Hunt's words, Lindsay "has turned a concrete, particularized grief into a generalized political statement" (1974, 94). Thus, Meg's lament, like several other such formal speeches throughout Arden's plays, serves as the site where the purely individual, monologic level blends into the social, dialogic level, where standpoints and attitudes are revealed and counterposed, thereby contributing to the generation of a complex pattern of emphasis in which shared experiences and structures of relationship, rather than isolated subjectivities, come to be foregrounded.

Arden's drama abounds in this kind of dialogic activity. In *Serjeant Musgrave's Dance,* for example, Annie's sudden but categorical response to the Serjeant and his militarism stems from what we later discover to be a traumatic personal experience. It is expressed, however, in the impersonal form of a ballad which—like Meg's lament—places a thematic knot in a sharply defined critical perspective.

> ANNIE (*confronting him*): Serjeant you are.
> MUSGRAVE: That's right.
> ANNIE: You seem a piece stronger than the rest of 'em.
> (*He nods.*)
> And they call you Black Jack Musgrave?
> (*He looks at her.*)
> Well I am looking at your face mister serjeant. Now do you know what I'd say?
> MUSGRAVE: What?

ANNIE: The north wind in a pair of millstones
Was your father and your mother
They got you in a cold grinding
God help us if they get you a brother.

(I.ii)

She reminds us of this again when, horrified by Hurst's obsession with gloom and depression, she remarks, "My Christ, then, they have found him a brother" (II.iii). The Serjeant's response to Annie, given in another encounter between them, is equally sharp, definitive, and critical.

MUSGRAVE: (*calling Annie*). Lassie.
ANNIE: Hello.
MUSGRAVE: These are my men. They are here with their work to do. You will not distract them.
ANNIE: I won't?
MUSGRAVE: No. Because *they* know, whether you know it or not, that there's work is for women and there's work is for men: and let the two get mixed, you've anarchy.
ANNIE: (*rather taken aback*). Oh? And what's anarchy? You, clever grinder—words and three stripes.
MUSGRAVE: Look, lassie, anarchy: now we are soldiers. Our duty. It's drawn out straight and black for us, a clear plan. But if you come to us with what you call your life or love—*I'd* call it your indulgence—and you scribble all over that plan, you make it crooked, dirty, idle, untidy, *bad*—there's anarchy. I'm a religious man. I know words, and I know deeds, and I know how to be strong. So do these men. You will not stand between them and their strength! Go on now: take yourself off.

(II.i)

These encounters demonstrate how two dramaturgic agents in Arden are usually able to confront each other, despite their marked differences, and to freely and fully articulate not just their responses to each other individually but their different perceptions of a common or general question or issue.[4] This unites them, structurally and dialectically, in a contrapuntal relationship based on exteriorized attitudes. In the above example, this contrapuntal relationship between Annie and Musgrave constitutes one of the major poetic elements in a play that has a strong folkloric, balladlike flavor and embodies a complex structure of agential relationships.

Thus, while the level of individuation (or, perhaps better, particularization) is not altogether absent from Arden's dramaturgic agents, it is not conceived of in privatizing terms. On the contrary, even at this level the personal merges with the social, the particular with the general, allowing the main emphasis to remain focused on shared social relationships and the agents' ontological status to remain firmly circumscribed by the fictive world of the play. The agents are clearly revealed to be artistic constructs, emblematic of various forms of human existence, behavior, and/or attitudes within some historically specific context of social relations. As a result, the focus of the action in a play is never on individualities in private conflict but on a dynamic interplay of attitudes and perspectives in relation to some specific shared situation or issue.

Superficiality

Because they lack the psychological "depth" and "complexity" that is valorized in bourgeois individualist aesthetics, Arden's agents may appear flat and superficial. However, their superficiality is clearly of a specific kind, drawing on a different tradition and value system. In other words, it is not a deficiency but a conscious ideological and artistic choice, which can be understood only in terms of the traditions that Arden builds on—that is, in terms of the medieval, the Elizabethan, and a myriad of other plebeian dramatic traditions that he, like other radical alternative writers from Mayakovsky to Dario Fo, draw upon and seek to renew.

Among the early influences on Arden, acknowledged by the author himself, is Ben Jonson, in whose "bricklayer's skill," he says, he found a "pattern book" that he was "very much in need of." Recognizing that no modern play is constructed in a way that he "would care to imitate," he decided that if he were to write social comedy, "Jonson was the man to follow" (Arden 1977, 25–26). Interestingly, what Arden calls Jonson's "bricklayer's skill" is described by T. S. Eliot as "poetry of surface," which "cannot be understood without study" because it is so deliberate that "we too must be deliberate, in order to understand" it. In this kind of poetry, Eliot remarks, "the emotional tone is not in a single verse, but in the design of the whole" (1967, 88). Such composition is also reminiscent of Breughel's epic paintings in which each figure possesses its own distinctive features and yet is inextricable from the overall pattern.[5]

The composition of Arden's drama is precisely of this kind. Its supposed superficiality is deliberate, cognitively significant, inclusive, and complex. It requires that his individual agents be conceived primarily as social types or figures in a foregrounded complex pattern of shared relationships in which they actively participate and which they collectively embody. This makes them, clearly, designs or relational constructs. This perception of their status and role is further reinforced by the fact that, by constantly exteriorizing themselves in speech and action, these dramaturgic agents emphasize their own lack of individualist closure and, as it were, direct our attention away from their separate selves toward some larger world of the collective, thus urging us toward a more complex perception of the dramatic action as a whole.

However, this exteriorization of agents, instead of divesting them of life and energy, as the individualist aesthetics would have us believe, releases in them a kind of energy and vitality that is both theatrically exciting and cognitively enriching. For, on the one hand, it frees them from illusionist hang-ups about naturalness and verisimilitude in speech and action and allows them a wide range of verbal and gestural activities, all of which (as we shall see in a subsequent chapter) enhance the ludic quality of the theatrical experience. And, on the other hand, it enables them to participate more fully and actively in the external world of dramatized social relationships. Unlike naturalist characters, these agents come across as active doers rather than passive victims, and in this sense they are truly agents rather than "patients" of the action. What they lack in psychic complexity, they make up in energy and ingenuity. Unlike their individualist counterparts, they are seldom found merely complaining about or lamenting a cruel fate, or merely railing against the injustices of a hostile environment. No matter how difficult or serious the situation, they usually respond to it actively, categorically, and boldly. Krank's remark to Butterthwaite in *The Waters of Babylon*—"I, Krank, am no longer in this a man of defence. I am to attack"—is emblematic for most of them. This is why—from the Krank-Butterthwaite plan to rig the municipal lottery, or the old people's successful conspiracy to reverse an unacceptable medical experiment in *The Happy Haven*; to the soldiers' rebellion and colliers' strike in *Serjeant Musgrave's Dance* and Butterthwaite's ingenious undertaking against a hostile situation in *The Workhouse Donkey*; to various violent and nonviolent counterhegemonic projects in the later historical-legendary plays—Arden's drama abounds in the images of energetically struggling groups of men and women. In the early plays, the struggle is often for mere survival under a hostile system.

But in the later plays it becomes more revolutionary as we see increasingly large bodies of people engaged in trying to forcibly alter the conditions of their existence.

The result of both the agents' energy and the situation-bound nature of Arden's dramaturgic focus is that the overall issue comes to be perceived simultaneously in its larger social aspect as well as in terms of the variety and diversity of responses that it evokes. We can illustrate this point by taking a closer look at Serjeant Musgrave—the agent and the play.

Musgrave is commonly regarded—within certain limits, correctly—as the central character of the play named after him (or, more precisely, after his "dance"). He is also one of the relatively more complex and seemingly more individualized agents in Arden's opus. Yet we know almost nothing about his background, save that he is a sergeant in the British army and has deserted it after the bitter experience of a colonial war. Nevertheless, his temperamental and behavioral traits—his religion, his discipline-ridden consciousness, his morose aloofness from the "life and love" of ordinary men and women, his maniacal zeal and sardonic humor, and, alongside these, the determination and courage that he demonstrates by turning against and desiring to avenge an unjust war—give him an extraordinary, contradictory personality and make him a complex "character." In the hands of a naturalist dramatist (for example, Osborne) this could easily have turned the play into a psychological, if not psychopathic, character drama. But Arden, first, so exaggerates these traits that they become comic and theatrical rather than exclusively tragic and psychological. Second, these traits are exteriorized in Musgrave's speeches and actions, for example, in his encounters with Annie (I.ii, II.i); in his prayer to God for help and guidance, and the Bargee's simultaneous parody of that prayer (I.iii); and in his comic end-of-the-world nightmare, which is accompanied by comic references to him made by Annie and others in a physically separate but simultaneous action (II.iii).

His traits, then, are event generating and constitute an integral part of the play's narrative design. What comes to be stressed in such a design is Musgrave's role or function. Our interest in his personality is channeled into textually manifest and narratively significant aspects only, with the result that the experience the dramaturgic agent Musgrave communicates cannot be isolated from the experiences bodied forth by the other agents in the play. It has to be viewed in the context of, and in relation to, them, as part of a complex structure of diverse experiences and perspectives.

This structure includes a variety of responses both to Musgrave himself and to his project in the play. They range from the categorically contrary response of Annie, through the skeptical but awed compliance of his own soldiers and the suspicious and wary interest of the colliers, to the compassionate but also critical response of Mrs. Hitchcock. These responses place Musgrave, firmly and inextricably, in a dialectical and critical perspective "in the round," so that no easy, moralistic, character-based assessment of his role is encouraged. This complex perspective on Musgrave's role, excellently explained by Forsas-Scott (1983), is encapsulated in the last scene of the play in a discussion between Mrs. Hitchcock, Musgrave, and Attercliffe.

MRS. HITCHCOCK: All wrong, you poured it out all wrong! I could ha' told you last night if only I'd known—the end of the world and you thought you could call a parade. In control—*you!*

MUSGRAVE: (very agitated). Don't talk like that. You're talking about my duty. Good order and the discipline: it's the only road I know. Why can't you see it?

MRS. HITCHCOCK: All I can see is crooked Joe Bludgeon having his dance out in the middle of fifty dragoons! It's time you learnt your life, you big proud sergeant. Listen: last evening you told all about this anarchy and where it came from—like, scribble all over with life or love, and that makes anarchy. Right?

MUSGRAVE: Go on.

MRS. HITCHCOCK: Then *use* your logic—if you can. Look at it this road: here we are, and we'd got life and love. Then *you* came in and you did your scribbling where nobody asked you. Aye, it's arsey-versey to what you said, but it's still an anarchy, isn't it? And it's all your work.

MUSGRAVE: Don't tell me there was life or love in this town.

MRS. HITCHCOCK: There was. There were hungry men, too—fighting for their food. But *you* brought in a different war.

MUSGRAVE: I brought it in to end it.

ATTERCLIFFE: To end it by its own rules: no bloody good. She's right, you're wrong. You can't cure pox by further whoring. Sparky died of those damned rules. And so did the other one.

MUSGRAVE: That's not the truth. (*He looks at them both in appeal,*

but they nod.) That's not the truth. God was with me . . . God . . .
(*He makes a strange animal noise of despair, a sort of sob that is choked off
suddenly, before it can develop into a full howl.*)—and all they dancing—
all of them—there.
    MRS. HITCHCOCK: Ah, not for long. And it's not a dance of joy.
Those men are hungry, so they've got no time for you. One day
they'll be full, though, and the dragoons'll be gone, and then they'll
remember.
    MUSGRAVE: (shaking his head). No.
    MRS. HITCHCOCK: Let's hope it, any road; Eh?

                                                     (III.ii)

This scene clearly indicates that the focus of interest is not Musgrave as a
character but Musgrave as a dramaturgic emblem for an ideological position. For he is but a bourgeois (puritan) variant of the type of the life-
destroying soldier also found in Feng in *The Workhouse Donkey,* Nelson
in *The Hero Rises Up,* and Arthur in *The Island of the Mighty.* As such, he
is shown to have internalized and become obsessed with the deadly
principles of discipline and good order that Arden associates with political and ideological control and oppression (cf. the preface in *The Hero
Rises Up*). In other words, he is the site of—indeed, he personifies—the
conflict between an oppressive militaristic system and "life and love,"
which that system regards as anarchy and therefore as inimical to its
interests. In him we see the bourgeois hegemony and its puritan heritage
in operation. But as a character Musgrave also shows the positive trait of
being able to rise in protest against an unjust and inhuman social order.
This allows his role to be viewed with partial sympathy in the play. The
play is so designed that we, in Arden's own words, "find ourselves
understanding [an agent's] problems, but not necessarily approving his
reactions to them" (Marowitz 1965, 44). Criticizing Musgrave from a
sympathetic position, Mrs. Hitchcock dialectically integrates both these
responses—the responses between which the play has been alternating
throughout.
    But then, in another, more fundamental sense, neither Musgrave
nor any other agent can be perceived as *the* focus of audience interest in
the play. As the action moves from scene to scene, different agents or
their different groupings come to occupy the center of our attention—
often, as in the scene cited above, upstaging Musgrave himself and presenting different perspectives on the main theme.

These responses and perspectives in Arden's work are usually arranged in what may be described as a multifocal and relational structure of significance, wherein each response receives its own full and direct emphasis and yet becomes meaningful only in relation to all the other responses within a given play. In other words, we find in Arden what, in another context, Jameson has described as "a rotation of character-centres which deprives each of them in turn of any privileged status" (1981, 161). This reinforces, and is reinforced by, the episodic composition of Arden's dramaturgy, which allows the focus to shift continuously from situation to situation, with each situation embodied by its own specific set of agents and relationships and governed by a specific response (or set of responses) to the central issue of the play. Such a dramaturgic structure discourages uncritical emotional identification with any individual character or point of view and instead encourages the spectator to reflect on the dramatized events from a position of critical distance. This multiplicity of experience, however, does not imply a liberal celebration of plurality for its own sake. Rather, by presenting values and positions in active and constant contestation, and by clearly rooting them in the disparities of material existence, Arden encourages us to focus simultaneously on the unjust nature of a given social order and on its historicity or potential for change.

Collective Relationships and Agential Groupings

My argument here is that a web of agential relationships, rather than the individual character, is the pertinent cognitive and analytical focus of Arden's dramaturgy. It is strictly within this collectivizing focus that the relatively finer and more particular definition and differentiation of some central agents as characters takes place. Furthermore, since the agents and their roles are socially rather than psychologically defined, the dramatized relationships in Arden are perceived, in supraindividual terms, as relationships between different collectivities or social groups. This perception is reinforced by the fact that Arden's agents usually function in clusters, forming themselves into distinct groups on the basis of similarity and difference in social status, vocation, and sociopolitical interests and ideals. Each such group emblematizes a potentially larger and socially more significant category than that of the domestic nuclear family, which is the main concern of individualist drama (and itself a compromise between "pure" atomized individualism, such as occurs later in

Absurd drama, and the bourgeois myth of social harmony stemming from an earlier, ascending social phase).

A division of dramaturgic agents according to the social groups to which they belong has existed in Arden's drama from the beginning, but the magnitude and scope of such groupings have undergone significant development over the years. In what follows, we will look at the nature and function of agential groupings in both his early plays and his later ones.

As mentioned, the earlier plays tend to concentrate on some local and historically marginal group or segment of the socially underprivileged. The central focus in these plays is on some specific conflict of interest between such a counterhegemonic (or deviant) group and the dominant social and moral order. The hostile Establishment is as a rule represented in these plays by its official representatives or functionaries who, insofar as they *objectively* represent or defend the interests of the dominant order against the divergent interests of an unassimilated (and often inassimilable) group, came across as a single group, or at least as representatives of various subgroups within the unity of a hegemonic order.

In *The Waters of Babylon,* for example, the central conflict of interest is between an alien (largely immigrant and non-English), morally "deviant" group of crooks, pimps, and prostitutes and a hostile social system (represented in the play by a municipal councillor, two MPs, and a policeman). In *Live Like Pigs,* likewise, a freely constituted household of irrepressible gypsies conflicts with the established middle-class environment into which it has been forcibly moved and with which it is socially and morally incompatible. The dominant order is represented in the play not only by its official administrative and political functionaries (the Housing Estate Official, the officially appointed doctor, and the policeman) but also by the Jackson family whose preoccupations with stability, security, and respectability exemplify the hegemonic power of the dominant ideology. Similarly, in *The Happy Haven,* a group of elderly but mentally active patients in a medical institution find themselves in conflict with the interests of their doctor and, beyond him, with the interests of a larger social group signified in the play by the politically and economically powerful patrons of the doctor's research.

The early plays thus focus upon the antagonism between some specific, and foregrounded, category of the socially underprivileged and the framing social and moral order. As for relationships within the socially lower group, they usually involve some collective endeavor, some collaborative undertaking in defense of the group's interests. For example, *The Waters of Babylon* dramatizes a collaborative and complicated process of conceiving, planning, and executing (albeit unsuccessfully) an ingenious scheme to rig a municipal lottery, while the main action in *The Happy Haven* is concerned with the process whereby several elderly people of different temperaments and backgrounds, faced with a common enemy, come to realize their common interests as a group.

Arden's subsequent plays continue the practice of dividing the agential space both horizontally, into the upper and the lower socio-ideological realms, and vertically, into subgroups within a shared but diversified sociopolitical space. They also continued to foreground the lower realm by focusing mainly on groups of ordinary people in struggle against the hegemonic order. However, plays like *Serjeant Musgrave's Dance* and *The Workhouse Donkey* also mark a significant step in the direction of a fully developed political drama. In these plays one finds an expansion of the dramaturgic focus to include the whole community (not only some specific and marginal fragment as in the previous plays) and a corresponding increase in the range of the dramatized relationships. This development also involves a significant cognitive shift as the main agential divisions come to be perceived increasingly in class terms. While *Musgrave* marks the first appearance of this class-based emphasis in Arden, its first full articulation is found in *Donkey*.

Set in an imaginary coal-mining town, *Serjeant Musgrave's Dance* presents social conflicts arising out of the existence of an unjust order that produces bitter class conflicts at home and conducts brutal colonial wars abroad. The main agential polarization in the play, therefore, is between the hegemonic order—represented by the Mayor, who, significantly, is also a mine owner (thus signifying the identity of economic and political powers), the Parson (who is also a magistrate), the policemen, and the dragoons—and those opposed to that order.[6] The latter are divided into three groups—Musgrave's soldiers, the coal miners, and the women—each with a distinct perspective. The conflict between the conscience-stricken soldiers and the unjust system is thus juxtaposed, in a complex relationship of unity and contradiction, with a bitter class conflict in which the same political order is seen to protect the interests of the mine owners against the local plebeian majority of colliers. The women are distinguished from both the soldiers and the colliers by their ability to see things more clearly. Represented in the play by Mrs. Hitchcock and

Annie, who embody and articulate the aspirations, fears, and experiences of the community, this third agential force embodies a more positive position—a position in which moral questions (of war and peace) and the political issues (of economic oppression and exploitation) are dialectically integrated within a robustly humane and unmistakably plebeian perspective of "life and love."

Each of these groups is involved in some specific project, and these projects provide the main body of the play's action. The soldiers' secret plan to avenge the brutalities of an imperialist war constitutes a pivotal project. It is juxtaposed, even counterposed, with both the colliers' struggle and officialdom's plan to keep the colliers at bay until the arrival of military reinforcements. These projects, each of which is collective and collaborative in nature, cut across each other in a complex narrative design.

In a somewhat similar strategy, the community of an isolated coal-mining town in *The Workhouse Donkey,* and therefore the play's agential space, is explicitly divided into four blocs or groups: the Labour politicians, their Conservative counterparts, the police, and the electorate (which itself comprises a variety of social groups—the workers, the press, and so on—and individuals). Although the play is centered on the pivotal figure of the colorful and ingenious Labour alderman, Charlie Butterthwaite (the workhouse donkey of the title), the action is made up of a complex network of intrigues and counterintrigues, involving various degrees and forms of contradiction within and collaboration between the main groups.

On the surface, *The Workhouse Donkey* is a comedy satirizing corruption in municipal politics. As such it focuses on the conflict of interest between the two organized political factions. On closer examination, however, the play reveals itself to be more complex in design and import. It becomes an indictment, from an expressly and cheerfully plebeian standpoint, of the "legitimate" political alternatives in postwar Britain as well as an acknowledgment of the necessity—indeed, the possibility—of finding a different, genuinely plebeian, revolutionary alternative. As such it marks an important stage in Arden's development in terms of political radicalism.

We can identify in the play a hierarchy of three related levels of increasing scope, within which the action and its significance is perceived and the agential relationships are defined. Only the surface level deals with electoral rivalries and intrigues in local municipal politics, involving the two political groups, the police, and their associates. The plebeian majority of the electorate, represented by the stonemasons, drinkers, waitresses, and so on, plays only a marginal and incidental role on this level, and Charlie Butterthwaite is perceived as no more than a particularly corrupt and ingenious politician whose maneuvers eventually bring him down.

As the action progresses, however, another, cognitively higher level of conflict begins to take shape, which has to do with the larger and more fundamental conflict between social classes. The focus shifts from electoral rivalry to class struggle. The Conservatives believe that "today / Class-struggle is concluded" (II.i), and the narrow political and social perspective of the orthodox section of the Labourites (which triumphs by disowning Butterthwaite at the end of the play) amounts to an agreement with this view. Butterthwaite, alone among the politicians, insists that "By solid class defence and action of the mass alone can we hew out and line with timbered strength a gallery of self-respect beneath the faulted rock above the subsidence of water!" (III.ii).

This is an entirely new voice in Arden's work. In *Sarjeant Musgrave's Dance* he touched upon the class question, but he could not fully reconcile it with the play's overriding pacifist moral stance. Here he foregrounds it. For, as we move from the surface to this deeper level, a different kind of polarization of the agential space comes to the fore. We see the two political factions, the police, and their bourgeois allies as belonging to the same side of the conflict—the side that directly or indirectly supports and perpetuates the existing class structure.[7] It is significant that the play begins with an agreement between Labour and Conservatives on the choice of Feng as the new police chief, a gesture signifying their common interest in law and order, and ends with their common rejection of Butterthwaite and their reconciliation with each other, which is highlighted in the metaphor of whitewash. Blomax's direct narration in the last scene underscores this: "You'll observe the general sense of bygones be bygones." The whole trajectory in between confirms the basic unity of the two political parties, despite bitter electoral rivalries. The Epilogue, sung by all who remain after Butterthwaite and his plebeian supporters have been forcibly removed from the stage, translates this unity into a striking audiovisual image.

The other side of this class conflict is represented by Butterthwaite and his plebeian supporters. He brings into a legitimized and "orderly" power struggle within the bourgeois system the officially unacceptable discordance of class conflict. Conceived as a colorful embodiment of the spirit, interests, and historical experience of the working masses, he, even when actively involved with the Labour party, never loses his class perspective. He describes himself to Boocock as a plebeian Messiah (II.vi). Outmaneuvered by Mrs. Boocock and other orthodox elements in Labour, he prepares himself for the final conflict (and on May Day, too) by activating the hitherto dormant plebeian sections of the electorate within a horizon fusing politics and ethics, revolutionary hope and carnivalesque license.

> Community? What's community? *You?* 'Oh no,' you said, 'not me,' you said—and rightly said by Judas—'leave it to the mugs,' you said, 'we're lousy.' Well. Charlie's lousy too: and Charlie bears in mind that the first day of May is not only a day of Socialist congratulation but also a day of traditional debauchment in the base of a blossoming hedgerow. (III.iii)

Finally, he leads a carnivalesque procession of his drunken followers into the new art gallery, a symbol of the hegemonic culture as well as the renewed Labour-Conservative unity in the play, disrupting what was officially envisaged as a polite, formal, and restricted ceremony. For a brief moment in this last scene, the existing social order is turned upside-down. As Charlie clearly points out to Boocock, the real conflict is not between the different power groups struggling for a greater share within the hegemonic system but between the dominant power structure as a whole and the plebeian masses. This conflict between a reigning hegemony and the plebeian masses who continually challenge and oppose it is a recurrent motif in Arden's drama. However, as noted, what is new here is the expressly subversive and revolutionary class bias.

After *The Workhouse Donkey*, first performed in 1963, Arden turned increasingly to historical and historical-legendary, subjects. This orientation did not signify an escape from the problems of the present nor a desire to write historical spectacles or commemorative documentaries. Rather, Arden's main concern seems to have been to study the past in order to better understand the present and draw inferences for the future. In depicting sociohistorically past periods, these later plays emphasize both change and continuity. They often demonstrate how at various junctures in history certain alternative possibilities were set up, missed, or deliberately thwarted.

Again, Arden's method of dramatizing history is radically different from that of the individualist dramatists. For example, in *Luther,* John Osborne took a historical subject and, through a curious mixture of surface devices from Brecht and psychology from Erik Erikson, turned it into a psychopathological character drama. This approach to history is based on a widely shared belief that history in the theater

> means people rather than events. What they do is less important than what they feel and suffer while doing it. Their success or failure isn't measured in worlds conquered or lost, but *in the private battlefield, in the vale of soul-making as Keats called it.* (Fry 1977, 86)

Contrary to this, Arden's emphasis in his historical-legendary plays remains firmly oriented toward doing rather than suffering. He focuses on conflicts, turmoils, and developments that have, at specific and significant junctures in the past, so intervened in the course of European history that everybody's "soul-making" was deeply affected, making any division between public and private untenable. Agential relationships in these plays are conceived in such a way that they evoke the impression of huge collectivities in conflict, a sharply polarized political order in transition. At the same time, his folkloric, storytelling style prevents these plays from becoming mere historical spectacles or documentary chronicles. Rather, they come across as parables drawn from the historical and/or legendary past and invested with sharp contemporary import.

In *Armstrong's Last Goodnight,* Arden's approach to the material of an old tale, derived from a sixteenth-century Scottish ballad about the treacherous killing of a bold and colorful border outlaw, was informed by his reading of Connor Cruise O'Brien's book *To Katanga and Back.* Arden found "a basic similarity of moral . . . problems" between the imperialist political enterprise in the modern Congo and the story in the old ballad. He wrote the play in unmistakably historical terms but without losing the dialectal diction, folkloric flavor, or episodic rhythm of the old song. He went beyond the song's simple, commemorative, and idealizing focus upon the individual protagonist, concentrating instead on a central tension of a specific historical period of centralization and absolutization of political power. In other words, he combined historical fact and folkloric fiction in a form in which the pleasure of storytelling communicates a comprehensive view of the sociopolitical contradictions that characterized that period. The simple tale of a legendary hero is thus transformed into a complex, multidimensional, political parable.

Arden presents the hostilities between the state and Johnny Arm-

strong of Gilnockie (who represents the general category of the freebooters) as a political conflict arising from the contradiction between two
sets of social and material interests: monarchy's concern with the consol-
idation and absolutization of its power, obliging it to suppress and bring
under its own political control the traditional lairds of the areas along the
border; and the border freebooters' resistance to the royal attempts to
deprive them of their traditional sovereignty. This power struggle is not
only related to the conflict between England and Scotland but also involves antagonisms and collaborations between several power groups
within Scotland. Chief among these is the nobility. The aristocratic
houses of Scotland are shown to be so many rival factions, which protect
and use the freebooting gangs to further their own interests. These factional interests not only result in bloody feuds, like the one that lies
behind Armstrong's betrayal of Wamphray (I.iii), but, as the Scots
clerk's comments at the beginning of the play imply (I.ii), they are also at
variance with the interests of the King. To this already complex set of
sociopolitical relationships, Arden adds, in a deliberate departure from
strict chronology, an ideological conflict—namely, the one between Lu-
theran "heresy," represented by the Evangelist, and official religion.

The complex configuration of forces is not just a backdrop against
which the legendary tale of Armstrong is played out. Rather, it is an
immediate and dynamic context of historical compulsions operating
within the central sequence of events. For example, the bitter animosity
between Lord Maxwell and Lord Johnstone is the ultimate cause of
Armstrong's betrayal of Wamphray. Nonetheless, the solidarity and collaboration between these two lords and the Cardinal, in their successful
endeavor to disgrace Lindsay in the eyes of the King, is one of the
important causes of the reversal of approach from an honorable policy,
based on an enlightened understanding of the border problems, to a
treacherous and dishonorable one, based entirely upon expediency and
therefore more compatible with the sociopolitical ethos of the period.

The play's main dramaturgic and cognitive focus is precisely on this
complicated dialectical process of power struggle in a historically defined
situation. It centrally involves collusion and contradiction among divergent social and institutional factions. This is why it is wrong to focus
only on the relationship between Lindsay and Armstrong as individuals
rather than mainly on the sociohistorical relationships between large
groups that come to a head in it. This is a common critical error. Even an
otherwise perceptive critic like Hunt makes this error when he concludes

that "*Armstrong's Last Goodnight* is about the barbarity of a civilized, humane man—a barbarity that is forced on him by the nature of the game he is playing" (1974, 98). While the play is about this, too, Arden's dramaturgic design requires us to be more concerned with "the nature" of Lindsay's "game"—a game that is clearly shown to be rooted in sociopolitical constraints and expediency—than with anybody's personal barbarity and its moral implications.[8] Arden's concern goes beyond personal motives, attitudes, and their moral implications. His play dramatizes a brutal power struggle. Moreover, as Lindsay's concluding address to the audience indicates, we are encouraged to view this power struggle critically and parabolically, "as one dry exemplar to the world" in which one may read "the varieties of dishonour, and determine in your mind how best ye can avoid whilk ane of them, and when" (III.xvi).

Left-Handed Liberty, which was commissioned by the City of London to commemorate the 750th anniversary of the Magna Carta, has a similar thrust: similar multiplicity of agential groups; complexity of situation, conflict, and relationships; blending of folkloric and historical interests; and preoccupation with the historical contradictions within an established power structure. Like *Armstrong,* this play, too, is analytical rather than commemorative. It is concerned not so much with a chronology of events leading to the signing of the charter as with making a critical examination of a myth in English political history pertaining to law and power. As Arden stated in his preface, it was only after he had got sufficiently interested in the historical implications—in fact, in the "apparent complete failure"—of the charter, and the problematic nature of its implications in liberal mythology, that he could make sense of this theme.

The play shows a complicated pattern of political conflicts and alliances between several powerful groups and institutions, each motivated by its own class or factional interests rather than by any concern for the general good of the commonwealth. This pattern is organized around two powerful, contrasting protagonists: King John and Pandulph, the Papal Legate. In John we are shown a high-handed and devious, though not entirely villainous, king who doggedly tries to foil attempts at curtailment of his autocratic power, which is centralized but not codified in written law. Pandulph is placed in a contrapuntal relationship to John, with whom he also shares the function of the narrator. His world view is fanatically consistent, uniting as it does extreme theocentric and absolutist centralization of power with the sacred law of the Scriptures. As an official representative of the Roman Catholic Church, whose authority and point of view he asserts throughout the play, he possesses tremendous political clout.[9]

It is against this horizon of sharp polarization of power between the King and the Church—each a law unto itself and wielding immense power over the people's material and ideological lives—that the main events of the play are enacted. We see the rebellious barons as a group of feudal tyrants who, despite their bitter inner contradictions and rivalries, act as a class, fighting not for any libertarian principle but for their own narrow political and economic interests. The interests of an integral "life-and-love" freedom, decentralized (or person-centered) and not entirely to be encompassed by written formulae, are adumbrated in Lady DeVesci and —by ironical contraries—in the plebeian ballad of the London prostitutes (III. v). The City of London, represented in the play by its mayor, stands for the interests of the nascent mercantile class. This class, which is yet to grow into the main agent of the epochal shift from feudalism to capitalism, is here seen to vacillate between the two main antagonists, the King and the barons. However, in its attitude to the political crisis within the feudal setup, it seems to be closer to the common people than to the privileged classes insofar as it shares the people's skepticism toward the value of the liberties offered by the charter, on the one hand, and the sincerity of the parties clamoring for those liberties on the other. The royal family of France, its claim to the English throne, and its war of succession with the temporary support of the barons, represents yet another factor in this already complex agential design.

Thus, rivalries, conflicts, and collusion between social and political factions—none of which stands predominantly for any general or public interest—constitute the primary material of *Left-Handed Liberty*. However, not content with depicting the situation in terms of its surface politics alone, Arden significantly incorporates into his text the plebeian standpoint. The inclusion of the singing girls of London and the village folk of Gotham is actually the inclusion of the alienated common people of England in a play that reexamines a bitter struggle for political control in the upper realms of the established social order. It allows us a glimpse of that order's underbelly. By showing us the indifference and cynicism with which ordinary men and women view the struggle between the King and the nobility Arden is making a significant political comment. This comment becomes explicit in the ballad that sums up the popular position in relation to the charter and mocks the promised liberties.

Good people of London
Come listen to me
And I'll sing you a song
of our free liberty—

　Liberty sign it and seal it
　Liberty who dare repeal it?

It was wrote out on paper
What can we want more?
Who cares for the Frenchmen,
Who cares for the war?
. . . .

Who cares for the Pope
With his horns like old Moses,
Or the King's hairy legs
In a garden of roses?
. . . .

Who cares for the larder
All empty and bare,
Who cares for the children
With lice in their hair?
. . . .

For they gave us sweet liberty
To cuddle and love:
What fairer companion
Will dance to your grave—

　Liberty sign it and seal it
　Who dare repeal it
　Touch it and feel it
　Meat drink, and fire
　True-lover's desire
　Liberty all in the mire.

(III.v)

The Mayor's comments on this satirical song—somewhat like those of
Lindsay's on Meg's grief in *Armstrong's Last Goodnight*—reiterates and
underscores this popular criticism of the charter.

It's not only that particular ditty, there's others as well, worse: there's a bad feeling in the streets. And I can't say that I blame them: they've heard enough pious pronouncements about liberty over the last twelve months to make the Fleetditch mud larks vomit. . . . But what have we got—in practical terms to show to the people? What bales of cloth, as it were, to lay upon my counter? (III.v)

Another instance of this satirical view from below is found in the revised version of Act Two, Scene Four, where Arden offers us an adaptation of the old story about the wise men of Gotham. The scene shows how the folks of this proverbial village, alarmed by the news of the King's proposed journey through their village, suddenly realize one of the things the charter should have included but does not.

> PARSON: There's another point to be made out of that, goodman farmer. It's a matter of Law. Now I don't know and I've never heard it proved, according to the document and precedent, and I don't hear that it was ever wrote down in pen and ink: but custom, I'm told it is, a Norman custom brought by old King William, that wheresoever the King should ride, be it harvest corn or champaine pasture, that very road for ever after becomes a public road—the King's High Road, no less. Now some call that prerogative of royalty. I call it just plain abuse. But how do we prevent it?
> MILLER: It should have been prevented in that Charter they made him set his seal to.
> PARSON: Not in so many words it wasn't, Miller—I raed it . . . it wasn't there.

Scenes like these have the effect of underscoring the socially and politically restricted nature of a particular power structure and of the conflicts within it. As for the charter itself, the clash between the narrow factional interests made for vagueness and ambiguity in the compromise document and thus for a potentially double-edged weapon. Subject to contradictory interpretations, the charter was, on the one hand, quite useless both in immediate politics and as the basis for the liberal myth of English constitutional freedom. On the other hand, the principle of public and accessible law, beyond either the unwritten whims of an amiable autocrat or the written institutionalization of a collective ruling class, could become an instrument of social justice. This duality of historical implications is clearly brought out in the argument between Lady DeVesci and her husband, a leader of the baronial party (II.ii). It is also presented through John's direct address in which he discusses the charter from an explicitly modern standpoint (II.vii).

Thus, *Left-Handed Liberty* is—ironically, in view of its commissioned genesis—not a chronicle of the events surrounding the sealing of a liberal Magna Carta. It is a comprehensive and critical overview of a complex period in English history from the point of view of a modern skepticism toward centralization and written (bourgeois) legislation.[10]

The implications of the nonsubjective, collectivizing, and expressly sociopolitical emphasis of Arden's dramaturgy are profound. As against ahistorical and idealistic perceptions of reality, it encourages a historical and materialist perception that does not view any given condition as final, absolute, and universal. Nor does it regard human relations as static, homogeneous, or harmonious but rather as a dynamic, diversified, and polyvalent balance of forces within a time and place that is historically defined because it is oriented toward the modern spectator.

Ideologically, Arden's focus on the social rather than the psychological, on collectivities rather than individuals, implies a rejection of the bourgeois-liberal notion of the autonomous individual, as it also suggests a redefinition of the term *individual* in its original, prebourgeois (and also the modern Marxian) sense of an *indivisible* member of a collective (cf. Williams 1976b, s.v. "Individual"). Equally, the incorporation of a finer definition and differentiation of the agents on the individual level within the overall framework of supraindividual emphasis suggests a rejection of what Jameson describes as "the tendential law of social life under capitalism"—namely,

> that structural, experiential, and conceptual gap between the public and the private, between the social and psychological, or the political and the poetic, between history or society and the individual which . . . maims our existence as individual subjects and paralyzes our thinking about time and change just as surely as it alienates us from our speech itself. (Jameson 1981, 20)

Chapter Four

Drama as Ludus

All is painted, all is cardboard
Set it up and fly it away
The truest word is the greatest falsehood
Yet all is true and all is play
　　　　　　　　—John Arden, *The Royal Pardon*

In chapter 1, we mentioned that illusionism constitutes an important characteristic of bourgeois theater. It is the manifestation in artistic practice of a naive and mechanical approach to the relation of art to empirical reality. This approach, emerging with the rise of the bourgeois world view and developing through a complex history of artistic and technological innovations, became the orthodox norm in the nineteenth century and remained strong until quite recently in Europe and America. It consists in a literal-minded preoccupation with the exact reproduction of everyday life, with the authenticity and accuracy of physical, social, and psychological details. In other words, it bases itself on what Francis Fergusson has described as "the pretence of unarranged and untheatrical actuality" (Fergusson 1955, 191).

This pretense, evident in all aspects of dramaturgic and theatrical production, has a profound effect on audience response. First, it undermines the spectator's perception of the artfulness and fictionality of the dramatized experience by concealing or suppressing the distinction between the signifier and the signified (see Barthes 1972, 74–75). Second, it encourages the spectator to get emotionally involved in the stage action so as to identify with the characters. Emotionally as well as intellectually captivated, she or he is usually reduced to the role of a mere receiver, or consumer, rather than an active arbiter, or coproducer, of the theatrical experience. By convention, he is simply treated as the absent proverbial fourth wall.

It is not surprising, therefore, that illusionism has in the past proved to be successful mainly in dramatizing such socially restricted situations as are correlative to an emotional intensity focused on exclusively individual and individualistic experiences. It so severely restricts the artistic and cognitive potential of the theater that the latter can no longer deal with complex and epic kinds of action or experience. It can present before us—and, indeed, often does so with great power and apparent authenticity—a privatized slice of life in all its isolated intensity. But it cannot, with equal success, dramatize the entire, complex, multilayered loaf. Since human existence in any given situation is characterized by a complex plurality both on the material and experiential levels, an adequate presentation of anything larger and deeper than isolated private sorrows or pleasures requires a correspondingly complex approach. Such a presentation will not be confined to the illusionist preoccupation with superficial verisimilitude and will probably use an emblematic style— that is, a style that, to quote Barthes again, "signifies" rather than "expresses" (1972, 74) and involves a frank recognition of the essentially playful and artificial nature of the theater.

Perhaps the biggest weakness of illusionism is not only that it fails to deal with larger issues of collective human existence but that it historically grows less and less entertaining. One of the important reasons for the individualist theater's reduced popularity, its socially restricted appeal today, is precisely its inability to provide what may be described as a wholesome aesthetic experience in which the elements of serious or critical contemplation and robust, gutsy pleasure are not divorced but integrally related. Unable to provide such an experience, the illusionist theater is also unable to draw in large, socially varied cross-sections of the people, particularly the plebeian masses who even today are notoriously addicted to various popular, albeit debased and commercialized, forms of entertainment.

Theater is a form of entertainment above all else. If we look back in history, we find that the vitality of the medieval and Elizabethan theaters derived precisely from their ability to provide varied and wide-ranging kinds of experience in forms that invariably included and emphasized the principle of vigorous pleasure. These traditions, like popular dramatic traditions all over the world, regarded theater as a form of game or sport. The very terms that were used to designate a dramatic performance indicated this ludic approach. For example, during the Middle Ages the terms commonly used for this purpose were *game, play,* and *sport* in English, *ludus* in Latin, *Spiel* in German, and *jeu* in French.[1]

This ludic emphasis was not merely a matter of medieval terminology. It lies at the very base of all popular or plebeian dramaturgic and theatrical practices everywhere in the world. It is evident in the robustly playful style of acting and staging, in the active and open interaction between performers and their audiences. Dramaturgically, it is evident in the wide range of freedoms taken with respect to style, technique, and subject matter. Such freedoms allow playwrights to deal, with ease, dexterity, and inventiveness, with subjects of such vast magnitude as historical chronicles, the entire biblical story from Genesis to Revelation, and the epic narratives of the *Ramayana* and *Mahabharata.* It allows them also to mix within a single text kings and clowns, tragic and comic experiences, casual and formal styles, morally serious and merrily frolicsome tones, and critical and celebratory impulses. In speech as well as in activity, it can range freely between the everyday and the stylized, creating a delightful interplay of the empirically verisimilar and the artful. Using such devices as direct comment, and aside, it can involve spectators directly and actively in the performance.[2] Such freedom, made possible mainly by an expressly ludic approach to the art of the theater, makes for immense artistic and cognitive possibilities and richness. Indeed, just as the illusionist theater is marked by its artistic and cognitive restrictiveness, the popular ludic theaters tend to be characterized by their creative extravagance and abandon.

In Europe this popular dramaturgic and theatrical tradition is best exemplified by the medieval and Elizabethan dramas, which usually dealt with serious religious, political, or moral subjects but nevertheless preserved and—as in the case of Shakespeare—even enriched the element of play and frolic found in the popular tradition. As John Russell Brown has observed,

Although miracle and morality presented issues of life and death, destiny and choice, good and evil—themes which in other ages have proved inimical to laughter—they had been given comic servants and midwives, coarse jokes, horseplay and grotesque combats; successive revisions augmented rather than pruned the low comedy. The later interludes on moral and social subjects were often most dramatically alive (and more effectively didactic) in incidents of parody or ignoble conflict. And when theatrical conditions became more stable and individual dramatists emerged, this comic vitality was sustained without diminution. Pathos, propaganda, heroics and romance all coexisted with full bodied laughter. (1966, 103)

This popular dramatic tradition remained strong and vigorous during the Renaissance despite opposition from Latinate, neoclassical scholarship. This scholarship was contemptuous of the vulgarity and lack of decorum in the popular forms and advocated strict separation of styles in terms of "high" and "low," which are, as Raymond William points out, "characteristic class-metaphors" (1966, 25). The outstanding quality and richness of the Elizabethan theater derived largely from its freedom from such neoclassical prejudices. Erich Auerbach writes:

> However important the influence of antiquity may have been on Shakespeare, it could not mislead him, nor yet any other dramatists of the Elizabethan period, into this separation of styles. The medieval Christian and at the same time popular English tradition which opposed such a development was still too strong. (1974, 312–13)[3]

Drawing upon this so called vulgar, rather than erudite, tradition, Shakespeare and his contemporaries could enjoy the artistic freedom that alone could produce what Bethel has described as "the principle of multiconsciousness,"[4] for it alone enabled them to apply their great skills equally to the creation of lofty heroic figures and delightful clowns, to the writing of sublime poetry as well as bawdy, coarse puns, innuendoes, and jokes. And it alone could allow them to combine, with complete lack of inhibition, diverse levels of experience. As for dramatic illusion, these playwrights not only disregarded it, but they often, as in the case of Shakespeare, played with it, creating a delightful and poignant interplay of illusion and reality, life and art.[5]

Such range, richness, and theatrical vitality was lost in the modern theater of illusion. And with it was lost the theater's ability to delight meaningfully. This loss is related to the modern prejudice against laughter, which in turn is related to the puritan heritage of looking down upon and suppressing plebeian or vulgar cultural forms. For, in the words of Bakhtin, the bourgeois nineteenth century respected only satirical laughter, which was actually not laughter but rhetoric. (No wonder it was compared to a whip or scourge.) Merely amusing, meaningless, and harmless laughter was also tolerated, but the serious had to remain serious, that is, dull and monotonous. (1968, 51)

Some of the original gay spirit of the theater and its ability to entertain meaningfully survived, however, in different plebeian forms of entertainment. And it was to the styles and techniques of these popular forms, and beyond them to the more vital traditions of the medieval, Elizabethan, and oriental theaters, that some of the great performers, writers, groups, and directors—such as Chaplin, Meyerhold, Mayakovsky, Eisenstein, Reinhardt, Piscator, and Brecht—turned during the first quarter of this century in their search for both popular and radical forms of entertainment (cf. Schechter 1985). On the one hand, this allowed them to incorporate within a single performance a vast range of sociopolitical experience, and, on the other, it enabled them to restore to the theater its lost communality, gaiety, and cheerfulness.[6] Thus, these radical artists not only restored lost ludic emphasis to the theater, but they put it to new, cognitively enriching, aesthetically pleasing uses.

Almost all these artists and groups in the radical alternative tradition began with the realization that an emphasis on fun and playfulness was a prerequisite for any theater that wants to deal with the large issues of contemporary sociopolitical life and aims to draw popular, plebeian audiences to itself. Quite early in his career, Brecht wrote:

There seems to be nothing to stop the theater having its own form of "sport." If only someone could take these buildings designed for theatrical purposes which are now standing, eating their heads off in interest, and treat them as more or less empty spaces for the successful pursuit of "sport," then they would be used in a way that might mean something to a contemporary public that earns real contemporary money and eats real contemporary beef. (1964 6–7)

Almost half a century later, a radical Scottish playwright and director, John McGrath, made a similar observation.

Working class audiences like laughs; middle class audiences tend to think laughter makes the play less serious. . . . Compared to the bourgeois comedies of manners and intellect, the working class comedy is more anarchic, more fantastical, the difference between the wit and wisdom of the Duke of Edinburgh and Ken Dodd. (1981, 54–55)

Further, these artists in the radical alternative tradition, like their predecessors in the medieval and Elizabethan traditions, do not see the element of fun and pleasure as something nonserious, something that diffuses or trivializes a play's serious social, moral, or philosophical purpose. They regard it instead as an integral aspect of that purpose and as an element that encourages the spectators to a cheerful, objective, and active contemplation of the action on the stage.[7] By keeping the audience mentally alert but also in a pleasurably relaxed state of mind and body, the ludic theater, they believe, frees spectators from "deadly earnest" ideological preoccupations and fosters an awareness of the generic and historical bonds that make them into a community as well as a consciousness of the socioeconomic factors that divide them into antagonistic classes. As such, it persuades the spectators to look at events and human relationships in a new and critical, truly philosophical way. These spectators are prompted to a greater realization of their own potential collective strength and of the alterability of any situation. The result is that no particular experience or situation, no matter how grim or grave, is able to generate feelings of general gloom, pessimism, or helplessness.

Arden's Theater

"The pleasure is in marvelling how well it has been done, in enjoying a superb display of theatre-craft, not in submitting to an illusion," Arden wrote in 1961 (see Arden 1961a). Again, several years later, he argued that the "*sine qua non* of all theatre work is that the audiences should be continuously entertained and invigorated" (1977, 49). This conscious emphasis on fun takes the form of a deliberate but also delightful anti-illusionism in his dramaturgy, allowing his plays to presuppose a ludic and demotic sort of performance. This dramaturgic style has been the cause of a good deal of misunderstanding between Arden and his critics. As Hunt has suggested,

The confusion between Arden and his critics springs basically from this fact: that they go to the theatre unconsciously expecting one "style and type of entertainment," and he offers them another. And this other style which he offers them happens to be one which rejects the basic assumptions the cultivated theatre-going public holds about what makes "good" theatre. (1974, 22)

In other words, while critics and the "cultivated" (that is, middle-class)[8] theater-going public tended to adhere almost exclusively to the individualist and illusionist theater tradition, Arden offered plays that drew upon rich but scorned traditions of anti-illusionist (that is, ludic and often subversive) plebeian entertainment.

A crucial point in Arden's approach to the theater is his conscious recognition of its fictionality. "The art of the theater," he writes, "is exceedingly ancient. . . . *The actor on the stage pretends: and presents the pretence to the public.* To what end, and in what manner, the social conditions of the age and the occasion will determine" (1977, 11; emphasis added). When frankly acknowledged and foregrounded in the dramaturgic text as well as in the style and conditions of performance, this "pretence" becomes a game requiring an active and collaborative partnership between the performers and the spectators. As such, it is obviously different from the deception practiced by the illusionist theater. The success and vitality of the popular theater forms in the past as well as in the present, Arden recognizes, derive from their ability to provide gutsy entertainment, an ability that has atrophied in the modern theater of illusion. He also knows that, "Apart from the pantomime and the music-hall, it is quite a long time since the mass of English people could find anything in the Theatre to produce this effect" (Arden 1959, 42).

To recuperate some of this electric quality of the plebeian theater forms was Arden's persistent endeavor throughout his work in the professional theater. As early as 1959, when most young minds in the British theater were engaged in a passionate but confused debate about how to make the theater regain its popularity and social meaningfulness,[9] Arden's position was relatively the clearest and the most categorical. He argued that English theater could not be revitalized merely by putting on plays about lower-middle-class or working-class situations (which is what the new playwrights like Osborne, Wesker, Behan, and Delaney were doing at the time) but by developing a theater that "can really use these situations to stir up [people's] spirits and send them home so excited that they have to tell all their friends to come the next night and the next and never mind the telly or the local or anything else." The theater, he said, can achieve this effect only if it builds upon that plebeian tradition which is "buried deep down under several hundred years of puritanical falsification," but "the sad remains" of which are still there "as embers that are still susceptible of being blown into flames." Working in close relationship with this tradition is the only course that can enable English theater to put up plays that are "organic events—to get hold of their audiences by laughter, by pain, by music, dancing, poetry, visual excitement, rhythm: and occupy not merely the minds of the people . . . but their loins as well" (Arden 1959, 42–43).

Arden is arguing here—as in numerous other such interventions—for a thoroughly nonillusionist, and nonindividualist approach to theater. He sees theater primarily as a form of communal entertainment. His concept of entertainment, however, is not of the frivolous, uncritical, and escapist sort in which the commercial theater specializes. It is not divorced from the goals of human society or of enhanced cognition. For, he continued, the very form and quality of a truly popular theater serves the purpose of "bringing men together in a kind of secular Eucharist, so that they can leave the building feeling that they are a society, not just a collection of odds and sods who have been coincidentally killing time for a couple of hours on a wet evening." By putting forward plays that are "as whole—and wholesome . . . —as a Ballad or a well-cooked Christmas dinner or a happy marriage," the plays that enable people to "laugh, not only at other people, but at themselves, and the things that hurt them," such a theater is able to communicate a complete experience which is as much a critical examination of some serious social, political, or moral issue as it is a celebration of people's potentially human relationship to other people, of their generic and collective strength.

Thus, Arden recognized, like Brecht, that cognitive experience can be both enriching and sensually gratifying.[10] It was this kind of cognitive/artistic experience that he sought to provide in his own plays. However, a few years of work in the established theater were enough to convince him that bourgeois society with its puritan heritage could not permit such a reintegration of intellectual and sensual pleasures in artistic practice. It is only in a "true state of socialism," as he pointed out in an essay, that "the theatre will [once again] serve our mental and sensual satisfaction" (Arden 1964c, 31; see also his review of *Brecht on Theatre* in Arden 1977, 37–41).

Arden's emphasis on shared fun, his recognition of the relationship between sensual pleasure and cognitive enrichment, and his view that it is only through building on the neglected plebeian forms and traditions that the modern theater can recover its vitality and popular appeal reveal his persistent preoccupation with, and search for, a truly modern yet popular kind of theater, the essential attributes of which would be playfulness as well as artistic and cognitive unorthodoxy. This is, as his reference to the "true state of socialism" indicates, not only an artistic but also a political project. It is certainly more than a purely theoretical preoccupation. For his openly artful dramaturgy is a testimony to his continuous exploration of new possibilities in society as well as in theater.

Blatant Theatricality

According to Brecht, "whenever it failed in the business of deception the theatre still proved to be theatre. Restoring the theatre's reality as the theatre is a precondition for any possibility of arriving at realistic images of human social life." We have already noted that for Arden a fundamental principle underlying the art of theater is the principle of fictionality or pretense: "The actor on the stage pretends and presents the pretence to the public." This, as he correctly points out, is true of all theaters at all times. However, the manner in which the theatrical pretense is actually presented to the public is determined primarily by whether the theater's essential artificiality is sought to be concealed or it is frankly acknowledged. Illusionist drama seeks to obliterate or camouflage all traces of artfulness from its creations, while the nonillusionist dramas of (or derived from) popular traditions not only acknowledge their own fictionality but often emphasize it. Thus, while the former practice turns theatrical pretense into deception, the latter produces an enhanced perception of theatricality and playfulness that adds to the spectators' pleasure.

Arden's own drama is blatantly theatrical in this respect. Developing in a conscious and close relationship with popular traditions, an independent tendency later strengthened by Brechtian theory and practice, it employs a variety of expressly anti-illusionist dramaturgic devices and techniques, which function to foreground the essentially fictional character of the dramatized action and produce that "estrangement effect" that is simultaneously so pleasurable and cognitively enriching. In what follows we shall examine three main aspects of this blatant theatricality: autoreferentiality, speaking to the audience, and the role of the narrator. Although they are discussed here individually for the sake of analytical convenience, it is important to remember that these aspects are not mutually exclusive. They overlap and dovetail with each other.

Autoreferentiality

In the last episode of *The Waters of Babylon,* Krank makes this dying speech.

only a few minutes to live,
I must see can I not give
Some clearer conclusion to this play
To order your lives the neatest way

(Act IV)

Coming from a comic, unheroic character, these simply rhymed lines may seem to be parodying the splendid, high-minded eloquence with which Elizabethan tragic heroes often took their leave of this world. But they are also a dramaturgic coup d'etat against artistic illusion. For the explicit reference to the play as play is a deliberate dramaturgic gesture to subvert and dispel theatrical illusion, to burst open, as it were, the hermetic boundaries that enclose the play-world. The incidents that precede the speech are significant, too. The scene had already included the spectators as the local citizens attending the lottery drawing. From this dramatic role they were further recast by Butterthwaite, in his own gay little play within the play, as Austria, Prussia, and Russia. Thus, the spectators had, by the time of Krank's dying speech, already been in several ways included in the play-world. Spoken obviously out of character and addressed partly to the audience and partly to the other agents (or, properly, actors?) on the stage, this speech jolts the spectators into a sudden and pleasurable return to the awareness that they are in a theater, watching—and even participating in—a show. Rather than detracting from the play's theatrical effectiveness, this sudden impact adds to it. This effectiveness, as our qualifying term *theatrical* suggests, is of a very different kind from the effectiveness valued and desired by illusionist aesthetics. It is based on the delight of the estrangement effect and emphasizes the hypothetical and ludic nature of the dramaturgic construction. It implies that whenever a play or performance dramaturgically incorporates explicit references to itself, whenever the theater turns to itself,[11] and becomes autoreferential, it enables the spectators' greater

perception of a theatricality that is pleasurable because cognitively enriching.

Such autoreferentiality is the ultimate and most blatant form of
theatricality. Historically, it is associated with plebeian traditions as well
as with Elizabethan and Brechtian ones. It is also an important feature of
Arden's dramaturgic style. In addition to *The Waters of Babylon,* it occurs
in several other plays. Of these, *The Hero Rises Up* and *The Royal Pardon*
are constructed entirely on the principle of autoreferentiality and embody
complex structures of play-within-play. However, an example of Arden's best and most mature use of the device is found in *Left-Handed
Liberty.* Just before the last episode, the flow of the action is interrupted
to make a somewhat detailed examination of the significance and implications of the Magna Carta. The previous scene (III.vi) had ended with
King John declaring in a direct address to the audience that, although
"the liberation of Norfolk, completed in mid-October, 1216 . . . must
take its necessary place in any dramatization of the life and death of me,
no doubt we can leave it alone for the moment." With this, with John
still on the stage, the scene changes. Arden's stage direction reads simply,
"No picture—bright lights, possibly house-lights up," and John walks
further downstage and resumes his direct address.

> There comes a time in any stage-play, when the stage itself, the
> persons upon it, the persons in front of it, must justify their
> existence—and I think this is the time now: because on the 18th of
> October, I have to die, suffering from a surfeit of cider and peaches,
> which is a great joke of course, for I shall be taken short in the very
> moment of neither victory nor defeat—my frantic history sus-
> pended under circumstances of absolute inconclusion—King John
> yet again too late to control his situation. A time, I say, must come,
> when we stand in complete bewilderment as to what we are doing
> here at all. I mean—what use is this—
> *He takes off his sword and throws it away, out of sight.*
> Or this—
> *Same business with his crown.*
> Or this—
> *Same business with his mantle.*
> —as a means of convincing you of the human importance of what
> we are talking about? What use am I myself—a bogey-man or ghost
> seven hundred and fifty years old and still mouldering—set down to

prance before you in someone else's body? What in fact have you
seen tonight? (III.vii)

He continues in this vein for a while. Finally, he pulls out a copy of the
charter, remarking:

> Yes; you saw me tear it up at the end of the Second Act, but I kept
> another copy. I always twist around, you see, I plant one or two
> careful feet, carefully behind me, in my own footsteps as I walk.

What follows is a detailed discussion of the charter and its implications.
This discussion, which interrupts the narrative flow, is itself punctuated
by John's repeated references to the growing disturbance in his bowels,
which serve to return the spectators every now and then to the realm of
the narrative action only to have them called back again to the discussion
and the empirical space-time of the performance.

This scene not only "demonstrates Arden's complete confidence in
his own stagecraft" (Hunt 1974, 106), but it is a significant comment on
the nature of dramatic illusion. Like Cleopatra's remarks about Elizabethan boy-actors, it represents a deliberate, even mischievous, dramaturgic gesture of stripping the theatrical performance of its mimetic
trappings, of its tinsel "reality," by showing us the playful means
through which an artistic illusion is produced in the theater. By dismantling and then reconstructing that illusion in full view of the audience,
and, as it were, with their active complicity, it clearly indicates the
boundaries that separate the play-world and the empirical world, including those that separate twentieth-century England from the twelfth-
century one. But, simultaneously and by the same gesture, it also so
dissolves these boundaries that the stage and the auditorium, the past and
the present, the play-world and the empirical world, meet face to face in
a delightfully dialogic confrontation.

This theatrical gesture is also rich in cognitive significance because it
involves the performers and the spectators in a collaborative intellectual
enterprise to analyze and understand a specific historical past. It would
have pleased Brecht, because it is an excellent example, in dramaturgic
practice, of how "footnotes, and the habit of turning back to check a
point" may be introduced into playwriting in order to break out of the
"confines of the subject" and to be able to think "about the subject"
(Brecht 1964, 44). In the words of Albert Hunt, "in the image of an

actor, who plays a king, deliberately stripping himself of his role and making direct theatrical statement about the untenability of authority" the playwright's struggle "with theatre form and his political commitment come together" (1974, 106).

John describes himself as a centuries-old ghost "set down to prance before you in someone else's body." Arden and D'Arcy's musical melodrama on Nelson, *The Hero Rises Up,* is designed entirely as an open acknowledgment of this principle. We see actors playing the roles of the spirits or ghosts of historical personages of a past age. These artistically resurrected spirit-characters then present episodes from their "stories" in which they participate as their "real," living selves. The entire play is conceived on this principle of actors showing us the spirits presenting the show, as an open acknowledgment of the fictive and playful status of the performance. But at the same time—and because of all this—the authors are both theatrically vigorous and able to deal easily with a vast and complex body of sociohistorical events and experiences.

Speaking to the Audience

The above examples also reveal the digressive nature of Arden's dramaturgy. The action in a play of his usually does not move smoothly or exclusively through direct dramatization of activities and dialogue. Within the epic magnitude, diversity, and complexity of his stories, he usually punctuates dramatized sequences with various types of direct, formal speech. These speeches, which are deictically oriented toward the auditorium, either directly or semidirectly—that is, spoken "in full consciousness of the audience but without the marks of direct address" (Williams 1981b, 44–45)—serve as introduction, exposition, and commentary. They fill the gaps in the dramatized action and move it rapidly from episode to episode, covering a wide range of times, places, and issues. In performance, they emphasize the presentational aspect of the dramatized experience and thus enhance the spectators' perception of theatricality. They are like so many deliberately created openings in an otherwise enclosed structure through which the play-world and the empirical world are allowed to come into meaningful contact.

In terms of their dramaturgic function, such speeches can be classified for critical convenience into two interlocking kinds: those in which direct speech is used to introduce the characters and reveal their feelings and thoughts; and those in which it is used to relate the narrative, or advance it or comment upon it. As such, and together with autoreferentiality, they are but aspects of what we have here called blatant theatricality. All these functions can often be found within a single speech. For instance, they are evident in the examples from *The Waters of Babylon* and *Left-Handed Liberty* discussed above. Nonetheless, we will distinguish between them and discuss them separately here. When a speech introducing or revealing a character is given to the actor playing that role, it becomes an example of what we will here call direct self-presentation; and when it is used primarily to advance and comment upon the action, it becomes an instance of direct narration.

As we saw in the last chapter, Arden delights in exteriorizing his agents through speeches, usually in verse, song or formal prose. This, we suggested, increases our awareness of their fictive status and makes their stage presence more exciting, more theatrical. In most cases, these speeches constitute acts of formal self-presentation—that is, instances in which an agent presents him/herself, an emotion, an experience, or a predicament in a formal speech.

Direct self-presentation is a ludic convention, common in the popular theater, applied to the central dramaturgic category of agents. Its effect is similar to that of auto-referentiality, which may or may not include this element. By allowing the agents and their responses to be presented in a deliberate and formal manner, it theatricalizes and distances them. Though a traditionally plebeian dramaturgic device, it reaches from popular spectacle to Aristophanic comedies, Shakespeare, and Brecht. It is not possible in illusionist theater, which finds any form of monologue and direct address unnatural.[12]

Many examples of this convention can be found throughout Arden's opus. These examples range from simple, traditional usages to dramaturgically very complex ones. In its simple form it is evident, for example, in Henry Ginger's gag in *The Waters of Babylon*.

Henry Ginger quick and hot:
Against Conspiracy and Plot
Though the fool policeman sleeps
Henry Ginger wakes and creeps
He tracks down Subversive Threat,
And he'll rescue England yet

(Act II)

It occurs again in Doctor Copperthwaite's self-introduction in *The Happy Haven*: "Copperthwaite, I've been here five years . . ." (Act I). It is there, too, in Arden's later plays. For example, Lindsay's words at the beginning of *Armstrong's Last Goodnight*: "I am Lord Lyon of Arms, Chief Herald of the Kingdom of Scotland. It is my function in this place, . . ." or Armstrong's song in the same play:

> I slew the King's Lieutenant
> And garr'd his troopers flee
> My name is Johnny the Armstrong
> And wha daur meddle wi' me?

(I. vii)

Nelson's harangue to the audience with which *The Hero Rises Up* opens is but a variation of the same strategy.

> If you don't know who I am you ought to be ashamed of your-
> selves, God damn your eyes. You are, I take it, Englishmen? . . .
> (*He sings.*)
>> They set me on a pillar
>> At the north end of Whitehall,
>> For every inch of that great pillar
>> A Frenchman I did kill . . .

These, then, are examples of the obvious or simplest form of self-presentation: an agent identifies and introduces him/herself and/or boasts about her/his achievements in a direct address at the outset of the play, at his/her entry or exit, or at the beginning or end of an episode. It is in this obvious form of self-identification and introduction that this device is most commonly found in traditional theaters—such as in the English Mummers' Play, in which the agent usually enters with "Here come I, so and so." In the above examples Arden is obviously working very close to this tradition.

This convention is also used in subtler and richer ways, so that any deliberate and stylistically or gesturally formal articulation of a character's emotions, attitudes, or problems also becomes an act of self-presentation. Shakespeare's soliloquies and some of Brecht's songs are examples of this usage. A majority of the asides, monologues, songs, verses, and formal prose passages found throughout Arden's work testify to his dramaturgic predilection for this convention. For example, in *The Workhouse Donkey* alone we find it in Feng's formal statements and declarations (I.ii, II.iii), in Butterthwaite's songs (II.vi), in Blomax's song (I.vi), and in Sweetman's soliloquy (II.i).

Whether Arden explicitly says so in the text or not (although he usually does), in actual performance any such speech requires on the part of the speaking actor a correspondingly formal and deliberate gesture and tone directed toward the spectators. For example, in *The Happy Haven*, Phineus makes this beautiful speech.

> I'm an old lady
> And I don't have long to live.
> I'm only strong enough to take
> Not to give. No time left to give.
> I want to drink, I want to eat,
> I want my shoes taken off my feet.
> I want to talk but not to walk
> Because if I walk, I have to know
> Where it is I want to go.
> I want to sleep but not to dream
> I want to play and win every game
> To live with love but not to love
> The world to move but me not move
> I want I want for ever and ever.
> The world to work, the world to be clever.
> Leave me be, but don't leave me alone
> That's what I want. I'm a big round stone
> Sitting in the middle of a thunderstorm.

(III.i)

Since Arden gives no explicit stage directions here regarding the manner in which this speech is to be delivered, and since it is spoken in the play in response to Crape's insistent questioning, a Stanislavskian actor might feel tempted to perform it as confessional discourse of one character to another, made entirely within the bounds of the fictional world of the play. Such an interpretation would, however, be theatrically awkward as well as semantically wrong. Rather than a private confession, the speech is a public declaration. Its very formality (the use of rhymes and rhythm) indicates this. In speaking in this formal manner, Phineus breaks off the preceding naturalist (or conversational) engagement with Crape. Besides, she speaks not as a unique individual but as an articulator of the experience of "the old" as a general category. Therefore, the speech will clearly be more effective if it is addressed to the audience, if the formality of its verbal composition is matched by a corresponding formality of tone, physical posture and positioning, and gesture on the part of the actress-speaker, requiring her to turn away from Crape, toward the auditorium, and perhaps even to move further downstage. Thus delivered, the speech will become an act of direct and formal self-presentation.

Such direct and formal statements by an agent have crucial consequences. First, as we saw in the last chapter, they prevent the dramatic speech and the agents from becoming subjectively ponderous, introverted, or self-indulgent. This in turn discourages the spectators from becoming too involved with the inner lives of the individual "characters." Second, self-presentation contributes significantly toward making the dramaturgic style, and the implied style of performance, more brisk, more light-hearted or cheerful, more demotic. But, above all, the significance of formal self-presentation lies in the fact that it foregrounds the actor rather than the character, the element of presentation rather than representation. For, in effect, self-representation is an act of open theatricalization, self-confessed role playing. Any actor presenting his or her character in such a studied, direct, and formal manner necessarily draws attention to him/herself as an artist and compels the spectators to a keener awareness of the performative aspect of the experience. Self-presentational speeches thus constitute dramaturgic as well as performative signals of a play's openly fictional, ludic status.

Direct Narration

Another conventional usage of direct address in certain kinds of theater is narrative description, exposition, and commentary. In one of its common and easily recognizable forms, this usage can be seen in the opening and closing segments of most of Arden's plays. With the exception of *Serjeant Musgrave's Dance*, every major stage play of his begins and/or ends with some form of verbal activity directly addressed to the spectators. The opening speeches are expository. They introduce the initial situation and main agent(s) and help locate the subsequent action by indicating its time and place and providing the relevant contextual information. The concluding speeches, on the other hand, tend to be more of a comment or statement involving a formal summing up of the story's argument and import. Depending on the play, this summing up may be comical or earnest and didactic. for example, the songs with which *The Waters of Babylon* and *The Workhouse Donkey* conclude are clearly comical and ironical. But Lindsay's direct statement at the end of *Armstrong's Last Goodnight,* the old people's speech at the end of *The Happy Haven,* and Aneurin's song with which *The Island of the Mighty* concludes (or, for that matter, the songs and speeches with which each of the six parts of the Connolly plays ends) are all earnest and didactic in tone and stance.

These prologic and epilogic speeches—which may be in everyday prose, verse, or song, and may be delivered by a single speaker or by a group—have the implication of bracketing a play and underlining its presentational aspect. The opening speeches prepare the spectators for a nonillusionist response based on full consciousness of the events' fictionality and artfulness, while the concluding speeches have the effect of reminding them that what they saw was both fiction and yet not without implications for empirical practice, and that it should be examined as such.

The story itself unfolds in Arden's dramaturgy through exhilarating and frequent alternations between dramatized sequences and direct narration. In *The Waters of Babylon,* as noted in chapter 2, Krank's direct addresses break up the dramatized action within the act divisions into scenes set in different localities. Insofar as these speeches indicate changes in locality and establish the identity of each setting, and insofar as they prepare the narrative context for each subsequent action and report the developments between two episodes, they perform the functions of direct narration. Direct address is frequently used in Arden's drama for the purposes of carrying the story forward and enriching and/or explaining the implications of particular events. In the latter case, its functions include those of describing, reporting, interpreting, and commenting. Such direct addresses, like the other forms of direct speech discussed above, punctuate the dramatized activities and dialogue and separate as well as connect different episodes.

Role of the Narrator

Direct speech in all its forms or usages makes the action in a play come across as something that is being presented or related to the spectators in the sense in which a storyteller is said to tell, narrate, or relate the story. In other words, it suggests the presence of a narrator or presenter. This role is usually explicitly present in the traditional forms of theater. It is also frequently found—although often less explicitly and under such names as Prologue, Epilogue, and Chorus—in dramaturgies that developed in close relationship with popular dramas. It is significantly absent, however, from illusionist forms of drama, which depend entirely on dramatized activities and dialogue.

The presence or absence of the narrator has a crucial influence on the whole dramaturgic design as well as on theatrical experience. Kolve has stressed its significance in relation to the roles of *Nuntius, Expositor, Contemplacio* and *Poeta* in the medieval dramas. "Their function," he writes, "is to enclose the action, whether natural or mythic, in a frame of commentary which puts the playing unmistakably at a distance from reality." Comparing these roles to the French *meneur du jeu,* who "could be in the very middle of the action, holding the playbook in one hand and a baton in the other, conducting the game," he goes on to argue:

What matters is that a similar conception of genre is involved, one far removed from that later kind of the theatre in which the happenings on stage, once under way, have the air of being autonomous, inevitable, and independent of author or director. (Kolve 1966, 27)

As employed by traditional theaters, the narrator/presenter is one who presents and explains the action to the audience. He not only brings different episodes of the story together but also brings the play-world and the empirical world into a sharp encounter. In other words, he acts as a mediator between the fictive possible world of the play and the real world of the performance, bridging as well as accentuating the gap between the two.

This role and function is implicit in Arden's early plays in all those instances of direct speech mentioned above. But it is not formally explicated as a separate agent. In *The Waters of Babylon,* Krank and (in the concluding segment) Butterthwaite can be said to embody this role, while in *Live Like Pigs* it is adumbrated in the ballad singer whose songs open the scenes. Similarly, in *The Happy Haven,* the function is implicitly shared by Copperthwaite and (particularly toward the end of the play) the old people. It is only in his later plays that the function of the narrator becomes explicit and is assigned formally to textual agents.

Arden's narrators perform all the usual functions associated with their role. They describe, report, and comment on events. As we saw in the examples from *The Hero Rises Up* and *Left-Handed Liberty*, they facilitate imaginative manipulation of time and place not only within the fictive realm but between it and the realm of empirical reality. Through their comments, they often bring out some significant point or implication of an event and guide the spectators' attention to it, offering it, as it were, for their active contemplation. A good example of this is Lindsay's comment on Meg's grief in *Armstrong's Last Goodnight* (I.v), quoted in the last chapter, which explicates the sociopolitical implications of Meg's tragic experience and foregrounds it for the audience as another, historically more significant, perspective on the brutal power struggle that the play is presenting.

Lindsay's comment on Meg's grief also suggests his omnipresence as a narrator. He is commenting on an action that he, as a "character," did not witness. In *The Island of the Mighty*, as discussed in chapter 2, the main narrators (Merlin and Aneurin) are invested with a similar omnipresence, which enables them to describe, for example, simultaneous actions taking place in two distant locations (e.g., I.iv). However, Arden's narrators do not always possess this quality. Their vision and knowledge often remain restricted in space and time by their fictive status as dramaturgic agents. Moreover, they often combine direct narration with self-presentation in their discourses. This creates an interesting dialectics of objectivity vs. subjectivity and problematizes the narration. Thus, in *The Island of the Mighty* (I.vii), Merlin, having decided to dedicate his abilities entirely to helping an ailing Arthur attain his last great victory (even "Though it cost me my life / And my truth and my poetic integrity"), relinquishes the role of the narrator temporarily, declaring:

> I do not want to bother any more
> With Balin and with Balan.
> If you're interested to hear what happened
> Let him tell you who best can.

Such a clash of interests and functions between the character (whose commitments belong within the fictional world of the play) and the narrator (whose commitments lie outside the play, to the performance and the audience) bodied forth by the same actor has the effect of rendering direct discourse more dramatic.

Another factor working in the same direction is Arden's practice of dividing the function of the narrator between several agents who usually represent different and divergent points of view. In *Left-Handed Liberty* this role is divided between King John and Pandulph whose ideological positions and loyalties tend in different, often opposite, directions. Similarly, in *The Island of the Mighty*, it is shared between three poets—Merlin, Aneurin, and (in a few scenes) the Pictish poet—who as agents are clearly associated with opposed sociopolitical groupings in the play. Merlin's "liberal" perspective on the action dominates the first half of the trilogy. In the middle of Part Two, Aneurin's categorically plebeian perspective takes over and remains dominant until the end of the play. These conarrators often get directly involved with each other in argument and dialogue, correcting, disputing, or completing each other's reports, observations, or comments. This creates an interesting interplay within the narration—a conflict that belongs neither entirely to the fictional time and space nor entirely to the empirical ones of the performance—and makes narration a complex, shifting, and multivocal process, an excellent example of what Bakhtin called polyphony. Even when there is no visibly direct physical encounter between the conarrators, this sense of the narration as a conflict between competing points of view is usually there.

Examples of such narratorial shifts and conflicts in Arden's drama range from simple to complex. In its simple form it can be seen, for example, in *The Island of the Mighty* (I.ix). The Pictish poet, who has been acting as the narrator for the Balin-Balan story, begins to narrate and comment upon a new episode (that of Arthur's last campaign), at which point Merlin, a fellow narrator returning, as it were, from leave, interrupts his song.

POET: (*singing*).

Old men old men on their horses so huge
And their dragon so high on its pole
They never will believe that for them there is a grave
Just as deep as for those whom they kill.

MERLIN: Oh no, my heathen friend—not true. We are only too well aware of the depths of our graves.
THE PICTISH POET bows gravely to him and goes out.

In the comments of each of these narrators the traces of their respective biases and affiliations as characters are evident. The Pictish poet's unfavorable disposition toward Arthur's Christian army is informed by his prejudices and interests as a representative of the unassimilable tribesmen in the play, which is made explicit by Merlin's reference to him as a heathen. Merlin's intervention, similarly, is made from the position of a Christian partisan of Arthur's army, as indicated by his use of the first-person plural. At the same time, this encounter is not located within the limits of the play-world proper, nor can it be said to occur entirely in the audience's (or performers') empirical space and time. It belongs to a different dimension of fictive time-space, which forms, as it were, the borderline between the play-world and the empirical world.

A more complex example of this kind is found in *Left-Handed Liberty* (I.ii). The previous scene had shown, through a stylized dramatization, the last meeting between King John and his dying mother. As the scene changes, John comes downstage and speaks to the audience:

> JOHN: My mother, Queen Eleanor of Aquitaine, received her tardy visitor upon April the first, 1204—they call it All Fools' Day in England. And we buried her at Fontrevault. She was eighty-two years old. However rudely death came in unto her, and however directly he attempted to force her to walk, I have no doubt but that she remembered the name of the day and made a fool of him in the passage. Not on the first of April, but on the nineteenth of June, some eleven years later, there came together a large number of my subjects to try to make a fool of me—being, as I was, the son of my father, who would never be governed, never.

Here John is supposedly giving the audience a résumé of relevant developments during the eleven years that had elapsed between the preceding and succeeding pieces of dramatized action in the play. In terms of the sequential structure of the play, this speech occurs at the end of those eleven years and immediately prior to the meeting with the barons on 19 June 1215. But, as his use of the past tense even for events that have yet to take place in the play clearly indicates, the speech is really being made by a "ghostly" John who has come out of a remote historical past, as well as out of the fictional world of the play, to address the spectators from their own empirical time and space.

In an interesting dramaturgic complication at this point, John's direct discourse is interrupted by the Pope's Legate, Pandulph, who points out to the king that something has been left out of his résumé. This interruption itself becomes the cause of a diverting (both in the sense of

digressive and of entertaining) altercation between the two, in which
their distinct points of view and personalities as agents come into conflict.

PANDULPH: Your Grace, you have omitted something.
JOHN: Am I corrected? Does someone dare? Ah, Master Pandulph: the Legate of the Pope. (*He looks at Pandulph's chart.*) I mis-
trust these geometrical figures, Pandulph. They are altogether too
pat. If one of these circles here were to have a little kink in it, thus—
you would find perhaps Mars banging into Venus at a vulnerable
and tender point and your entirely perfect mechanism would be
wrecked by eccentricity.
PANDULPH: Exactly so. *If* there were a kink. But a kink would be
a falsehood, and a falsehood in the geometry of God is inconceiv-
able. But you are not the geometry of God, Your Grace, you are a
mortal man and very prone to falsehood. As I said, you have omitted something. In your account of your stewardship of the remote
English vineyard, you have failed to mention, did you not, that for
six whole years you yourself were excommunicated and your kingdom laid under Interdict. You chose to defy the Pope—
JOHN: Over a technical matter—
PANDULPH: The appointment of an Archbishop. Technical? Perhaps. But in the end, you were governed. You were compelled to
submit.
JOHN: I chose to submit. I viewed the matter in a larger perspective. I never make the mistake of elevating small disputes into questions of principle. Besides, I had to deal with the Baronial discontent
and a danger of invasion from France.
PANDULPH: Nevertheless, you surrendered your crown to the
Pope and received it back, upon terms.

It seems that here both Pandulph and John are speaking simultaneously
as narrators and as characters. Occupying, as it were, a liminal time and
space, they complete the narration between themselves. But the fact that
this bivocal narration is given in the form of dramatic dialogue or argument, involving a retrospective glance at events that are already past,
enhances its excitement and gives it the quality of a dramatic episode.
The theatrical interest of the scene and its complex play upon different
levels of illusion and reality reach a new height when this verbal argu-

ment turns, suddenly and in the middle of a speech, into a dramatized activity representing an action that, in terms of the retrospective stance of the argument, is supposed to have already taken place.

PANDULPH: Nevertheless, you surrendered your crown to the Pope and received it back, upon terms. Here it is. (*He holds the crown.*)

JOHN: I am glad to get it back. All my jewels are beautiful, this more beautiful than most, quite apart from its significance. You haven't abstracted any of the decorations, have you? No: that is just as well.

PANDULPH: (*withdrawing crown from John's reach*). Kneel, my son, and acknowledge your fault.

JOHN: Under pressure, and with all due calculation, I will kneel. (*He does so.*)
Having offended God and our Mother the Holy Church in many things, and hence being in great need of the Divine Mercy, we offer and freely yield to God and to the Lord Pope Innocent III and his catholic successors, the whole kingdom of England for the remission of our sins, so that from henceforth we hold it from him and from the Holy Roman Church our Mother, as a sworn vassal. And let this Charter of Obligation remain forever valid.

PANDULPH: Come then, exalted prince, fulfil the promises given and confirm the concessions offered, so that God almighty may ever fulfil any righteous desire of yours, enabling you so to walk amid temporal blessings as not to fail of winning of the eternal.
He places the crown on John's head.

JOHN: (standing up). And furthermore I swear that as soon as I have the means and opportunity I will lead an army to the Holy Land and redeem from the Paynim Turk, by force, the Blessed Sepulchre of Christ.

PANDULPH: (*producing a jewelled cross*). Wear this upon your breast in token of your sanctified intention.
(*He hangs the cross round JOHN's neck.*)

JOHN: Diamonds? Good. Silver-gilt. Not so good. Parsimonious, rather.

During this dramatized action the past of the narration suddenly becomes the present of a performed activity and the two conarrators of the play switch to their separate agential roles. The fictive world of this "flash-back" episode is itself often broken open by John's humorous remarks, which are clearly in the nature of asides, though they are not identified as such in the text. The result is a highly pleasurable interplay of illusion and reality, a complex to-and-fro movement between the fictive space and time of the narrative and the empirical or audience space and time of the performance.

This sequence is, in my view, one of the best examples of ludic dramaturgy to be found anywhere in twentieth-century drama. It is so pleasurable because all of its complex playing upon levels of fiction and reality, and all of its theatrical excitement, are of a piece with the cognitive significance. It is a gestic sequence in the Brechtian sense of the term, revealing certain historically significant attitudes and relationships. While imparting in a brief compass a lot of narratively necessary information, it also clearly shows, for example, that the relationships between a greedy and devious monarch and the Roman Catholic Church of the Middle Ages were based not on spiritual but on the purely materialistic grounds of fines and rewards, on a businesslike agreement to support and further each other's worldly interests.

Thus, Arden's dramaturgic use of the convention of direct address in its various forms grows, in his later plays, highly complex and playful. The instances of direct address function, as it were, as so many doors and windows in the otherwise enclosed structure of a play-world. Through these openings the agents move with ease in and out of their fictional habitats, making the fictive and empirical worlds come into dialogic interplay, while at the same time keeping them clearly distinct. The use of direct speech also foregrounds the play's performative aspect and presupposes a theatrical experience in which the spectators are held in an alert—but also, in a seeming paradox, cheerfully relaxed—state of mind. Each instance of such speech is an escape from the proscenium arch and an attempt to reach out to the spectators, to involve them more actively and collaboratively in this game of pretense.

Performances within Performance

"Diverse toys mingled in the same / To stir folk to mirth and game." This is how a medieval play, *Fulgens and Lucrece,* describes itself. Like all ludic types of theater, Arden's dramaturgy, too, aims to provide a richly variegated entertainment. Instead of confining itself to the everyday forms of behavior and activity, it includes a variety of expressly artful verbal and gestural forms, largely drawn from popular tradition. In other words, in his drama, not only speech but also physical activity often stops being casual and becomes formalized.

Sudden and frequent shifts of this kind within a play constitute a diversified, multilevel, performative structure—a structure of little performances within performances. Such a structure reflects the "off-hand approach" and the "principle of variety structure" that are characteristic of such popular entertainments as vaudeville and the Music Hall (McNamara 1974, 16). Arden has from the beginning believed that

> in a play, the dialogue can be naturalistic and "plotty" as long as the basic poetic issue has not been crystalized. But when this point is reached, the language becomes formal (if you like, in verse, or sung), the visual pattern coalesces into a vital image that is one of the nerve-centres of the play. (Arden 1965c, 127)

In his own work, the formalized segments—song, dance, game, and ritual—of a play stand out against the relatively more "natural" or normal sequences, and they function both as its experiential "nerve-centres" and as a way to foreground the essentially ludic character of the performance.

Songs

A prominent and persistent feature of Arden's dramaturgy is the use of songs. As a rule, every major play includes a number of songs in addition to numerous instances of spoken or recited verse. His characters often burst into verse or song when they have something narratively, emotionally, or cognitively significant to express, and sometimes for no obvious reason at all. Also, they sing when they are excessively happy or sad, jubilant or disturbed. As a result, the songs in Arden's opus cover a wide range of content and mood. There are gay and comic songs, like those sung by Blomax and Butterthwaite in *The Workhouse Donkey,* and contemplative and melancholy songs such as those sung by Krank in *The Waters of Babylon*; songs that are lyrical and romantic in nature, like the song of the Young Marshal in *Left-Handed Liberty,* and songs that are bawdy such as the duet by the Maid and the first Armstrong in *Arm-*

strong's Last Goodnight. There are also songs of direct and satirical political comment such as some of the scene-opening ballads in *Live Like Pigs,* the street ballad on liberty in *Left-Handed Liberty,* and the sailors song in *The Hero Rises Up. Left-Handed Liberty* contains four songs, *The Waters of Babylon* and *Serjeant Musgrave's Dance* six each, *The Royal Pardon* nine, *The Workhouse Donkey* and *Armstrong's Last Goodnight* eleven each, *The Happy Haven* twelve, and *Live Like Pigs* no less than twenty-five, including the songs that inaugurate fourteen out of a total of seventeen scenes in the play. Similarly, there is a great deal of singing in *The Hero Rises Up, The Island of the Mighty, Vandaleur's Folly,* and *The Non-Stop Connolly Show.*

On one level, these songs (like verse and heightened prose) are instances of formal speech, and, as such, they are expressly artful and artificial forms of verbal activity. They *say* whatever they have to say in a manner that is both emphatic and—because of the order and regularity of repetition and rhythm—pleasurable. They also "bring out and enhance the stylization" of the agents (Forsas-Scott 1983, 10). On the other hand, singing in theater is more than speech. It has musicality, tune, and its rendering requires on the part of the singer both skill and a conscious demonstration of that skill. This skill is, for the most part, a consciously cultivated ability to control and regulate certain parts of the body— particularly those connected with the vocal organs. Moreover, when singing for an audience (whether large or small, public or private), the singer invariably assumes a more or less deliberate, self-conscious physical stance, which differs from his or her ordinary or normal stance (say, during informal conversation). In other words, singing is deictically oriented toward an audience, which makes it a performance. As a performance, singing subsumes any particular song (even a sad one) under an aesthetically pleasurable experience.

Arden's songs are usually written in the ballad style and sung to the tune of folk and popular airs derived from Irish, Scottish, English, and, as in the case of some of the songs in the Connolly plays, American traditions. The tunes and their sources are generally specified by the playwright in the text. While it is beyond my competence or immediate purpose to attempt a musical analysis, it should be stressed that dramaturgically—like the songs of the pantomime or the Music Hall— these songs in Arden are so many cheerful little performances within the overall performance. As such, they have, besides their narrative usefulness, their own immediate theatrical excitement and pleasure. Finally, they mark transitions or breaks from "natural" everyday activities and thus interrupt the monolinear continuity of the plot.

Dances, Games, and Rituals

Just as speech in Arden's drama often abandons the casual form of the colloquial and the everyday and becomes formal, rhythmic, even tuneful, gestural activity, too, often takes on the stylized and openly artful forms of dance, game, and ritual. Arden's penchant for adapting these forms for theatrical purposes has been evident from the beginning. In his first play, *The Waters of Babylon,* the first act ends with Krank suddenly, and for no obvious reason, bursting into a merry step-dance while singing a melancholy song. The play also includes a sequence in which the action (dramatizing the prostitute Bathsheba's successful seduction of the puritanical councillor, Caligulla) shifts from the ordinary and conversational to an enchanting, highly stylized game involving answering rhymes and a circular chase around the stage (Act Three). Similarly, *Serjeant Musgrave's Dance* includes, in addition to Musgrave's own weird dance from which the title derives, a vigorous group dance led by the irrepressible Bargee to the accompaniment of a children's circular song. In *The Workhouse Donkey,* besides a gay dance by Blomax and Gloria (I.vi), the narratively crucial episode of the town-hall burglary—which would have formed the most intense, climactic moment in any illusionist rendition of the story—is presented largely through song and dance, which estrange and distance it. Dances occur also in the later historical-legendary plays. For example, in *Armstrong's Last Goodnight,* a group dance is performed to traditional music and singing, while *Left-Handed Liberty* includes three dances: a vigorous and noisy shepherds' dance—"a grand stamping dance" called Morpeth Rent (II.ii), a street ballad danced to tambourine music and singing (III.v), and a Morris-like dance (revised version of II.iv).

Whatever its significance in the overall context of the play, a dance is always a show, a set of stylized and ordered body movements and gestures. It invigorates the performance and enhances its ludic quality. The use of games and rituals has a similar effect in Arden's drama. Such actions may be predominantly verbal, predominantly gestural, or mixed. The verbal as well as the mixed games usually employ rhymes. For example, in *The Happy Haven,* Act III, the old people constrain each other to tell the truth by swearing thus in rhyme: "Truth or lie till the day I die / Strike me dead if I tell you a lie." This verbal game, which obliges everyone who plays it to answer truthfully the questions of the opposite player, is used by the authors to foreground a significant cognitive element. It highlights the process through which the characters become aware of their real responses to Dr. Copperthwaite's scientific scheme of restoring youth to the aged. Phineus's beautiful speech, quoted earlier, is made in the course of this game. Nonetheless, the game has its own immediate delight as a fanciful activity reminiscent of children's games. The compulsion that the players feel stems not from any superstitious belief in the content of the swearing rhyme but is related to the need to respect the rules and injunctions of the game.

Sequences such as this, like the seduction scene in *The Waters of Babylon,* have an unmistakable folkloric flavor. They transform the stage into a playing area and elevate the dramatized action to the level of some enchanting game, resulting in much enhanced pleasure. In a revised version of Act Two, Scene Four of *Left-Handed Liberty,* appended to the main text, Arden adapted a children's folktale about the wise men of Gotham as a theatrical game involving a group of villagers who enact some of the incidents of this story to fool the king's messenger into thinking that they are daft. The story thus becomes a veritable play within the play. What the spectators see are four actors playing thirteenth-century villagers playing characters in a folktale.

Arden's interest in traditional, folkloric forms also includes an interest in the theatrical possibilities of ritualistic actions. The Bathsheba-Caligulla seduction scene in *The Waters of Babylon* and the truth-or-lie rhymes in *The Happy Haven* are early examples of this interest. Another is found in *Live Like Pigs,* where the Old Croaker is presented as an embodiment of a primitive, superstitious, and anarchic spirit (which, as we shall see, makes her a prefiguration of the Old Morgan in *The Island of the Mighty*). Through most of the play she is seen to be involved in some striking action such as obsessively tearing paper or cloth into strips and singing or chanting rhymes or snatches of ballads, which make bawdy, mischievous, or sarcastic references to the happenings around her. All this adds to her theatrical interest. For example, in Scene Fourteen, she fears that the furious mob outside will break in through the windows, so she performs an old superstitious ritual. Taking the little girl Sally with her, she goes from one window to another, flattening her palms on the panes and chanting:

Window close and window true
In and out and who comes through?
Mary and Jesus and the Twelve Tall Riders
Nobody else nobody else nick nack noo!

Performed repeatedly throughout the scene, this "old rubbish," as her daughter, Daffodil, calls it, has its own immediate, diverting interest and theatricality. The session of evangelical praying and hymn singing, building up to a rhythmic ecstasy in speech and movement, generates a similar interest in *Armstrong's Last Goodnight* (III, vi).

Besides its immediate theatrical interest, its ability to energize and vary a performance, Arden's use of songs, dances, games, and rituals (like his use of autoreferentiality, self-presentation, and direct narration) also has cognitive significance. These forms function as distancing devices and create an estrangement effect (which is essentially a cognitive effect). The interplay of distancing and delighting that flows out of their openly artful nature emphasizes and clarifies significant themes, implications, or aspects of the story and enables the spectators to view it from a cheerful but also critical position.

This is particularly evident in Arden's later plays. These plays evidence an artistic and political maturity, combining a better grasp of the Brechtian practice and theory with a more militant political commitment. The use of street ballads and the fable of the wise men of Gotham in *Left-Handed Liberty* is a good partial example. However, it is in the plays like *The Island of the Mighty* and *The Non-Stop Connolly Show* that Arden's ludic dramaturgy finds its best expression.

Traditional forms found in Arden and D'Arcy's trilogy on Arthurian Britain are probably unparalleled in modern drama in range and variety. In a previous chapter, we noticed this range and variety in relation to Part One, Scene Three, of *The Island of the Mighty*. Dances, masks, primitive rites and rituals, verbal riddles, magical happenings, and superstitious practices, which the play as a whole includes and which profoundly influence its dramaturgic style as well as the type of performance it presupposes, make for a drama that "plays" a lot. Combining influences that are geographically as wide ranging (although, in terms of artistic practice, related) as Celtic folklore, traditional Indian theater, and Brecht, the play calls for a light and racy performance in which the stage is uncluttered by heavy scenery and the acting is unfettered by individualist preoccupations with "building character." Its agents are conceived

in an epistemologically comic (that is, distanced) mode—a basic fact that
David Jones, the play's first director, seems to have missed (cf. Hunt
1974, 168–72).

However, within such a dramaturgic form, theatrical playfulness
and cognitive seriousness come together in a complex experience. Part
Two, Scene Five, illustrates this adequately. The scene, which depicts
the marital/sexual encounter between Arthur and Gwenhwyvar as a
ferocious combat between two monstrous antagonists, is remarkable for
its vigor and excitement. Its theatrical energy is in large part the result of
a rich combination of masks, mime, song, music, dancing, ritual, and
direct commentary. The wedding rituals and the first sexual encounter
between the two characters are presented as dumb shows that are eluci-
dated in Merlin's and Aneurin's direct commentaries.[13] Basically, Arden
and D'Arcy's dramaturgy in this scene fuses influences derived from two
distinct traditions: first, the British folk tradition of the Mummers' Play—
particularly what Alan Brody calls the Hero Combat Plays (Brody 1970;
Forsas-Scott 1983, 3–7); and, second, certain traditional forms of Indian
epic theater. For example, while Arthur's boastful speeches and some of
Goddoddin's asides are obviously comic and resemble similar situations
and speeches in the traditional St. George Play (see also Arden and
D'Arcy's adaptation of this form in *The Royal Pardon*), the masks, the
warlike dance, and the music are, as we shall see, strongly reminiscent of
an Indian traditional form of dance-drama called the Chhau.

The very idea of presenting the scene as a battle between gorgon and
demon seems to have been derived from the conventional Chhau motif
of the combat between the ferocious goddess Kali and the demons she
destroys. Also, in the Chhau, as in the play, the combat is presented in
the form of a vigorous stamping dance all over the acting area, accompanied by thundering drum music. That the masks, too, are conceived in
the Chhau style becomes obvious when one compares them with Arden's own descriptions of the masks that the goddess and the demons
traditionally wear in the Chhau.[14] In an essay on the Chhau dancers of
Purulia, he writes:

Some of the characters were demons with tusks instead of teeth, and
ferocious whiskers. . . . All had bare feet and ankle-bells. . . . The
great goddess Kali—mother and destroyer—wore a black jumper, a
mini skirt, a necklace of human skulls, a long wild hair wig, and her
red mouth was contorted into a wide snarl, her tongue stuck out

between her teeth. . . . She was very dangerous and stamped on the men whom she killed. (1977, 144)

The tusk teeth, long wild hair, protruding tongue, and red mouth are all reproduced in the masks that D'Arcy and Arden prescribe for Arthur and Gwenhwyvar in the play.

> Arthur's mask is a grinning demon—great tusk-teeth—bright red face—staring eyes—hair like a golliwog. Gwenhwyvar's is a kind of gorgon—protruding tongue—green hair of great length—staring eyes—livid white face.

Staring eyes, although not mentioned in Arden's essay, is also a characteristic of the Chhau masks, as are the thundering vigor and rhythm that the authors recommend for the Arthur-Gwenhwyvar dance.

Arden and D'Arcy found in this highly stylized and traditional form not only tremendous theatrical energy and spectacularity but an emblematic richness that made it suitable for expressing and foregrounding the central cognitive implications of the scene (further explicated by the two poet-narrators). The destructive nature of the Arthur-Gwenhwyvar marriage is from the beginning based on an obstinate stance of mutual hostility rather than love. By presenting the sexual act as a violent physical combat, the playwrights could show, too, the corrupting influence of war and brutalization on normal, indeed, on the most intimate, human relationships. More significantly, this depiction of the Arthur-Gwenhwyvar relationship encapsulates the central conflict of the trilogy—the one between the patriarchal principle of oppression, control, and slavery and the matriarchal principle of freedom and love, between the liberatory principle of erotics and the repressive principle of imperialist politics. For, while Arthur is throughout associated with the patriarchal principle of repression, discipline, control, and good order, Gwenhwyvar is conceived as an embodiment of the matriarchal principle of what Musgrave criticized as "life and love," and, as in this particular scene, Arthur's attitude toward women equals his attitude toward the land—he strives to master them both—just as Gwenhwyvar's defiance of the Roman General has larger utopian implications.[15]

The scene is of crucial significance for the play's narrative structure as well. The antagonistic relationship between Arthur and Gwenhwyvar shown here is directly related to the subsequent sequence of events, involving the latter's assumption of the role of the Daughter of Branwen and her betrayal of Arthur in favor of Medraut, and leading to the disintegration of Arthurian Britain. Since Medraut's military strength derives precisely from his having become Gwenhwyvar's chosen champion, the battle between him and Arthur can be said to be a continuation and final form of the battle that began with the marriage of Arthur and Gwenhwyvar. The scene thus has a function similar to the induction or the dumb show in Elizabethan theater: it gives us, in an imaginatively abbreviated form, a foretaste of events to come.

Opening Out the Stage Space

As Michael Bristol has pointed out,

> The institutions of theatre affect forms of artistic production, of social interaction, and of the creation of meaning; by favoring certain styles of perception, representation, and understanding, institutional constraints determine how meaning will be created by the audience's experience of the text in performance. (1983, 637)

Arden's dramaturgy, with its collectivist and ludic emphasis, was clearly incompatible with the social as well as the artistic complexion of the theater in which his plays were produced. Even his early plays reveal a powerful impulse to open out the conventional stage space in order to connect it with the auditorium in a more fluid, more actively collaborative and dialogical, and therefore socially more meaningful, relationship. Dramaturgically, as we saw above, this is evident in a number of conventions and devices that he characteristically employs, particularly when, as in *The Waters of Babylon* (III), *The Happy Haven* (II.i), and *The Island of the Mighty* (I.x), the spectators are cast into the play. These are essentially conventions of the open, comic (historically plebeian) dramaturgy and stage, and they clearly contradict the illusionism of a picture-frame stage.

Thus, Arden's refusal to allow himself to be restricted by the conventional proscenium stage, which is the commonly available kind of stage in England, was clear from the beginning. No doubt, in the course of his professional career he was often forced to adapt his writing to such a stage, but he did not like it. He felt that the conditions such a stage imposed were not suitable for his dramaturgic style or for the kind of experience he wanted to generate through his plays. Such a stage, he believed, was too static, too enclosed and illusionistic, to allow him and the performers the freedom to explore new possibilities. In his prefatory note to *The Happy Haven* he lamented the circumstance.

> At the Royal Court, the play had of necessity to be played within the proscenium arch. This is a necessity that will doubtless be imposed upon most productions of *The Happy Haven* in this country, but it is nonetheless a regrettable one. The unsatisfactory organisation of the English theatre in general and the archaic design of its buildings hamstring any attempts on the part of the dramatists and directors to open out the conventions of the drama.

Even when writing for production on a conventional proscenium stage, Arden sought to transcend its illusionism and formal restrictions dramaturgically by inserting into the plays, as we have seen, direct addresses, asides, and songs. He also sought to emancipate the scenography from proscenium restriction and to recover something of the openness and versatility of traditional popular staging.

In terms of scenography, his preferences—as expressed in the prefatory notes and stage-directions in his plays—show growth from what Brecht called "partial illusion" to complete nonillusionist or an emblematic scenography (Brecht 1964, 219). In *The Waters of Babylon,* Arden required that "the sets should in no way be realistic." Wherever necessary, the locality should be indicated "rather by suggestion than by outright illustration." In writing this play, he said, he had in mind "the sort of scenery" that was used in the eighteenth and the early nineteenth centuries, "which involved the use of sliding flats or drop curtains which open and close while the actors are still on stage—a method still in use in provincial pantomimes." The play requires that the stage be divided into two areas—one a permanently open forestage area, which throughout remains neutral and unlocalized; and the other an inner, curtained area, which opens from time to time to reveal different specific locations (Krank's house, the architect's office, a public lavatory, and so on). To transport him/herself from one location to another, an agent simply walks downstage to the neutral area while talking to another agent or directly to the audience. In the meantime the scene behind closes, reopening a little later as a different location. The agent then just walks into it. For the identification of any specific location, Arden indicates only the

minimum and most characteristic objects. There is no attempt at outright illustration. Thus, all that we have by way of physical objects to tell
us that we are in an architect's office is a drawing table with some
instruments, papers, and a telephone on it; and of these the telephone is a
necessary piece of property because it is used during the action. It is
mainly through direct narration and dialogue that a locality is dramatically established. This method of using stage space, which already implies a virtual abolition of the proscenium arch, is significantly reinforced
by a bold dramaturgic gesture in the last episode when the spectators are
cast into the play as the public attending the lottery draw.

    This early dramaturgic preference for "partial illusion," for keeping
the property and sets to the necessary minimum, and for reshaping the
stage space so as not to allow the proscenium arch to exercise an illusionistic effect is also found in *Serjeant Musgrave's Dance,* wherein Arden
recommends stylized scenes and costumes and specifies that "scenery
must be sparing—only those pieces of architecture, furniture and proper-
ties actually used in the action need be present." It was with *The Happy
Haven,* his first play in collaboration with D'Arcy, that Arden got his
first opportunity to see a play produced on a stage radically different
from the conventional proscenium stage. It was written during Arden's
fellowship at the Drama Department of Bristol University and, as the
"author's note" in the published version informs us, was initially presented there on "an open stage, following roughly the Elizabethan
model." Arden found the experience of working on this stage useful and
stimulating. It gave him an opportunity to prove to himself that "the
leanings [he] had long had toward the open stage and its disciplines were
justifiable in practice as well as theory." The effect of this first experiment with the open stage can be seen clearly in the text of the play itself,
in which the stage is used, as Hunt points out, "partly as a music-hall
platform and partly as a lecture theatre, in which Copperthwaite demonstrates scientific experiments which are also magic conjuring tricks"
(1974, 67). The play includes fantastic elements, (for example, a grown
man is transformed into a baby and an imaginary dog is chased all over
the stage). With its use of masks, games, songs, direct addresses, and
elements of fantasy, the play endeavors to attain a form and style completely free from illusionism.

    The Happy Haven was first produced in 1960. In the same year,
Arden and D'Arcy wrote a nativity play, *The Business of Good Government,* for an amateur production in a small Yorkshire village where they

were living at that time. Producing the play in the village church, the playwrights discovered that the chancel steps of most churches provide a natural open stage. The play is clearly designed for open-stage production. "Indeed I recommend," says Arden in his preface to the text, "that where a proscenium stage is to be used, the producer should start by removing the proscenium frame, curtains and footlights." Except for the Holy Family and the three Wise Men, the cast enters through the audience in a carol-singing procession at the beginning and leaves similarly at the end. Throughout the performance, the cast is to remain visible, sitting in "unassuming" chairs, which must clearly seem to be "the furniture on the stage rather than fittings in, say, Herod's palace or the Bethlehem inn." They thus wait for their cues in full view of the audience and "in a relaxed and natural way." The acting area at the center of the stage, entirely free of furniture, is divided into two sections: a wide, lower space, and a small, slightly raised platform (or rostrum, as Arden calls it) at the back. Without any furniture or sets, the scenes are located entirely by means of identifying the agents through their direct description and/or action, their gestures, and their movements.

These experiences outside the professional, metropolitan theater deeply influenced Arden's development. All the major plays that he (or he and D'Arcy) wrote during this period are, as we know, cognitively more serious, based as they are on historical-legendary materials of significant political import. But they are also more playful, "theatrical," and emblematic in style. In terms of artistic interests and preferences, there is a similarity between these plays and amateur experiments such as the one exemplified by *The Business of Good Government*. On the other hand, the freedom to experiment and to follow and realize one's own ideas and notions necessarily showed up the relatively restrictive and rigid structure of the professional theater. It is not surprising, therefore, that the period of Arden and D'Arcy's increasing dissatisfaction with London's professional theater coincided with the period of their increasing involvement with amateur and fringe theaters.

In *The Workhouse Donkey,* written in 1963, their interests and notions anticipated the month-long arts festival they hosted at their residence in Kirbymooreside the same year and the day-long antiwar event called "War Carnival" in New York in 1967. The play, as the author's preface informs us, is conceived as a festive, full-throated entertainment celebrating "the old essential attributes of Dionysus: noise, disorder, drunkenness, lasciviousness, nudity, generosity, corruption, fertility, and ease." Arden wanted the play to last for something like the whole day, allowing the audience "to come and go throughout the performance, assisted perhaps by a printed synopsis of the play from which they could deduce those scenes or episodes which would interest them particularly, and those which they could afford to miss." To present such an entertainment, the theater would obviously have to "offer rival attractions as well, and would in fact take on some of the characteristics of a fairground or amusement park: with restaurants, bars, sideshows, bandstands, and so forth, all grouped around a central playhouse." He regretted that the conditions under which the "regular" theater operated did not permit such forms of public entertainment.[16]

Arden was fully aware that such a radical alteration in the makeup and function of the existing theater was desirable but not immediately possible. He recognized that such a transformation would require changes in some fundamental economic and political relationships within the theater as a public institution as well as in society at large. Over the next few years, he and D'Arcy were to grow increasingly conscious of and uneasy about this tie between established cultural forms and institutions and the sociopolitical power system. They were also growing progressively more alert to the lack of freedom and unacceptable working conditions that such a system produced for the artist, particularly the playwright. In their major plays of the period—*Left-Handed Liberty*, *The Hero Rises Up*, and *The Island of the Mighty*—they did away with sets completely, using instead emblems in the form of backcloths, charts, and projected or displayed titles to differentiate and locate the scenes. Freeing it from illusion-creating and movement-obstructing architecture and objects, they sought to make the stage space more fully a playing area that is open, versatile, dynamic, and rich in creative possibilities.

Arden and D'Arcy have continued to explore these possibilities in different ways, drawing largely upon the conventions of popular theater forms from Europe and Asia but always within the terms of an emphatically ludic performance. Although in recent years they have turned increasingly to radio drama, the few stage plays that they have written since *The Island of the Mighty* testify to the fact that they continue to work toward achieving some of the characteristics of popular dramaturgy and theater.

Chapter Five

Toward a Theater of the Oppressed: Plebeian Bias in *The Island of The Mighty*

[M]ost of history in fact consists of gaps. To fill them in would be to direct the flow of interpretation from a comfortable "mainstream" into a series of eddies representing the socalled "losing" side in one historical conflict after another. "Mainstream" is winners' history: eddies and backwaters are where the losers still survive, refusing to be entirely written-out.
—Margaretta D'Arcy

At a time when *commitment* was the catchword and the main yardstick by which the relevance of a new play was measured, Arden's work was found wanting in this regard. What was meant by commitment in the fifties, however, was a response to the postwar situation communicated mainly through moralistically conceived characters and situations. John Russell Taylor's statement in 1962 that "Arden permits himself, in his treatment of the characters and situations in his plays, to be less influenced by moral preconceptions than any other writer in the British theatre today" was both a defense of the latter's craft and an explanation of the hostility of his early audiences and critics (Taylor 1963, 84). It was correct as far as it went, but it did not go far enough. Instead of raising and facing the questions of world view and ideological bias in Arden's dramaturgy as a whole, Taylor remained entangled in the question of a moralistic vs. nonmoralistic conception of characters and situations. In effect, he attributed to the playwright a liberal position that defended eccentricity and assigned equal value to all causes—or, more precisely, to all sociopolitical interests—and implicitly denied the possibility of qualitative change. What Taylor and many others like him failed to grasp was that the author's world view and position need not necessarily be located

in or identified with a particular agent or point of view within a play—
although it may sometimes find a sympathetic echo in some particular
dramaturgic element or aspect. It can be determined only in relation to
the totality of the dramaturgic structure and in terms of the tendencies
that it embodies.

This study has so far focused mainly on the diversified nature of
Arden's dramaturgy. In the preceding chapters, we saw how his drama
was richly variegated in terms of its eventual, agential, and performative
components, and how this affected the experience of a play in performance. I have also suggested that this diversified structure is held together by a unity of approach, or standpoint, which not only allows the
components of a single play to cohere but unites Arden's diverse works
into one coherent dramaturgic opus—one dramaturgy.

This bias shall be our main concern in the following pages. We will
focus on *The Island of the Mighty* and examine it at length with a view to
arriving at a better understanding of the new ideological and artistic
directions in Arden's dramaturgy.

Social Polarization and the View from Below

All art is political insofar as it implies some assumption or belief about
the way people actually *do* and ideally *should* live together. However, in
every age some works are felt to be more profoundly political than
others. In postwar British drama, the underlying emphases of Arden's
dramaturgy are more deeply and lastingly political than, for example, the
merely emotional anger in Osborne or the equally emotional and desperate clinging to hope in Wesker. This is perhaps why, while Osborne
soon lost his "anger" and became part of the established bourgeois theater, the trajectory of Arden's artistic and political career shows a contrary movement through an increasingly conscious involvement with
radical politics, leading finally to a position so revolutionary that it could
no longer be accommodated by the established theater.

We argued in chapter 2 that society rather than the individual, history and politics rather than private psychology, constitute the main
focus of Arden's dramaturgy and that the personal aspects become significant in his plays only in terms of their larger sociopolitical implications.
We saw that the emphasis on shared relationships constitutes a fundamental dramaturgic principle in his plays and, furthermore, that the
action in almost every play, implicitly or explicitly, suggests a universe

polarized between the privileged and the un- or underprivileged, the powerful and the powerless, those who are included and those who are left out of societal power—in short, between the upper and lower realms of political-economic existence in a class-based society. Thus, the action in *The Waters of Babylon* and *Live Like Pigs* was seen to dramatize the shared life and struggles of a specific underprivileged group within a hostile social order. This order divides people, attitudes, practices, and life-styles into the mutually exclusive categories of respectable and unrespectable, acceptable and unacceptable, and it is represented within the play by such familiar functionaries as politicians, officials, and policemen. Similarly, we saw that the later historical plays, which focus mainly on contradictions and rivalries within the privileged sociopolitical realm, include some significant comment that suggests a plebeian perspective, a view from below. Meg's lament and Lindsay's direct comment on it in *Armstrong's Last Goodnight* and the street ballad on liberty and the "peasants of Gotham" scene in *Left-Handed Liberty* are notable explications of this perspective.

Arden's dramaturgic practice of setting the action within, and in implicit or explicit relation to, a sharply polarized sociopolitical universe has the significant consequence of dialogizing every viewpoint and voice within the multivocal structure of a play. It also points to the fact that a fundamental tendency of his dramaturgy has from the beginning been a critical perception of the oppressive and antipeople nature of the class-based power structures and a quest for an ideal alternative. Every play turns directly or indirectly upon the conflict between repression and freedom, a conflict that is often also formulated poetically as the antithesis of Carnival and Lent, or, in Arden's own terminology, between "curvilinear" and "rectilinear" forces and tendencies. In their preface to *The Hero Rises Up,* Arden and D'Arcy note a continual opposition in British history between what they call the rectilinear emphasis on discipline, order, and moral rectitude—which they associate with the state administration of troops and the perpetuation of hegemonic interests—and the curvilinear disposition toward disorderliness, nonconformism, and freedom—which they associate with plebeian classes and attitudes, and which they trace back to tribal, matriarchal society.[1]

Arden's approach to this subject has developed with his artistic and political experience. In his earlier plays it was more vaguely humanitarian than precisely political. There seemed to be present even a romantic fascination with "low life." The humanitarian approach can be perceived in *Serjeant Musgrave's Dance* as well, but by this time it had already become problematic. The fact that the play juxtaposed, and in some ways attempted to link, foreign colonial wars and internal class struggle showed up the inadequacy of a purely humanitarian response to political issues and the desirability of a more conscious, complex, and class-based approach. However, the clash of perspectives—of ethical humanitarianism and class politics—that lay at the core of this play's dramaturgy remained unresolved, and the link between imperialism and capitalism, although strongly felt, remained unclear. Writing about it eighteen years later, Arden would suggest that Musgrave's failure resulted from "his inability to understand the political implications of the labour movement" (1977, 155), yet the play itself failed to articulate these implications with precision or clarity.

It was in *The Workhouse Donkey* that the conflict between these two early tendencies—the one toward liberal humanitarian values and the other toward a more directly class-based analysis—was resolved and became integrated in a robust and expressly plebeian form of humanism. Thereafter, Arden's approach grew increasingly more political and historical-materialist. In plays like *Armstrong's Last Goodnight* and *Left-Handed Liberty,* the perception that social and cultural life has its basis in material life, that people are in fact guided not by lofty ideals or moral principles but by concrete material interests, is very strong.

From the early to the later plays Arden developed a more clearly articulated plebeian bias, that is, a bias in favor of the common, disinherited multitudes. For example, his practice of deliberately incorporating a view from below into events and developments in the upper social realm, which we noticed in *Armstrong's Last Goodnight* and *Left-Handed Liberty,* was not an idiosyncratic departure from the "authentic" facts of history but a conscious and profoundly significant dramaturgic gesture of viewing history critically—even subversively or "left-handedly"—from a plebeian stance. This stance not only revealed the class-bound nature and significance of the dramatized power structures but also implied that the true human values lay with society's oppressed. A logical extension of such a value judgment could envisage not only axiological but also pragmatic inversion indicating in favor of which social groups might the course of history be radically altered.

The first open expression of this radical plebeian alternative to existing history dates back to *The Workhouse Donkey,* but its best and most categorical presentation came in the epic trilogy *The Island of the Mighty.*

This work marks the culmination of a period of Arden and D'Arcy's artistic and political development, as also their break with the "legitimate," metropolitan theater of London. It is in these three linked plays that, for the first time in Arden's professional career, the revolutionary potential of the disinherited multitudes is directly articulated and celebrated.

Arriving at "The Island of the Mighty"

The compositional history of this trilogy covers almost the entire period of Arden's career as a dramatist and is closely bound up with his and D'Arcy's lives and times. A subject of active contemplation and several practical attempts for seventeen years, it epitomizes their artistic and political development thus far. Its genesis was in the very first play that Arden wrote. In 1953, four years before his first professionally produced play, he was inspired by Malory's *Morte d'Arthur* and Robert Graves's interpretation of poetic myths in *The White Goddess* to write an unpublished play on the Arthurian subject. The play, being one of his first attempts at playwriting, was, as Arden himself tells us in his preface to the trilogy, "pretty ponderous and pretentious."[2] His main difficulty seems to have been with "relating the political plot (of jealousies among British generals leading to the breakdown of resistance to the Anglo-Saxon invaders) to the Gravesian theme of the survival of pre-Christian cultural and religious practice and belief." He had naively tried to overcome this difficulty by using "a travelling group of minstrels and irregular actors," which became a "pastiche of the 'player-scenes' of *Hamlet*." Nobody was interested in producing this play, and the script was shelved.

A few years later he rewrote the play, making several changes in dramaturgic style and structure as well as deepening its political and historical significance. In writing this second version, Arden benefited from his recent exposure to the work of Brecht, which, he tells us, "enlivened [his] dialogue and stage-craft." He also found David Jones's First World War epic *In Parenthesis* of great help in intensifying the play's political and military realism. On the political front, the Suez crisis of 1956 made him aware that "British imperialism in decline had much in common with its Roman precursor." Nevertheless, although this new version was "more competent" than the first one, Arden still could not find anyone to stage it.

A decade later, he returned again to this "early obsession" with the Arthurian subject. In 1966, when the BBC offered him a commission to write a trilogy for television, Arden decided to rewrite and expand the earlier play. This allowed him to include a lot of new material, corresponding to a crucial expansion of his and D'Arcy's artistic and political experience. His development had already acquired the maturity that is manifest in *Left-Handed Liberty*, which, as we saw, is one of the most brilliant examples of epic dramaturgy outside Brecht. He was also deeply influenced by the radical, activist, political climate of the late sixties, with its growing antiwar movements, widespread disillusionment with U.S. policy among intellectuals, the discovery of the CIA's nefarious presence in and control of intellectual and academic bodies and institutions, and the growing realization that the United States was "the greatest single extant threat to the peaceful future of the world." The result of all these experiences, the major political context for which was the war in Vietnam, was that the

> social-democratic middle-class intellectual consensus . . . went into a condition of crisis. . . . Dissent became subversion, a broad-based-liberal-outlook became the licking-of-the-ass-of-LBJ, experimental art became a method of keeping the student untainted by any sort of precise thought, and sexual liberation became the means by which the younger generation was distracted from politics.

The experience of this "new and alarming" climate gave Arden the idea for Merlin, who would embody the newly revealed contradictions of the contemporary liberal intellectual. His conception of Merlin was derived mainly from the old Welsh legends where he is presented as "a poet who went mad and ran wild in the woods as the result of 'a great slaughter.'" In portraying Merlin, whose story was to develop eventually into the main focus of the third part of the trilogy, Arden also drew upon the pre-Norman Irish legend of Crazy Sweeney.

The trilogy took three years to complete, and when it was ready the BBC rejected it. Following an invitation from the Welsh National Theatre, Arden attempted to convert the television script into a stage play. He soon realized that the play as it stood would be weak and boring on the stage. In consultation with D'Arcy, who was to coauthor the final version, he also recognized the need to revise the text in light of the new political and artistic insights that they had acquired since 1966, when the television version was undertaken.

The period of 1968–70 was a significant turning point for Arden and D'Arcy, as it was for many others in Western Europe and America. As Arden himself wrote later, in 1968 many things "had come to a head" politically. He goes on to list the student-worker revolt in France, the brutal police attack at the Chicago Democratic Convention, the Russian invasion of Czechoslovakia, and the massacre at the Mexico [sic] Olympics. Within Britain,

> There was the prohibition by Stormont unionism of a perfectly reasonable Civil Rights March in Derry, the incorrect accusation that Northern Irish Civil Rights was a front for the IRA, the savage attack on the marchers who had the nerve to defy the ban, and the inexorable slides of the largely-forgotten Irish problem into the maelstrom of blood and bitterness which to this day swirls wider and wider. (Arden 1977, 83)

The period witnessed a powerful resurgence of revolutionary activity, with large numbers of men and women—Marxists, Maoists, Trotskyites, anarchists, pacifists, feminists, propagators of free sex, hippies, beatniks, Black Panthers, and numerous other counterhegemonic movements and groups—agitating for a radical and democratic reordering of the capitalist social order and its institutions. This brought in its wake an explosion of countercultural creativity. An active, and activist, concept of culture—culture as a political weapon, as an ideological intervention in the existing reality—flourished in every field of creative endeavor.

The infusion of revolutionary ideas and ideals energized the theater by effecting a radical alteration in both its concept and its practice. There were heated discussions in theater circles about the political function of art in general and of drama in particular. There was an exciting intermingling of the twin concepts of political action as performance and performance as political action. As a result, theater became bolder, more innovative, more flexible, more portable, more community based, and, above all, more directly involved with the material and emotional life of its audience. Theatrical activity itself broke out of the conventional, architecturally enclosed space and relocated itself in the socially (as well as physically) more open spaces of streets, neighborhoods, shop floors, fairgrounds, parks, and marketplaces.

Radical theater groups that had emerged all over Western Europe and North America were not only looking for alternative audiences—

specific social groups of underprivileged and/or disaffected people: women, proletariat, immigrants, ethnic minorities, youth—but also for a new, more active, and more immediate kind of contact with the audience. Theater, they believed, should help raise the spectators' awareness of the issues of their time and, as Brecht had once suggested, prompt them to "intervene actively in life."

Arden and D'Arcy's work in the theater, too, received a new impetus from the antiauthoritarian spirit of the period. In 1967, they staged a theatrical event called *War Carnival* at New York University. The daylong program, involving students in the university's theater department (where Arden was at the time a visiting lecturer), was improvisational and largely unscripted. It included dramatic skits, films, songs, and games of chance, all adding up to a statement against militarism in general and the war in Vietnam in particular. The experience, in Arden's words, proved "to be something of a turning point" in his career as a playwright. Until then, although he had already come to recognize that "spontaneous ensemble improvisation is perhaps the only way to jerk the theatre forward from the successive ruts in which it sticks year after year," he had "a horror of the extempory buried deep in my subconscious" (1977, 47).

Soon after their return from New York, Arden and D'Arcy collaborated with Roland Muldoon's committed socialist group called CAST (Cartoon Archetypal Slogan Theatre) to create *Harold Muggins is a Martyr*—a political satire inspired, as Arden suggested later, by the condition of Britain under Harold Wilson's Labour rule, which "began to remind us more and more of the lessees of a sleazy restaurant who must pay protection money to LBJ and his neighborhood mobsters" (1977, 46). The production, which occasioned a movement for greater unity and contact among left-wing artistic groups and individuals, was, according to Catherine Itzin, "one of the classic legendary events in political theatre" (1980, 20). The approach to the London Unity Theatre (where the play was staged) was turned into an "environment," and, in addition to the sideshows in the foyer, the event included "street performances, and improvised shows by local children instigated by D'Arcy" (Kershaw 1992, 125).

One of the prominant features of the radical theater of this period was that the established, conventional forms of cultural production and dissemination were widely regarded as instruments of bourgeois ideological manipulation and control. Through their own experience in the "regular" theater, D'Arcy and Arden, too, had come to recognize this with increasing clarity. In 1968, they found themselves involved in a bitter quarrel with the Institute of Contemporary Arts (ICA) over the production of their play *The Hero Rises Up*. This "Doorstep-Brawling" (as their "Asymmetrical Preface" to the published edition of the play calls it) arose out of seemingly minor differences about the management of the production. Nonetheless, the experience made the playwrights realize just how much (or how little) freedom bodies like the ICA (which, as the authors point out in their preface, gets its "money from Roman sources—i.e., any official body, with its inevitable subservience to a military requirement") allowed the artist. Later Arden described the experience in these words.

> Libertarianism if it trod too far out of line—could be chopped off by the neck by those whose public postures had always been so erect in its defence. We quarrelled with the ICA on specific professional issues: our right as co-author-directors to compose our own publicity material, our right to manage the production the way we wanted it managed, and our right to determine the type of audience we thought would be best served by the show we were putting on. In isolation the argument could be regarded as ephemeral and unimportant. But taken in conjunction with the general mood and events of the time it seemed an ill augury. We were genuinely if naively flabbergasted by the sudden and fearful rigidity of the ICA officials: had the day at last arrived when the gentlemanly accommodation of artistic and administrative differences in the theatre would be no longer possible? And, if so, what did this bode for our work in the future? (1977, 83)

The main orientation of Arden's thinking (more precisely, rethinking) at that time found a powerful expression in his autobiographical radio play, *The Bagman, or the Impromptu of Muswell Hill*. The play is set within a dream (or, rather, a daydream) of the author-narrator who identifies himself as

> John Arden (thirty-eight) of ancient family,
> Writer of plays for all the world to see,
> To see, and pay for, and to denigrate:
> Such was my work since 1958.

Through a sequence of supernatural adventures, this narrator finds himself in a strange land, which is sharply polarized between a privileged, politically powerful, and complacent minority, living within the heavily fortified enclosure of a city, and a vast, dispossessed majority starving in the harsh conditions of the wilderness outside the city. Captured by the powerful rulers of the city, he finds himself faced with a difficult choice between becoming a court entertainer, enjoying a life of complacent comfort, indolence, and supposed freedom, and aligning himself with the rebels and helping them in their struggle to reclaim political power for the dispossessed by force.

Although he initially feels a greater sympathy with the struggling revolutionaries, and although his experience of the brutal repression to which they are eventually subjected has clearly shaken his earlier notions about the nature of art and the role of the artist, he is too cowardly to commit himself to their cause and ends his narration by obstinately asserting the greater value of his liberal fence-sitting. This ending is clearly meant to be taken ironically. The entire play is written in a detached and self-critical style. It presents, as Hunt correctly points out, a "very painful statement about the state of mind Arden found himself in during 1969" (1974, 143). Through the figure of the artist-narrator, Arden critically examines his own earlier position in this admittedly autobiographical play. He comes to recognize how he has hitherto allowed himself to be manipulated and used (or, in the words of the Unpopular Minister in the play, "encouraged" and "controlled") by the political and cultural Establishment. He sees himself, too, in Hunt's words, as "a reprehensible coward" (p. 143).

Thus, *The Bagman* investigated, more directly and boldly than ever before in Arden's opus, the relationship between theater and politics. The play also formulates the playwright's growing recognition of the political potential of theater, which the authorities seek to thwart in a variety of direct and indirect ways, as well as his awareness that in the conflict between the privileged few and the disinherited masses the artist cannot be a mere onlooker but is willy-nilly aligned with one side or the other.

In the same year, Arden and D'Arcy visited India, where they spent several months and traveled widely through the country, seeing theater and discussing politics with pacifist Gandhians as well as militant Maoists. The visit had a deep and lasting impact on their thinking about art and society. In Arden's own words, they returned from India "more inclined to see the direct connection that the theatre should have with the struggles of everyday life—shall we say, more alienated from the professional theatre" (quoted in Hayman 1980). This visit to a country where "the war between the fed men and the hungry men, the clothed men and the naked men, the sheltered men and the exposed men, is being waged with great ferocity" also strengthened these playwrights in their already more committed, more openly partisan view of sociopolitical conflicts (see Arden's preface to *Two Autobiographical Plays* [1971]).

Arden and D'Arcy's Indian experience familiarized them with class and ethnic oppression, as well as revolutionary resistance to that oppression, and the festive forms of traditional Indian theater as well as the contemporary political theater there, which has consciously built upon popular forms and traditions. It is not surprising, therefore, that they were no longer satisfied with the BBC version of the Arthur trilogy. They painstakingly rewrote it in light of their new artistic and political consciousness. The result was what is, by any standard, one of the major twentieth-century plays in the English language—a play that has, alas, yet to receive a proper production on the stage.[3]

The compositional history of *The Island of the Mighty* is, then, closely linked with the life histories of its authors and the political circumstances of their time. In more than one way it marks the culmination of an important period in Arden and D'Arcy's development, in which influences as wide ranging as English, Irish, and Indian; contemporary history, folklore, and politics; traditional European and Indian theaters; and the peace movement, Brecht, Marx, Mao, and the New Left, all converged.

An Antithetical Universe

> [E]very thing that is ever done in the name of God and good order becomes done against us.
>
> — *The Bondwoman* (I.v)

We have already noted that it is characteristic of Arden's dramaturgy that it invests history with a storytelling interest and invests folklore with sociohistorical significance, thus encouraging each to fertilize and enrich the other. We cited some examples of this from *Armstrong's Last Goodnight* and *Left-Handed Liberty*. However, the best example of this practice, and of his and D'Arcy's dramaturgic skill as a whole, is *The Island of the Mighty*. Most of the narrative material for this epic trilogy is derived from a variety of Irish, Welsh, and English sources, which are woven into an intricate and significant narrative. Profoundly informed by their understanding of history and politics, the trilogy also comes across as an enormous political parable whose vehicle is a plebeian rewrite of the Arthur story and whose tenor is of our own times. It comprises a large number of subsidiary parables strung together by the unifying theme of the conflict between the oppressor and the oppressed. The result is that the play can be understood—indeed, must be understood—on the basis of political thematics and organization deployed as a cunning use of both the folkloric and the storytelling interest.[4]

Arden and D'Arcy's trilogy is an imaginative journey into a remote, legendary past with important sociopolitical significance for our time. Merlin's opening song is, in effect, an invitation to the audience to undertake this journey.

> O Christian men, are you aware
> How once an Emperor controlled
> The going-out and coming-in
> Of every man in all the civil world—
> So hard he toiled?
> Around his boundaries he set
> A ditch, a wall, a palisade.
> The wild men outside were kept
> Outside, until one day he was betrayed,
> Or so he said.
>
>   (I,i)

This return to an only seemingly dead past is concluded and reinforced by Aneurin's final song with, as we shall see later, its openly plebeian and revolutionary appropriation of the biblical story of Lazarus. These two songs bracket the whole trilogy, and, as it were, put it within quotation marks. Together with all the other instances of direct address, they distance the action from the audience while at the same time cognitively connecting the play's experience to contemporary history (by suggesting, in Arden's words, that "British Imperialism in decline had much in common with its Roman precursor.") They are thus sharply marked conduits between the overall parable's vehicle and its tenor.

Merlin's song lays down the basic terms of the trilogy's overall structure. Its oppositions between inside and outside, identical to a certain notion of civilization vs. wildness, indicate the main theme and point to the conflict between the privileged rulers of the imperial "civil world" and the "wild" dispossessed masses. Furthermore, Merlin's reference to walls and fortifications suggests the exclusive nature of political power, just as references to the smashing of the "golden crown" and the "kicking over" of the throne with which the song ends suggest the carnivalesque activity of uncrowning, the plebeian pleasure in turning the world upside-down.

The universe of the play is—as in Arden's other plays but more clearly—divided into two antithetical groupings. The first, the politically dominant group, is that of the rulers, comprising Arthur, his Roman army, and the native princes. These are perceived in the plays as the oppressor class. The other, politically lower but axiologically higher, is the plebeian grouping of the disinherited masses, represented by Garlon, Dylan, the Picts, Caradoc, the Bondwoman, the Cowman's wife, and almost all the other women. Arthur's half-sister Morgan belongs to this level by choice rather than by birth, and she represents the collective memories and dreams of the masses.

These antithetical groupings remain locked in an actually or potentially conflictual relationship throughout the trilogy. They not only divide the play's agents into two divergent groups but provide all its main themes, motifs, and emphases, making for two mutually contradictory perspectives, attitudes, values, and orientations. The various forms that this polarization takes can be condensed in a table thus.

Dramaturgic Category	Oppressors	Oppressed
Social horizon and present value system	Class society, patriarchal	Tribal communism, matriarchal
Hierarchical level	Upper	Lower
Characteristic stance	Coercive, authoritarian	Subversive, anarchic
Mode of existence	Official, open	Popular, secretive
Attitude toward history, time horizon	Linear time, backward orientation (toward the historical past of the Roman Empire)	Curved time, forward orientation (toward utopian future ending the "bad" linear time)
Associated space	Inner: bonded, fortified, exclusive space of cities, forts, palaces, military camps	Outer: open and wild space of forests, valleys, hills

Dramaturgic Category	Oppressors	Oppressed
Division by age-cum-vitality	Aging, in the process of decline and death	Youthful, in the process of becoming
Religion	Christianity	Paganism
Source of knowledge	Desensualized intellect: learning, books	Sensual body: memory, experience, observation
Protagonist	Arthur	Gwenhwyvar
Ideological mouthpiece	Merlin (also Taliesin)	Aneurin (also Morgan)

These binary oppositions are readily found in the text, and all of them should be substantiated in the discussion that follows. But a few require some immediate explanation.

First of all, the division by age is only partly and imperfectly related to the physical ages of the main agents. No doubt, even at this demographic, or empirical, level, a broad division of this kind can be detected in the text: the ages mentioned in the list of dramatis personae as well as various references within the text show that Arthur and most of his companions are to be presented as old. Arthur is the oldest of them all and near death. "Why you poor old man—I never guessed you were so near death," says Balin when he first sees Arthur's face (I.iii); and "Old men, old men, on their horses so huge," sings the Pictish Poet (I.x). In contrast, most of the active plebeians are young (for example, the recruits of Medraut's new regiment are repeatedly referred to as "young soldiers" [cf. II.v]). However, this division on the basis of the supposed physical ages of the characters is imperfect. It does not, for example, hold true of the princes of Strathclyde and Gododdin (who are young but belong to the oppressor class) or of Morgan (who is clearly associated with the plebeian spirit but is older than Arthur).

As befits a parable, our category is therefore principally based not on physical age but on the state of what, for want of a better description, may be called their allegorical age or historical vitality. Thus, while Arthur at seventy is old and physically failing, Morgan at seventy-five possesses something like eternal youth: she dies laughing, jumping, and racing through the mountains (III.viii). In other words, while the world of the rulers is perceived as decaying (even visibly), that of the plebeian masses comes across as full of undying spirit, vitality, and tenacity. The latter survives and will continue to survive various historical vicissitudes (although not without great suffering), while the former disintegrates and is destroyed at Camlaan (the "end of all great men" [I.v]). This undying vitality of the people is fully evident in Aneurin's concluding song, the message of which is that no matter how much you push them "out" and "under," how often you "muffle" and "bury" them, the people will come back, again and again, and turn the world upside-down or inside-out.

Attitude toward history and time horizon (our table's fifth category) refers to the different historical horizons and social times (cf. Gurvitch 1964) from which the two groups derive their inspiration. While the agents of the dominant group look back to the history of the Roman Empire as a fixed and linearly continuing paragon of civil order (in other words, of a class-based society), the plebeians are moved by the utopian dream of possible liberation (that is, of a classless society), which, in this spiral time, is simultaneously the return of the Daughters of Branwen. Thus, while the rulers' group is oriented toward an unchanging past, which is also ethnically alien, the ruled are inclined toward a native utopian future repristinating a golden age.

As for the first category, the value system (in some ways consubstantial with the social horizon), the native tradition is obviously matriarchal. The Picts are ruled by a queen who, like the Hindu goddess Kali or Durga, is both a terrifying goddess and a mother figure.

> POET: Jesus. He was a God and a King. His mother was the star of the Sea, and when we travel in our fishing boats that is also the title that we put upon our own Mother.
> QUEEN: True . . .
> POET: He died in Her service, as our own God and King every year must face death in *your* service, upon the island.
> QUEEN: True . . .
> POET: But here is where the mistake lies. The Roman conquerors stole Him from us. He belonged to all men, and in particular to men like ourselves who have a true veneration for His Blessed and Most Terrible Mother.
> QUEEN: Such men in such times are of necessity poor and hungry.
>
> (I.viii)

Later (in II.vii), when Gwenhwyvar introduces herself to Strathclyde as his "uncle's wife" and traces her family back to a common female ancestor, the prince is bewildered and appalled by it.

STRATHCLYDE: Oh . . . I have never heard of a pedigree before that consisted of nothing but women.

TALIESIN: It is customary among the Picts—

Furthermore, the Picts, the women, and the other plebeians (all of whom are also Celtic natives) derive their inspiration from the Branwen legend, which poetically embodies the collective memory of a matriarchal golden age when "huge ladies of great beauty" ruled over a happy and prosperous people. The patriarchal value system of the politically dominant group does not need to rely only on the Branwen legend, important as it is, since the value system is present in its social organization (Arthur himself is a self-appointed patriarch of the island), its attitudes toward the powerless (particularly toward women, as in Arthur's attitude toward Gwenhwyvar), and its religion (with the predominance of God the Father in Christianity, which is made explicit in the Pictish Poet's comment about the Roman appropriation of the tribal matriarchal religion).

Finally, and perhaps the most important, the dramaturgic spaces—which are, as Arden and D'Arcy's production notes point out, both emotional and geographic—are likewise mainly antithetical. To the oppressors belong the built, bounded, or walled-in, and therefore exclusive and restrictive, spaces of the cities, forts, palaces, and military camps (for example, the Balin–Chief Porter encounter cited in chapter 2). To the tribal and plebeian agents belong the open, wild, and "uncivilized" spaces of the forests, hills, and valleys. This spatial division is implied in Merlin's opening song and continued by the repertory of emblematic backcloths prescribed by the playwrights. These backcloths are to be "painted in bold colours and clear lines; no perspective or naturalistic chiaroscuro" and are "not to be taken as realistic scenery, indicative of particular places; they are *emblems* of the kind of environment, emotional and temporal as well as geographic, required for each scene" (emphasis added). The sequences in which the plebeians predominate are usually set against the backcloths designating open, natural spaces (Woodland, Seascape, Snowscape), while those in which the action is dominated by the rulers are played as the enclosed and man-made spaces of Fort and Camp.

Restrictive spaces are thus associated with rulers and former Roman conquerors and their "rectilinear" (that is, coercive and antifreedom) attitudes. Arthur is presented as the embodiment of a condition that finds succinct expression in the spatial image of "the spiked encampment" (II.v). The Picts, a mountain tribe, refer to Carlisle as the City of the

Wall (I.iv), while Balan finds a Roman fort "Much in the nature of a prison . . . a cruel gridiron where our liberty must burn to death" (I.iii). On the other hand, the plebeians are associated with "curvilinear" (that is, free and freedom loving) attitudes. Morgan, although born in the restricted space, has made the wild forests and hills her home: conversely, she represents the wildness, freedom, and depth of non-"civil" nature.

The opposition between these two kinds of space is implied throughout the trilogy. Thus, speaking of popular faith in the Branwen legend, Morgan says, "Not in the palaces of the princes believed, but in all the secret places where people are thin and small"—in what she had a little earlier described as "little dripping cottages and forest shelters from the Firth of Clyde to Bodmintor" (II.viii). It is implicit also in the contrast that Merlin makes between Aneurin and himself.

> He remained constant from the day of his birth
> To the wild forests and the rain soaked earth.
> I in my youth ran shamelessly for shelter.
>
> (III.viii)

This somewhat romantic division between open (free) and closed (bounded) spaces, and between their attitudinal and emotional implications, is also suggested in the antithetical imagery that dominates the discourse in the trilogy as a whole.

	Oppressors	Oppressed
Temperamental	Orderliness	Wildness
Oppositions	Propriety	Madness
	Politics	Erotics
Spatial	Inside	Outside
Oppositions	Above	Below

Thus, the contrast between the two kinds of space is related simultaneously to the contrast between sheltered and the unsheltered men, orderliness and wildness, sanity and madness, oppression and freedom, and between a desensualized existence and a fully sensual one. All of these are concrete dramaturgic aspects of the conflict between the oppressors and the oppressed that polarizes the universe of the trilogy.

There is also a third kind of space in the trilogy, represented by the backcloths called Mill and Ruins. Its position is intermediary (or, pessimistically, synthesizing). It functions as both a connection between and a separation of the other two spaces. It emblematically signifies the conflict in which the restrictive, oppressive space is progressively disintegrating, a "built" or civil space being reclaimed by nature—in other words, the increasingly and inevitably shrinking space of the oppressors' order.

> BALIN: What kind of a house do you imagine this was once before the bushes grew all over it?
> BONDWOMAN: House of a great man—some Roman very probably. Birds live in it and badgers. End of all great men.
>
> (I.v)

Thus, this intermediary space is related to the inevitable "end of all great men." It is also implied in the trilogy's opening and concluding songs: for, nature taking over or reclaiming the bounded, fortified space is semantically related to the idea of wild men jumping over the wall and destroying the imperial city (in Merlin's song) as well as to the idea of the return (from a dormant or buried state) of the oppressed masses in Aneurin's song.

It is this potentially explosive sociopolitical space of a sharply polarized universe that the action in the trilogy actualizes. Its antithetical categories permeate the structure at the eventual as well as the agential levels: they are the two existential alternatives between which the central agents in the three major stories of the trilogy—Balin and Balan (Part One), Arthur (Part Two), and Merlin (Part Three)—have to choose. All three stories involve a set of two closely related agents (brothers in blood or spirit, alter egos) making a dramatically opposite choice, thus:

	Part One	Part Two	Part Three
Oppressors	Balin	Arthur	Merlin
Oppressed	Balan	Morgan	Aneurin

In the following sections we will discuss at some length each of these major stories with a view to demonstrating how the fundamental sociopolitical division operates in it.

Arthur and Morgan: The Dialectics of
Utopia and Practice

> Then be the servant: pay attention to the desires of your employer. He
> lives in a thatched hut, acknowledges no Emperor but the chief of his clan.
> —Medraut (II.ii)

Arthur's defeat and death, although it becomes the main focus of interest only in Part Two, is the main or pivotal story to which the other two— those of Balin and Balan, and of Merlin—are directly and crucially related. As conceived by the authors, this story focuses mainly not on the marvellous adventures and tragic defeat of a valiant hero but on the secret and subversive life of the people under an oppressive system, that is, on the utopian content of their folklore and its power, under particular historical circumstances, to inspire them to rise against oppression. Arthur himself is conceived not as a chivalrous hero but as a sincerely ruthless militarist who sees making war as his divine duty. "I am a soldier, I make war, with good conscience, and that's it," he tells Gwenhwyvar, who later taunts him about how different he was before it "came into [his] mind that making war / Was all the work that needed to be done" (II.v).

Arthur is an authority figure who is completely alienated from the people. In their eyes he represents all that is alien, oppressive, and unacceptable. He is popularly regarded as a traitor who has willfully disowned native traditions and identified himself with the imperial Roman heritage of "the long sword" and the "spiked encampment" (I.ii). Once a people's hero, he reneged and freed himself from that role with great brutality (II.x). He chose for himself a new political role, which aligned him with the oppressors. He appointed himself the defender or champion of civility and Christianity from one end of the island to the other (I.ii)—a role that requires the defense and perpetuation of a system of political, cultural, and economic oppression. He derives his authority from his Roman title, his Roman sword of Magnus Maximus, and his pseudo–Roman army—all, as Medraut reminds him (II.ii), relics of a dead and hated past. Although he claims to be only a servant and not "the master" (II.ii), he is authoritarian and domineering. This becomes particularly evident in his relationship with the native, hereditary princes whom he claims to defend but treats with great contempt. He often imposes his will on them and uses them to fight his own wars (I.i, vii).

He destroys Pellam, a sovereign prince, to keep his "lines of communication to the fortresses in the South" open, and threatens Strathclyde, another sovereign prince, with the same consequences.

> If you attempt to interfere with my headquarters in Carlisle, or with my lines of communication, you will be served the same as Pellam. Make no mistake about that; you are one of the hereditary rulers whom we are bound to defend, but defended you will be, though it cost you your life and your crown and every acre you possess.
>
> (I.vii)

However, Arthur's relationship with such princes is not only one of contradiction but of collaboration. He offers them protection, and in return they support and maintain him and his army by paying regular tribute (III.iv) as well as by allowing him the use of their territories, palaces, and forts. Both Arthur and the princes are, at any rate, one in their contempt for the native pagan masses, although the princes seem to be relatively less alienated from the people (see, for example, Strathclyde's disapproval of Latin terms [II.vii]).

Arthur, who once possessed the potential to become a people's hero, is counterposed in the play with Morgan, his half-sister, who embraced that alternative. Both are portrayed in dimensions larger than life and therefore come across not as *characters* in the strict sense of the term but as typical—though personalized—embodiments of two mutually contradictory values or perspectives: one official and repressive, and the other plebeian and subversive. While Arthur is hated or rejected, Morgan is a widely loved heroine of the masses: "God help us, that old Morgan, she was the queen of the heart of the lot of us!" the Blacksmith's Wife is reported to have told Gwenddydd (III.viii). Her wildness and madness is counterposed to Arthur's civility and orderliness: "I cut my hair short, I turned myself back into a cool-headed Roman," he tells Merlin (II.ii). He is overincluded in the system (he can use any territory, fort, or palace for his army), while Morgan is brutally excluded from it.

> The prince of Strathclyde is my nephew, my own dear sister's son, and he will not even grant me a little dingy corner in his fort where I could sit and dip my bread into the soup and curse him for his sovereignty!   (II.viii)

Just as Arthur sees himself in the role of the sole remaining custodian of an alien and imperial culture, Morgan personifies the spirit and endurability of the native, plebeian culture. She is a veritable repository of all its secret and subversive songs, folklore, collective memories, and dreams. Where Arthur looks backward to a solid orderly past, Morgan looks forward to a decentralized utopian future. While Arthur remains strongly committed to a deadly and coercive existence governed by "the long sword," "the spiked encampment," orderliness, and desensualized intellect (knowledge derived from books, discipline, and efficiency)—Morgan, living in an old mill between the fort and the woodland, is ardently dedicated to the open, free, and subversive condition represented by the wild forest, the rain-soaked earth, and the sensual, fertile body.

Arthur and Morgan represent the opposite poles of the play's great existential divide. Arthur, associated with the master class (the oppressors, both alien and alienated from the people), is a figure of Lent (and, as such, has precursors, in Arden's opus, in Musgrave and Feng). Morgan is associated with the people and their indomitable desire for freedom and happiness. Personifying the principle of Carnival, she derives her artistic lineage from Charlie Butterthwaite and the Old Croaker. They are, thus, no longer characters from folklore but the principal, antagonistic agential forces in an expressly political-allegorical discourse. Together with the other antithetical agential pairs, but in a central way, they personify the two extremes between which not only the story of Arthur's defeat and death but the entire universe of the trilogy unrolls.

To dramatize the main Arthurian story of Part Two, the playwrights use not only the material derived from Malory and Geoffrey of Monmouth but also draw upon the legendary traditions of the Celts. From the latter they fabricate a myth of a matriarchal golden age and its promised return. By combining this myth, which is connected with the Celtic folk hero Bran the Blessed, with the conventional Arthurian narrative, they are able to superimpose the motif of a popular revolt on the traditional narrative of Arthur's last and fatal battle with his illegitimate son Medraut. This matriarchal utopia—which is believed "*Not* in the palaces of princes . . . but in all the secret places where the people are thin and small" but "not necessarily ignorant"—is shown to express the people's perennial desire and hope (in Ernst Bloch's sense; see Bloch

1973) for a happy future. The legend itself is perceived in the play as a myth or fairy tale whose significance is poetic rather than literal. It is reconstructed and interpreted differently by different agents but always with obviously utopian implications. Speculating about the conditions of life during the time when "huge ladies of great beauty" inhabited the island, Gwenhwyvar and Gwenddydd emphasize the element of economic communism.

> GWENDDYDD: There was neither division nor degree upon the digging of the land—
> GWENHWYVAR: No one for their own self held any title to the ground—
> GWENDDYDD: Indeed it is most doubtful whether any digging was done at all. Hunting and fishing and the gathering of fruit from trees and everyone did their share of it and everyone shared what was obtained.
> ANEURIN: Are you certain of that?
> GWENHWYVAR: Good God, poet, what's wrong with you, we are amusing ourselves with fairy-tales, we don't have to talk truth, you know!
> ANEURIN: I don't know that it is truth, either what I said or what you said. But I am glad to discover that whatever happens *now* you both agreed at once that it should not have happened *then*. Which is, I suppose, the main purpose of a fairy-tale, even when we laugh at it . . .
>
> (II.v)

A little later, Morgan, describing the folktale as it is reconstructed and interpreted by the "thin and small," but not necessarily ignorant, people, emphasizes its subversive and insurrectionary content, its message that the rule of "the long sword" must be overthrown and the dragon standard broken (II.viii).

This utopian myth triggers a sequence of events leading to the battle between Arthur and Medraut. Morgan helps Gwenhwyvar recognize herself as the Daughter of Branwen. In turn, Gwenhwyvar chooses Medraut (who, on Arthur's instructions, is trying to recruit young tribals to fight against the English) as her champion. This champion, after he has fought with and destroyed the usurpers of the Branwen kingdom, would be "the secret king of the Island of the Mighty," or

"Bran reincarnate" (II.viii). As a sign of her choice, Gwenhwyvar makes a deep cut on Medraut's forehead with her thumbnail. With this mark, Medraut—till now the lieutenant of the hated general who had failed to find young tribal recruits—instantaneously becomes a popular hero. Dylan, a tribal chieftain, insists on calling him Lord General and declares that the long-hoped-for utopia has arrived.

DYLAN: Lord General! With that mark upon you, you can travel the valleys of Strathclyde and Gododdin, every man will join your Army, every woman will fall at your feet, kiss the corner of your plaid, they will—God, they would get into bed with you if they were not afraid of the anger of the Great Lady—!
ANEURIN: You are made joyful by what you have seen?
DYLAN: (in an ecstasy). Here is a great lord and a brave soldier who has remembered what everyone else of his house has so long forgotten—why should I not be joyful? Bran has come back to us— the Buried head has risen up—the Princes and the Priests and the Conquerors are all of them to be killed! I will go out and tell your soldiers, lord, the whole Island belongs to them all—! (he rushes out).
(II.ix)

This sets off a massive popular revolt against all the princes, priests, and official bards. It is represented by the "eruption" on the stage of a crowd of men and women who, wild-eyed with wonder, are carrying weapons and chanting "Bran lives again." They kill the Prince of Strathclyde, Medraut's brother, and attack the conservative bard Taliesin, saying,

Here is a poet who forsook his duty
He did squat across Our Lady sleeping
He befouled all her beauty—

(II.ix)

But the people's utopia is doomed to fail. Although the ordinary people do not know it yet ("they will discover it" soon enough [II.x]), it was over the moment it began because Gwenhwyvar chose the wrong champion.

There is one reason and one reason alone why the Daughters of Branwen be called home

There is one reason, it is the same reason, why the battle-standard
    be broken:
For how else can I believe that justice will ever be done
The very names of their tribes by some conqueror have been
    imposed,
Forced under is their ancient language by an alien tongue that will
    not flow,
Generation after generation while the long sword has been
    walking over,
They have lived and lurked under—altogether without hope
Except that they have constructed this foolish hope of their own:
Queen Branwen, they will say to you, once ruled through
    nothing but love—
She had no need of General and need of no soldiers
Her lovely land was held in common, no landlord gathered his
    gold,
All of the people ate what all of the people did grow,
And on the day that her huge power once more shall be made
    known
Once more shall the life of the Island of the
Mighty be exactly as I have told.

                                              —Aneurin (II.ix)

This is how Aneurin, the people's prophetic bard and one of the play's
narrators, describes the only valid reason for "calling home" the Daughters of Branwen and for smashing the dragon banner. He goes on to ask:
"Is it possible that the Chief Dragon's Lieutenant will be the man to
bring that power?" The answer clearly is in the negative. The new power
that Medraut has acquired as a result of the Branwen sign on his forehead
has gone to his head. He clearly wants to use it to increase his military
might. It has given him such dreams of power and domination that he
has turned against his own father and erstwhile superior. Thus, far from
being a true people's hero, Medraut turns out to be a megalomaniac, a
usurper who wants not only to take Arthur's place but to make himself
the emperor of the island—a position that even Arthur declined in his
youth (II.ii). All this makes him a false hero who, as Morgan points out,
still carries a long sword and "does not go to break the Banner of the
Dragon" but "to take it for his own."

An explosive sociopolitical situation thus becomes the main focus of interest in the play, upstaging the conventional tale of Arthur's last battle. The myth of the Branwen golden age is itself historicized. It proceeds simultaneously through a dual process of construction and deconstruction—that is, its mythical aspect is continually undercut and criticized as different agents, drawing upon their memories and interests, piece it together and interpret it. The main voice in this process of reconstruction is that of Aneurin, who emphasizes throughout a poetic rather than literal-minded reading of the legends (for example, in II.i and ix). He maintains that only in this way does the mythical material become historically and cognitively useful. He explains why the Morgan-Gwenhwyvar-Medraut attempt to bring back the golden age could never have succeeded and articulates the most crucial and ponderable problem emerging from that attempt.

> ANEURIN: . . . The power of Branwen cannot be brought forward unless the people themselves demand it. But they cannot demand it unless they have first seen it, with their own eyes and quite close to them. And who is to show them this?
> GWENDDYDD: Why not yourself, you are a poet?
> ANEURIN: Yes, but I can show them nothing till the banner is broken in two. Who can break it—except Medraut? And upon whom will be the burden of breaking Medraut in his turn—?
>
> (II.ix)

This simultaneous process of construction and deconstruction of a popular myth, of celebration and criticism of the people's utopian dream, suggests a dialectical perspective that is neither exclusively utopian in a weak sense (such as the one represented by Morgan) nor exclusively empiricist and pragmatic (such as the sense represented by Arthur). Rather, it embodies a dynamic fusion of the positive aspects of both: the values of utopian communism and the practicality of empirical power. In other words, it suggests a perspective that is *not only* utopian *but also* historical and "scientific" (see Suvin 1976). It is this perspective that comes across as cognitively the most valuable one of the entire trilogy—and, indeed, as the whole play's organizing final horizon.

This dramaturgic practice of historicizing legendary and folkloric elements and presenting them in an expressly sociohistorical perspective, so that the primary focus of interest remains the struggle between the oppressors and the oppressed, is equally evident in the other two parts of the trilogy.

Balin and Balan: Whom to Fight For?

So many weapons and not one day of good fortune.

—Merlin (I.vi)

Arden and D'Arcy derive the story of Balin and Balan from the *Morte D'Arthur*. In Malory, it concerns mainly the fantastic adventures of two valiant knights of Arthur's court. In one of these adventures, Balan kills Garlon, a treacherous knight with the gift of invisibility, and his brother, King Pellam. The death of Pellam brings on an earthquake, which kills the damsel whose lover was treacherously killed by Garlon and for whose sake Balan had undertaken this adventure. Later, in a castle of "fair ladies," Balin and Balan joust, each unaware of the other's identity, and kill each other.

This tale, as told by Malory, abounds in the elements of chance, fate, and magical manipulation. In Arden and D'Arcy's dramaturgic reconstruction of it, however, these elements are only vestigially present as poetic reminiscences within a tale constructed upon a refunctioned sociopolitical logic. The Balin–Balan strand becomes a political-historical parable. Not only is its narrative skeleton subsumed under a radically different kind of motivation, with many different details, but its whole horizon and tenor is in the way of a counterproject to Malory. Rather than knights seeking adventure, Balin and Balan are conceived as petty princes rendered homeless as a result of an English raid. Further, as we noted in chapter 2, they represent two distinct attitudes toward Arthur and other such "great" men, indicating different levels of political con- sciousness. While Balan wants nothing to do with Arthur and his Roman army, which he sees as inimical to his freedom, Balin sees in Arthur a powerful ally. Even the minor characters are altered by the playwrights. Garlon is no longer a knight but a peasant victim of princely oppression, which has forced him to become a violent and angry outlaw. As he tells Merlin,

I have suffered far too much from these Kings and these Princes. Every one of them is my enemy. Though they don't know it till

they feel my weapon. . . . I had a cornfield and an orchard, five
pigs, and a black-and-white cow. But the Prince of Gwynedd took
them off me, grabbed my wife to be his mistress, turned me out of
my cottage. For what reason? I was in debt to him, rent and so
forth. Interest upon money lent me. Said I was to be bound to him
as a serf for evermore if I could not pay it. My grandfather had been
a serf—but there was a Roman Emperor in those days. Not one of
our own hereditary princes. For a Roman it was natural he should
enslave the men of Britain. My grandfather bought his freedom
with hard work. Died of it moreover. Spitting blood all down the
blanket. Not for me. Here's my liberty—(He flourishes his knife.)
Secret, from behind a cloak. Gwynedd's bailiff had this in his
kidney—ah! (I.iv)

Thus, what was in Malory Garlon's magical gift of invisibility becomes
in the play an oppressed and wanted man's need to be sly and secretive.
Similarly, the damsel of Malory's story becomes the Bondwoman, another victim of the oppressive system, who was once Taliesin's slave.

She had a brother who was my pupil, about ten years ago. He stole a
very valuable book from me and eloped. I demanded the price of the
book from his father, who was of course unable to pay. He was
some sort of small holder, there were poets in his family, but neither
gold nor silver. So I took the girl. She was a bad bargain. A thief and
a runaway just like her brother. (I.vii)

The Bondwoman runs away with Garlon into the freedom of the forest
where she seeks not only a life of peace for herself but the social and
political salvation of her class. As for Pellam, he is conceived as a small,
poor prince with an overlarge sense of ambition. He claims to be the
divinely ordained savior of the island and declares Arthur to be the anti-
Christ. His death at the hands of Balin is followed not by a super-
naturally caused earthquake but by a well-planned, brutal attack by Arthur's army in which the Bondwoman is trampled to death. Similarly,
Malory's castle of "fayre ladies" becomes the land of the freedom-loving,
matriarchal tribe of Picts who practice a kind of primitive communism.
It is their seasonal fertility customs that cause the deaths of Balin and
Balan at each other's hands. Moreover, the tribal customs and rituals of
the Picts are themselves demystified rather than romanticized. They are

shown to be leftovers from an earlier period in their social history. Like
the Branwen legend, they often evoke critical remarks. The Pictish war
leader doubts their usefulness and validity (I.iv, I.viii), while Balan twice
refers to the "ill customs" of the Picts (I.iv, I.ix). When both the old and
new kings are dead, the Pictish Poet remarks:

> We make our King lame so that he cannot escape. And then after all
> his pleasuring the next King finds it easy to kill him. Until now the
> custom was good. But certain people came to believe it should be
> put an end to, and I think that is what the Goddess has now done.
> Whether or no we turn Christian as a result of it, is a matter to be
> considered. (I.ix)

The Pictish Queen's direct remark about the comparable potencies of
Christianity and tribal paganism is also ironical. It suggests the heady,
intoxicating quality of religions and recalls to mind the well-known
Marxist dictum that religion is both the opiate and the consolation of the
oppressed masses.

> What need do we have of Christ—for we have the red heather
> Wherefrom we can distil our own strong potent liquor—
> Neither your ale nor beer nor wine
> It makes us drunk enough in our good time.
>
>   (I.iv)

The new meanings that Arden and D'Arcy have given to dramaturgic
agents and actions have, thus, drastically altered the cognitive content of
the old tale. Even the adventures of Balin and Balan have changed radically in their implications. Instead of belonging to the realm of the supernatural, they are clearly shown to stem from the different choices the two
brothers make and are held up, as it were, for a comparative evaluation.

    Balin, obsessed with the idea of joining some great army, embarks
upon one misadventure after another, only to end up with several
weapons that "stick" to his hand (I.vi). We have seen (in chapter 2) how
he decides to join the Roman army in spite of Balan's advice to the
contrary. Unable to acquire the necessary discipline of the Roman army
(which is alien to his native wildness), he is driven out of Arthur's court
and goes to join Pellam's new army. On his way he meets the Bondwo-

man and Garlon, beats the latter in a fight, and wins the slave woman. At
this point another alternative is offered to him. The Bondwoman suggests that they forget about great men and their wars and live peacefully
in the pleasant surroundings of the forest.

> Look you, we have a great big sack
> Full of gold to put on your neck
> And embroidered cloth for your strong back
> We have a whole great island full of trees and mountain water.
> And no one to control us wherever we shall wander.
> Neither poet nor king knows who or where we are.
> In the summer we can lie down bare
> Upon the mosses and beneath the briar,
> In the winter we can huddle close and kiss each other warm—
> A little hut you can make for us out of branches of
>   blackthorn . . .
> The wind comes cold already—
> Why don't we build a fire—
> I don't think we can cook any food
> But I have some nuts and apples
> I found growing wild in the wood . . .
> Don't go and be a soldier—
> I will love you forever.
>
>   (I.v.)

Balin is offered a life of freedom, pleasure, and love away from the
oppressive society ruled by princes and warlords. But, blind with the
thought of vengeance against the English, he rejects the offer and continues on his perilous course. Outside Pellam's house, the Bondwoman
suggests another, more revolutionary, alternative.

> For you to help a little King to grow into a bigger one—what good
> is that to me? . . . Look, forget you are a nobleman. If you must live
> a life of fighting, why not fight in defence of me? There are so many
> like myself—everything that is ever done in the name of God or
> good order becomes done against us. The best thing of all would be
> if you could make friends with Garlon. He is not always clever but
> he has had dealings in his time with every outlaw gang through the

breadth of the forests of Britain. What—yourself and himself—
good friends and good fighters—you could soon have a thousand
men! (I.v)

As pointed out earlier, the Bondwoman typifies the victims of the
existing oppressive system who desperately seek to find a life of freedom
and happiness. Here she advises Balin to create an oppressed people's
army instead of joining the army of the oppressors. But, once again,
Balin chooses to ignore her advice. The significance of this choice is
underscored when, after her death, he realizes the truth of her words and
how, if he had heeded them, it "might have changed it all" (I.vi). Balin is
deeply affected by this experience. Consequently, he is already a changed
man when he arrives, half drowned, in the land of the Picts.

Poor men and hungry,
I did not know why they were so angry
So angry that their thoughts run thick and mirk
And every blow they strike must miss its mark.
Salt water in my mouth.
I vomit out with a great oath:
For such good men that their bellies may be full
I strike my blows alone and strike them with good will.
I am no more a nobleman.
I am quite other and out of the law.
Garlon I have been
And Barabbas and branded Cain.
Direct will be my hand.
Clear will be my brain.

(I.viii)

The choices made by Balan, in direct contrast to his brother's, reveal
greater foresight and political consciousness. He is clear about his values
and priorities. His first priority is freedom. We noted in chapter 2 how he
refused to have truck with Arthur and his great Roman army. In the land
of the Picts, unencumbered as he is with his brother's concerns about
nobility, Christianity, and vengeance, he has no difficulty identifying
with them. In response to their request for help in defending against
Strathclyde's attack, he argues his position thus.

I told a Roman poet that I would not be commanded.
I would fight for my wild liberty
Until the run of my blood was ended.
Liberty from those who attacked me
And also from those who defended.
I stood alone when I told him, on a hill outside a stonewall fort
It seems to me now that you likewise stand alone
You look for no strength to help you that is greater than your
    own
For fear that it should spring back to you, and then are caged and
    caught.

                        (I.iv)

He feels that his freedom is linked with the freedom of the oppressed
people.

So long as you are free
There is some hope for me.

He agrees to fight in defense of the Picts. Balan's position is, thus, not
very different from the one represented by the Bondwoman.

All this has the effect of transforming the traditional magical tale of
Balin and Balan into a political parable exemplifying two distinct responses to political oppression and militarization. The cognitive significance of this parable goes beyond the narrative vehicle of Arthurian
Britain. It has, for example, a parallel in contemporary political history
of which the authors, writing in the charged political climate of the late
sixties, were fully aware. The different courses chosen by the two
brothers are akin to the two attitudes found among Third World countries toward a superpower like the United States, or, nearer to Arden and
D'Arcy, among the Irish toward the British government and army.
Furthermore, the war methods of the Picts are strongly reminiscent of
the guerrilla warfare that the Viet Cong were waging at the time the play
was written.

I will tell you how they fight—not like
The power of Rome or blundering pride
Of Christian swaggerers from Strathclyde—

But like the mountain cats themselves who hide
And glowering glide
Among the rocks and golden gorse
They wait to spring and then run back
Into their holes and none can find
Upon the stony ground that secret track
Of their attack.

(I.iv)

Similarly, the parabolic significance of the victory of the Picts over the superior forces of Strathclyde, explicated by Merlin in terms of the victory of the weak over the strong, anticipates the victory of the Vietnamese over the world's mightiest power.

And so the strongest soldiers go
Betrayed, defeated, all in tears.
The weaker ones who conquered them
Have conquered all their weakness and the fears
Of a hundred years.

(I.iv)

This is how, and just how much, Arden and D'Arcy's dramaturgy has altered and historicized what was in their source a feudal tale of chivalric love, heroic adventure, and marvellous happenings.

Merlin, or the Two Kinds of Poetry

> The poet without the people is nothing . . . . The people without the poet will still be the people.
>
> —Aneurin (III.x)

The story of Merlin—for which, as we noted, the authors drew upon old Irish and Welsh sources, reinterpreting them in the light of contemporary political experience (particularly that of Vietnam and Northern Ireland)—reformulates the conflict between the oppressor and the oppressed, in cultural terms, as a conflict between two kinds of poetry, between two distinct courses or attitudes available to a poet: namely, to align with the rulers or unite with the people.

The cultural space in the trilogy, like its political and economic space, and in direct correlation to it, is divided into two mutually contradictory power levels. The hierarchically higher, or dominant, level is governed by values derived from Christianity, the imperial Roman heritage, and the learned tradition, while the lower, plebeian level comprises the oppressed people's collective dreams and aspirations as expressed in their oral culture (folklore). The plays make it amply clear that the dominance is enforced and maintained mainly through military prowess, ruthless repression, and ideological manipulation (witness Strathclyde's belligerence toward pagan culture in I.iii and II.ix). These two cultural levels produce two different kinds of poetry: the orthodox or official kind, and the popular. Orthodox poetry is represented in the trilogy by the chief poets of the princely courts who collectively constitute the College of Bards and whose main representatives are Taliesin, Strathclyde's chief poet (the conservative type), and Merlin, Arthur's chief poet (the liberal type). The other, plebeian kind of poetry is represented by poor, officially neglected, and scorned poets personified in the straightforward, blunt, and rebellious Aneurin whose vulgar patrons are politically weak but numerically strong (see his conversation with Merlin in II.i).

Both kinds of poetry are political. But, while the official kind is shown to be subservient to the interests of the oppressors (and only in rare and special cases, such as that of Taliesin on the eve of the Arthur-Medraut battle, capable of freeing itself from this subservience), the latter is committed to the people and their dreams of political salvation. While the former is based on the rigid rules derived from books—Taliesin and Merlin are referred to as learned—or desensualized intellect, the latter is more flexible and is based on lived experience and observation. For example, Aneurin prefers to describe himself as observant rather than learned (II.ix). The former, subservient to the oppressors, is forced to celebrate wars and death. "What am I? A Chief Poet? I ornament with polished euphony the coarse words of the General's thought. And the General's thoughts are always of dead men—you can't ornament *those,*" says Merlin (III.vi). The other kind of poetry celebrates the sensual life of the whole body, the body politic or the community. These two kinds of poetry remain in conflict throughout the play, and, indeed, they constitute a significant aspect of (and *not* a "superstructure" on) the main political conflict between the oppressors and the oppressed.

The most explicit example of this conflict is found in the scene depicting a meeting of the College of Bards (II.i). There the "old," "rheumatism-stricken" Chief Poets meet to decide upon Aneurin's application for the title of Chief Poet. To test his skill, they ask him to compose an ode on a specific topic in a specific meter. The given subject is a popular legend about the protective value of the buried head of Bran the Blessed. The meter, in keeping with the loftiness of the subject, is heroic. However, Aneurin not only ignores these specifications but actually turns them, as it were, upside-down, outraging the conservative cultural establishment. Instead of extolling the magical qualities of the buried head, he questions the literal truth of the legend in light of the historical fact that the Romans were able to successfully invade and occupy Britain. Furthermore, disregarding the specified lofty form, he produces a bawdy, mischievous, and, in Merlin's significant phrase, "low-class of satirical ballad." Shocked and infuriated by his impudence, Taliesin announces the unanimous verdict of the College: "Your candidature to the title of Chief Poet is disallowed. A few hundred years ago you could have been burnt for this."

Aneurin is rejected because he challenges the official standpoint. The official interest in perpetuating a patriarchal myth exemplifies ideological manipulation and control of the people's collective consciousness and memory by their rulers. Pointing out "the lack of logic" in Aneurin's argument, Taliesin—for whom the Picts, the ancient inhabitants of Britain who have continued to survive subversively outside the Roman-Christian hegemony, are the main threat to the island's security—goes on to justify the Roman conquest.

> The Romans did indeed come, and for four hundred years they stayed here. They intermingled with our people, they gave us government, built stone roads, and fortified towns, they provided us with the inestimable blessing of the Gospel of Christ. Not at all the sort of invasion against which we are defended by the Buried Skull of Bran.

Taliesin's argument has an unmistakably familiar ring, for the colonization of Africa and Asia was often justified in the name of its civilizing and modernizing effects on native populations and conditions. Contemporary imperialist domination and plunder of the Third World is also justified in similar terms.

The clash between Aneurin and the College of Bards thus signifies a clash between two different kinds of poetry, each inspired by a different sociopolitical orientation. The playwrights have conceived Merlin's story in terms of this conflict. Merlin, as Arden's preface tells us, is a "liberal intellectual who no longer knows what is liberality and what is tyranny, who is unable to draw a distinction between poetic ambiguity and political dishonesty." His story should provide an example (or indeed an exemplum) of how the inner contradictions of such a liberal position allow the artist to be manipulated by the rulers and how the association with power corrupts her or him further. In the first two parts of the trilogy, we are shown Merlin's degeneration as a poet. In Part Three we see his eventual regeneration.

As Arthur's official poet, Merlin is shown to have consciously sacrificed his poetic integrity to serve his master's political and military interests. For example, in a direct address in Part One—throughout which he is used by Arthur more as a spy, a gatherer of military intelligence, than as a poet—he articulates the contradiction in his position. Contrasting the untruth of his own poetic words to the truth of the crude words of the bandit, Garlon, he says:

> What word apart from his foul word
> Can now be trusted in these days?
> I am the General's poet—I make
> The words that make him famous in his age—
>
> War must he wage
> Poetry must praise
> Such wars until he wins
> How can he ever win
> Without blemish or sin?
> Dead men are carried in
> Praise the death and the killing
> My words are ever willing
> In the service of his sword

(I.vi)

In serving his militarist master, and by writing in praise of death and wars, Merlin has allowed his poetry to be degraded into falsehood. He has been guilty of sins of commission and omission. He has written, for example, about Arthur's military successes but not about his failures (see Arthur's remark to Gwenhwyvar, II.v). Moreover, he has done this consciously, knowing full well that he will pay for it with his life, his truth, and his poetic integrity (I.vii).

By portraying Merlin in this way, Arden and D'Arcy are offering a criticism of the liberal intellectual whose position (as Arden also showed in *The Bagman*) is based on moral cowardice and political opportunism. For example, in contrast to Aneurin's self-respecting bluntness, which prompts him to leave Gododdin's service (II.v), Merlin, though humiliated, cannot refuse to take his "pay," decides to continue serving Arthur, and even finds some justification for doing so (II.vi).

In Part Two, a sharp agential contrast between Aneurin and Merlin is established, which provides a measure of how far Merlin has strayed from true poetry. Aneurin has, despite material hardship and the scorn of the cultural establishment (cf. II.i), remained true to his vocation and to the people. He is a typical representative of all those plebeian wandering minstrels whose poetry is widely but secretly cherished by the people. His songs are those that, in Morgan's words, are "sung only in secret." As such, they "are not heard by everyone, even though everyone sings them" (II.viii). His songs are sung secretly because they are subversive. They say only one thing to the disinherited native peasants: "The dragon-banner must be broken and the Daughters of Branwen called home." Aneurin's constant loyalty to the people is placed in direct contrast to the opportunistic type of poet represented here by Merlin and Taliesin. When Morgan boasts that all poets belong to her, Aneurin reminds her of this other type.

> ANEURIN: They *were* yours, a long time ago. Not any more, old lady. I am the only one left, I think.
> MORGAN: And all the rest belong to Christ and to the men of the long sword.
>
> (II.viii)

Merlin's refusal to come to terms with the contradictions of his situation, his clever evasion of all disturbing thoughts about the injustice he is doing to himself and his poetry, is in direct contrast to Aneurin's ability to face and articulate such grievances. In an encounter (II.i) between the two poets, Aneurin raises a question that Merlin would rather not face, much less answer.

> MERLIN: It appears to me altogether you are not happy in your work.
> ANEURIN: Are you? For whom do you compose?

MERLIN: For my master the General Chief Dragon.
ANEURIN: Does he listen?
MERLIN: I thought there might be some small ebb-and-flow of something agreeable in you, but there is not. You live like this all your life, you ingratiate yourself with nobody, nobody!

As mentioned, Merlin's subservience to "the long sword" has killed his poetry: as he himself tells us, "The time has long gone past I should think of composing a *poem*" (II.vii).

It is with this knowledge that we approach the story of Merlin's madness and recovery in Part Three. This story operates on two distinct levels: the folkloric level of a magical narrative in which Merlin's madness is caused by Taliesin's curse and ends only when the curse has worked itself out; and, subsuming the folkloric material, the parabolic, functional level on which it examines the question of the function of a poet and poetry in class society.

The parable of Merlin's regeneration, his return to poetry, life, and the people, is constructed in three stages, which have significant correspondence to the three stages of human growth: childhood, youth, and maturity. At each stage Merlin is helped by (or associated with) another agent, and each stage is characterized by a dominant emotion. These stages may be expressed in a table.

	Childhood	Youth	Maturity
Helper	Morgan (mother)	Gwenddydd (lover)	Cowman's wife (friend)
Dominant Emotion	Self-love	Sexual love	Selfless, communal love
Object of Desire	Own body	Another's body	Collective body of the community

Merlin's regenerate life thus becomes a second life. However, in passing through a symbolic death and rebirth (his madness and reawakening), Merlin is first divested of his earlier, degenerate life. This is achieved by means of madness, which throws him initially into a state of forgetfulness. He goes mad as the result of the great massacre at Camlaan, which he not only willfully refused to avert but actually helped bring about by attacking Taliesin just when the latter had almost succeeded in preventing the battle. This act epitomizes the extent of Merlin's degeneration, the distance he has strayed from poetry and humanity. His wounding of Taliesin is carefully shown not as a sudden, isolated act of passion but as the culmination of a long process. For, as Aneurin remarks,

> You may think it took him but a moment
> To put out his hand and drive that spear.
> Great error. He had been in the doing of it
> Year after year after year after year—
> Driving his barb, you see, into his wife
> And into himself and into poetry—
>
> (III.iii)

However, faced with the large-scale devastation that his refusal to act as a "true" poet has brought about, he suddenly becomes aware of his degeneration not only as a poet but as a human being. This fills him with "all this turbulence and darkness, and fury, and giddiness, and frenzy, and flight, unsteadiness and restlessness, unquiet, disgust." His madness thus becomes an expression of his self-disgust and, as Gwenddydd remarks, "disgust with every place in which he used to be" (III.ii).

Merlin goes mad when his commitment to Arthur—to the culture of "the long sword"—is shattered. This commitment had alienated him from himself, from life, and, above all, from the people, true source and addressee of all poetry. So his madness also becomes a stage in his gradual return to the true vocation from which he had strayed. For it is only through his madness (or mad wildness), and with the help of an equally mad and wild Morgan, that he begins to understand what he had tried so obstinately to push out of his conscious mind.

> He had discovered
> Upon what road it was he staggered.

In the end, he will rediscover himself and reaffirm his loyalty to the sensual body and the people—to what, in an earlier play by Arden, was described as the "life and love" of ordinary humanity. But before this final regeneration,

> He must thread his own way home again
> Through thorns and bog and snow and rain,

He must put his bleeding feet
One by one where they did tread before
Until he comes once more
Upon the doorstep of the door
From which so long ago he strutted out—

(III.iii)

Merlin's recovery has to be slow and proceed in stages because he has strayed too far from that prelapsarian condition of his early life and poetry when, as Gwenddydd recalls, he wrote love poems and enjoyed making love in a muddy marshland. He must recover that ability to derive pleasure from the ordinary sensual things of life, from ordinary people. However, before the journey back is undertaken he must get away from the surviving men of the long sword—Bedwyr and his two companions—who see their only hope in "rescuing" Merlin for their own use (III.iii). His madness helps in this, too, for it puts him beyond their and everyone else's reach. He has reached a stage at which, as Aneurin says, he can no longer be of use to Bedwyr and people like him: "He has been used by far too many far too long" (III.vi).

Merlin is at the stage at which nobody can reach him—nobody, that is, except old Morgan. It is Morgan, the plebeian muse of the poets, alternating between motherly and sexual love, who helps him to begin again. It is she who wakes him up from his mad sleep by tickling him. When he does wake up, he is reborn. Believing that Arthur is still alive, he declares his determination to have nothing to do with men whose thoughts are only of death. Like a child, he rejoices in his nakedness, in the rediscovered sensuality of his body, from which he and his poetry had strayed since those early days of love in the marshland of Gwenddydd's father. He is now returning to that early stage. "I shall remain naked. I shall rejoice in it," he says, and "I shall look for a young girl— two of them—three—and astonish them by my virility." These joys and pleasures will lend to his poetry more strength and sensuality, more body. For the poetry that he will now compose will be written "Not only with music and words"—that is, not only with intellect—"But with every muscle and every nerve, / Touch and taste and hearing and sight and smell, / Never before will they say, / Has Merlin done his work so well."

Merlin's rediscovery of the physical body and all the pleasures that it can provide is thus the first significant step in his self-recovery as a poet.

His childlike laughter, which, along with Morgan's, resounds throughout this episode, is an expression of his new sense of freedom and joy.
This new freedom and rediscovery of the body is also signified by his
wild leaping with Morgan, at the end of which they leap out of the
millhouse and into the forest. For a time they live a merry life of
freedom—"laughing and leaping across the ridges of the hill . . . in
competition with one another like a pair of puppydogs, which could go
the farthest." And then Morgan dies. Left alone after he had rediscovered
his physicality and the pleasures of human companionship, Merlin re-
members and longs for Gwenddydd—"I remember a young woman. I
remember her body as though I had lived in it." But Merlin's way to
Gwenddydd is obstructed by Taliesin's head. He struggles with it and
pushes it out of his way. On the folkloric level this struggle signifies
Merlin's attempt to overcome Taliesin's curse. But viewed in the light of
Aneurin's remarks (quoted above) about the driving of the barb, and
Merlin's own statement that the "only true reason for driving a spear at
Taliesin is because he was a Chief poet just like myself" (III.vi), it signi-
fies a (successful) attempt to free himself of the last remaining effects of
his former life—as Arthur's Chief Poet—characterized as it was by an
excessive dependence on a desensualized intellect (emblematized in
Taliesin's disembodied head).

Merlin's memory of and desire for Gwenddydd is the second crucial
stage in his recovery. He has now returned to his youth and to the love of
another's body—traveling back to the time when he loved and wrote for
Gwenddydd, to that precise point in his past life where he went astray.
Having returned to that point, he is able to make a new beginning, an
alternate and opposed choice. His first step in the new direction—a step
that also marks the beginning of the third and final stage in his
recovery—is his respect and love for Aneurin, who, he says, has "remained constant from the day of his birth / To the wild forest and the
rain soaked earth." This indicates that Merlin is already moving toward
the "life and love" of ordinary humanity and toward a poetry that serves
the people rather than their masters.

The third stage in Merlin's recovery culminates in his new maturity,
as reflected in the encounter with the Cowman's Wife with which his
story (as well as the trilogy) ends. In this last episode, we find that the
culture of the long sword has given way to the culture of the Church.
Bedwyr, now a (perhaps self-appointed) saint, still wants to rescue

Merlin—no longer for the long sword but for God. He wants to tell him "all the truth of the Love of God." But Merlin knows better. As we saw, he has already acquired a different kind of love—the love of life, the love of humanity: "They will haul me in to Jesus," he tells the Cowman's wife,

> and I do not want to go. I know more about Jesus than any of them do. Jesus ran through the forest, stark crazy, making poems. And because he couldn't find any man or woman to hear his poems, had himself spiked up in public on the wide branches of a tree so that no one will ever be able to say they did not know he had ever lived. Merlin will not do that. Merlin has learned better. (III.x)

From his lonely wanderings he has learned that it is not enough to write; one must write for somebody. And he has chosen ordinary working people as the source as well as the audience for his poetry. His love, gratitude, and respect are directed not toward God and his saints but toward the laboring masses—toward the Cowman's Wife, her family, and her work. It is in the persons of such people and in their labors that he finds beauty. He wants to sing to them about themselves.

MERLIN:

> All this year all by myself
> In a world that to other men appears to be quite empty
> I have watched and I have seen so many things of such
>   beauty—
> But not even the beauty and revelation of the rainbow
> Was as bright in my sight as the line of milk that you draw
> From the udder of your cow.

And has one single poet ever thought to ask you what kind of song he ought to make? No. I am asking now. You tell me. I make it.
COWMAN'S WIFE: I—I—please go away.
MERLIN: Ah, you can't tell me—
ANEURIN: (addressing the audience from the corner of the forestage). What I said to Bedwyr about the loneliness of the poet is not true! MERLIN: I ought to have known. I took you by surprise . . .
ANEURIN: I told Bedwyr a stupid lie because I was frightened . . .

MERLIN: But none the less I will sing to you . . .

ANEURIN: The poet without the people is nothing. The people without the poet will still be the people . . .

MERLIN: To you, and for you, and for your husband and for your children . . .

ANEURIN: All that we can do is to make loud and to make clear their own proper voice. They have so much to say . . .

....

MERLIN: I know about your children. I have been watching them. Look, I brought some black berries. You give them when I'm gone.

ANEURIN; An impediment in their speech they very well have, but—mother of God—they are not dumb!

MERLIN: Sssh—ssh—here is the song. (*He sings.*)

>Mother of your children
>And wife of your good man
>Your face is pale with terror
>But you stand up tall and strong
>The green man from the thorny wood
>Wears neither wool nor silk
>But his chest is broad and his eyes are clear
>He has drunk your good white milk.

(III.x)

The significance of this new stage in Merlin is evident. Aneurin's direct commentary further underscores it. After a long and hard experience, Merlin has finally come to recognize that beauty resides only with the people, since it is created by them in their ordinary lives and labors. This experience of love for humanity and his mockery of the religion of the "saints" is the last act of Merlin before he is killed by the foolishly jealous Cowman. It completes the last stage in the process of his recovery. Although Bedwyr still tries to claim him for the Church—"I do pronounce that Merlin died at peace with God. Any poet that tells it different shall stand condemned as an enemy of the truth"—we know that he died at peace not with God but with himself, his poetry, and his community, thus celebrating the three most valuable things that he had rediscovered during his long journey back to a new and higher kind of sanity and maturity. He died a newly but fully awakened man.

The story of Merlin's madness and recovery is thus invested with profound cognitive significance in *The Island of the Mighty*. It comes across as a parable about the poet's place in society. Out of the great divisions between the oppressor and the oppressed, the desensualized mind and the sensual body, coercive authoritarianism and subversive plebeian poetry, and finally between death and life, Merlin had obstinately opted for the former and ruined himself and his poetry. When faced with the devastating consequences of his choice, he went mad—a state of oblivion, of limbo, of unlearning. He could not be rescued; he had to be *re*-formed, step by step. He went through a rebirth, and thence through what may be regarded as a second childhood and youth, finally arriving at a new kind of maturity. In his former life he had "run shamelessly for shelter" when he joined Arthur's court. In his new life he had to become a naked, hungry, unsheltered human being before he could rediscover his true identity and loyalty. As a "learned Chief Poet," serving a master who dealt only in death and destruction, he had neglected his own body, and Gwenddydd's body, as well as the unaging collective body of the community. So he has to return to them all, one by one. In the end he rediscovers himself, recommits and rededicates his work to the common people, and dies celebrating life and love.

People as the Protagonist

> What looks certain is not certain,
> The way things are will not last.
> When the ruling class has spoken,
> The ruled shall raise their voices.
> Who dares say: Never?
>
> —Bertolt Brecht

It is the people who, invested with the driving thematic force (and, indeed, heroism), are cast as the protagonist in *The Island of the Mighty*. Their perspective (the plebeian perspective) becomes axiologically as well as agentially the dominant one. Liberatory forces of poetry and erotics (for example, Morgan, Aneurin, Balan, and the reborn Merlin) belong to them. They are also the axiological and (at least potentially) empirical "mighty" to whom the island rightfully belongs. Their oppressors, all those who have kept them from their rightful inheritance, are only the warped and ironical mighty. While the militaristic might of Arthur and his Roman army is shown to be hollow and transient, the people come across as immortal. Though any particular agent belonging to the people is clearly vulnerable and/or foolish, it is the people as a collective protagonist to whom the future belongs. While the time of the oppressors in the play is perceived throughout the trilogy to be oscillating between "is" and "was," that of the people is experienced as "will be" and "yet to come"—in Ernst Bloch's term "the not-yet-here" (1973). All this is clearly indicated in Aneurin's concluding song, which marks the end of an imaginative journey into the "buried" past of Arthurian Britain (cf. Merlin's opening song) and summarizes the cognitive enrichment obtained from this collective journey by the spectators and performers.

In this play, Arden and D'Arcy present us with a harsh critique of the social system based on exploitation and repression, but they also celebrate the people's ability not only to survive but to learn from experience. In the course of the action we are shown economic, political, and ideological oppression as well as the people's suffering under such conditions, but we are also shown the people's powerful desire for change and, more important, their willed collective endeavor in that direction. In the land of the Picts we are even given an example of a different and in certain ways happier kind of social system. Perhaps the most significant agential opposition in the play is—as mentioned—that the rulers are shown to be decaying and dying while the people are presented as very much alive and in the process of becoming—in spite of but also *because of* their pain and suffering. "The end of all great men" emphasis is in sharp contrast to the emphasis on the people's ability to learn (cf. II.viii, II.x, and III.x). The revolt in the trilogy fails—nor could it be different in a parable applicable to the seventies. Yet its failure is clearly caused by the ideological and historical limitations of a particular, analyzed situation. It therefore does not necessarily foredoom such collective endeavor in the future. Instead, the play turns it into a cognitively enriching, and thus positive, historical experience.

It is this historical experience that we as spectators (or imaginary spectators, that is, readers) gain from our imaginative journey into a remote past. It is also the net result of Arden and D'Arcy's own artistic and political experiences. Aneurin articulates and accentuates it when, using the Lazarus image, he sings of the undying determination of disinherited people to come back and take possession of "the whole world."

And Lazarus he came up like a strange gigantic mole.
He tore the muffler from his jaw—
All rotten he was, with such an evil smell

They closed their eyes and down they fell.
And this is what Lazarus said to them all
When he came back to life so hideous and tall:
'Oh I found underground
A score or two
Of decent people
Just like you,
I found underground
Two thousand or three
Of stinking corpses
Just like me.
And when the big boots
Dance on the grave
It is the corpses
They will raise
For you went and you buried them
With all the life inside
That they could not live
While they were alive.
We are going to come back
And we are going to take hold
So hideous and bloody greedy
We take hold of the whole world!

(III.xiii)

Aneurin's song is simultaneously a threat of revolutionary apoca-
lypse and the promise of the plebeian millenium that will follow the
revolutionary activity of turning the world upside-down or—in terms of
the dominant image of burial—inside-out. However, this plebeian millenium is clearly not to be instituted from above (by God's ordinance, as in
the Grail legend). It is to be wrenched from history by a powerful and
willed collective effort of the many ("two thousand or three") who have
for centuries been "muffled" and pushed "under" by the few ("score or
two"). Thus, what had so far been outside (the wild men) will be inside
and what is inside (emperors, princes, warriors, and landlords) will be
outside or, indeed, nonexistent (empty). The people will be their own
masters.

Notes

Chapter One

1. The Berliner Ensemble visited London for the first time in August and September of 1956 with *Mother Courage, The Caucasian Chalk Circle,* and an adaptation of Farquhar's *Recruiting Officer.* It received lukewarm notices from the critics.

Although Brecht's name was frequently bandied around as a result of this exposure to his work, the full implications and significance of his theory and practice were not yet grasped. As Martin Esslin recalls,

> that Brechtian era had a great deal of talk and discussion about *Brecht* and what he was thought to stand for, but few valid productions of Brecht, little genuine knowledge about Brecht, and hence little evidence of any influence of Brecht's actual work and thought. (1969, 63)

2. "It is . . . a sad commentary of the state of the English theatre today that so few of Mr. O'Casey's plays should have been revived or indeed produced at all in London," wrote Richard Findlater (1952, 183). As far as the Unity Theatre and the Theatre Workshop are concerned, there seems today to be a revival of interest in their work and a retrospective acknowledgment of their contribution since the sixties when fringe, agit-prop, theater groups proliferated in England (as elsewhere in Europe and the United States) and consciously traced their lineage back to that period (see, for example, Goormay 1981; Itzin 1980; and Kershaw 1992).

3. Eliot himself recognized that he had failed to solve "any general problem" of form in *Murder in the Cathedral:* "it struck me that I was using a verse which would serve my purposes for this one play and subject, and for no other. . . . I had not solved any general problem" (from an interview quoted in Findlater 1952, 137).

4. "In bourgeois tragedy, as in the comedy of manners, the material of drama was coming, if still hesitantly, to be defined as *contemporary* (in contrast to almost all previous drama) and, in association with this, *indigenous,* in the sense that there could now be a normal expectation of congruity, when desired, between the time, place, and milieu of the dramatic action and of the dramatic performance" (Williams 1981a, 166).

5. "Where in other modern forms . . . secularism could be a merely neutral abstention from supernatural interventions or agencies, or even a negative awareness of the loss of such a dimension, in materialism it was a positive emphasis, which produced a quite specific new form" (Williams 1977, 203).

6. In fairness to Dryden it must be stated that his position was not consistently in favor of illusionism. In the same essay, he also says that "it is very clear to all who understand poetry, that serious plays ought not to imitate conversation too nearly. If nothing were to be raised above that level the foundation of poetry would be destroyed" (1912, 87).

7. Raymond Williams traces the use of colloquial prose as the form of dramatic speech back to the comedy of manners (see Williams 1981a, 162.)

8. In another context it would be necessary to distinguish between the more serious and critical form of naturalism and its lesser and complacent form. For, in the best examples of the former, there usually is a sense of tension or dissatisfaction with the conventional form. As Raymond Williams has observed,

> In Chekhov or Ibsen . . . what is visible and directly expressible is no more than a counterpoint to the unrealised life—the inner and common desires, fears, possibilities—which struggles to find itself in just this solidly staged world. When we speak of naturalism, we must distinguish between this passion for the whole truth, for the liberation of what can not yet be said or done, and the confident and even complacent representation of things as they are, that things are as they seem. (1976a, 180)

9. Brecht referred to such a theater by different names. He first referred to it as the narrative or non-Aristotelian theater, then as the epic theater. Toward the end of his life he often spoke of a dialectical theater and of a "theatre for the scientific age," which, he explained, is possible only on the basis of the earlier category of epic theater.

10. For a useful discussion of Brecht's term, see Bloch 1972.

11. Explaining his notion of a "gest," Brecht writes:

> Not all gests are social gests. The attitude of chasing away a fly is not yet a social gest, though the attitude of chasing away a dog may be one, for instance, if it comes to represent a badly dressed man's continual battle against watchdogs. . . . [The] social gest is the gest relevant to society, the gest that allows conclusions to be drawn about the social circumstances. (1964, 104–105)

12. In Arden's case, there was also a distinctly Irish component to this tradition. This influence, evident even in his early plays, was to grow increasingly pronounced in his and D'Arcy's later work as they became steadily more involved with the questions of Irish nationalism and British colonial dominance. In a personal communication, he once told me that

> Margaretta's Irish background, and my growing involvement with it ever since I first met her in 1955, means that what you call the popular English

tradition invoked in my work, and particularly our joint work, is often in fact more Irish than English, even though the ancient Irish never had a regular folk theatre in the ordinary sense of the word, though of course all the other aspects of popular tradition you refer to were historically very strongly represented. What you refer to as official or ruling class culture in this context, therefore, becomes colonial British dominating culture, and an element of national resistance is involved as well as class conflict.

Chapter Two

1. A similar typological distinction is found in Tzvetan Todorov who distinguishes between plot-centred and character-centred narratives (1977, 86) and in Seymour Chatman who differentiates between what he calls resolved plots and revealed plots (1978, 48).

2. It must be stressed, however, that these are analytical categories. As such, their value here is mainly differential or relative rather than absolute. They inevitably ignore the immense range of variations and many compromises, shades, and exceptions that might be found in any actual historical situation or individual example.

3. Lydgate's Mumming texts are written in the Chaucerian style and were originally presented in a storytelling form. His *Mumming at Hertford,* for example, presents two groups of six costumed actors who mime the actions described by the three speaking actors. Lydgate himself describes his texts as made "in wise of ballad" (Wickham 1976, 196). In Lydgate's texts as well as in the recently recorded texts of folk plays (see Cawte 1967, and Chambers 1966) we can clearly see an early attempt to accommodate into dramatic form material designed for narrative. The chief narrative device that these texts use is the figure of the "presenter," a folk equivalent of the Greek chorus or the Music Hall narrator. For a discussion of this see chapter 4 below.

4. For discussions of this practice and its influence on medieval and Elizabethan dramaturgy, see Doran (1954); Bradbrook (1955); and Bluestone (1974). Writing about the Elizabethan drama, Bradbrook points out that

> The main literary tradition in England as elsewhere was a narrative one, inherited from the later Middle Ages. The first problem confronting dramatic poets was that of transforming narrative material and traditions into dramatic form. Not only the stories, but also the organization of the stories, was based on narrative (p. 4)

5. For further discussion of the theory and method of the Elizabethan dramatic adaptations, see Bluestone (1974).

6. As Beckerman points out,

> Shakespeare's manuscripts, on the evidence of the printed quartos and the *Sir Thomas More Manuscript,* contained no structural labels whatsoever. They

consisted of stretches of dialogues introduced by entrances and concluded by exits, with a clear stage in between. (1969, 32)

See also Bradbrook (1960a, 32–34), and Hirsh (1981, 1–31).

7. Prejudice against plot, against what Edwin Muir calls an "irresponsible delight in vigorous events," is characteristic of the modern aesthetic attitude (cf. Bentley 1964, 18–20).

8. The term *chrono-logical* is borrowed from Chatman who uses it in this way to emphasize the temporal and logical nature of a narrative sequence (1978, 44).

9. "The whole spatial continuum in a text in which the world of the object is reflected forms a certain *topos*" (Lotman 1977, 231).

10. A few definitions are in order here. *Event* refers to the smallest significant and consequential segment of action. It is, as such, similar to Barthes's *function* about which he says: "The 'soul' of any function is its seedlike quality, which enables the function to inseminate the narrative with an element that will later come to maturity" (1975, 244). It is a consecutive (that is, it follows another event) as well as consequential (it generates another event) unit of action. As such, it may entail another event, which in its turn may entail another, and so on through an entire sequence. A plot must contain or imply at least one such sequence. However, at any point of a plot an event may generate more than one synchronic event and may thus become what Propp calls the initial situation for starting a new sequence or several new sequences (ibid., 25; also see Aristotle's *Poetics* 7:1450b). When a plot contains or implies several such diverse sequences, it can be called *multilinear,* and its discrete sequences may be identified as *narrative strands.*

11. Beckerman refers to this form as intensive and traces it through the Greek, French, and Ibsenian tradition (1970, 188). He contrasts it with what he calls the extensive structure of the medieval, Shakespearean, and Brechtian tradition (p. 189).

Chapter Three

1. It was out of this difficulty that the styles of expressionism, and more recently the Absurd, arose. In these dramas the inarticulateness and incommunicability of human experience, as well as the impossibility of any meaningful relationship between people, are elevated to the level of a universal, metaphysical truth. Pauses and silences rather than speech are perceived to be meaningful. This notion of the failure of communication between human beings, this haunting and agonizing feeling of the inadequacy of speech and relationships, seems to be related to the general crisis in the culture of individualism and liberalism in the twentieth century. Perhaps that is why it is a common motif in a good deal of contemporary bourgeois literature.

2. Arden himself often recommends an emphasis on socially typical aspects in the performance of his plays. For example, in his "Note on Sets and Costumes" in the printed text of *Armstrong's Last Goodnight,* he suggests that the

costuming should be such that "each of the characters [is] immediately recognizable as a member of his social class." In his earlier plays he usually included directions giving selective details of appearance, age, and so on. But after a frustrating experience with the established theater, he and D'Arcy, in their "Production Notes" to *The Island of the Mighty,* lamented that "Particular descriptions of characters involving details of dress and physical appearance, are liable to produce excessive attempts by some actors at 'involvement' with their roles in a way that inhibits a clear rendering of the stories of the plays."

3. The crucial significance of this connection between Musgrave and the bourgeois heritage is that, within a play modeled on the celebratory form of the Mummers' Play, it demonstrates how the popular cultural forms and traditions are, in Forsas-Scott's words, "being quenched by a new order which turns the theatre into a place for arid speech-making and sermonizing" (1983, 7). Confrontation between these two major sociohistorical traditions is a recurrent motif of Arden's drama with its most direct expression occurring in his 1979 radio play *Pearl.*

4. The verbal and physical responses of Arden's agents often arise from their confrontation with something or someone outside their private selves. In this respect, their speeches are rather like those memorable speeches in Shakespeare about which A. G. Kiernan has observed: "[they] are likely to grow directly out of men's feelings for one another: those of other dramatists are likelier to be inspired by men's feelings about themselves" (1964, 48).

5. It is significant that both Brecht and Arden admire Breughel's work. See Brecht (1964, 157–59); and Arden (1977, 11–16).

6. There are significant references within the play to the roles of the Mayor, the Constable and the Parson. Playfully impersonating the Mayor, Mrs. Hitchcock says:

I am a proud coalowner
And in scarlet here I stand
Who shall come and who shall go
Through all my coal-black land?

About the Constable the Bargee sings:

Constable alive or dead
His head is of leather and his belly's of lead.

The Bargee's words to the Parson (in I.ii) are also significant: "You're a power, you are; in a town of trouble, in a place of danger. Yes. You're the word and the book, aren't you?"

7. It is interesting to note here that the decade preceding the writing of Arden's *The Workhouse Donkey* was characterized in British politics by Labour-Conservative consensus on issues of the welfare state and Keynesian economic strategies. The general elections of 1955 and 1959 were contested "not on the

issue of capitalism against socialism, but on the question of which party could better administer a society organized on the principles of welfare-capitalism" (Davies and Saunders 1983, 20; see also Harvey 1989, 132–40).

8. P. Dodd makes a similar mistake although from a different perspective. He correctly recognizes that "the play is not organized . . . to study and render the characters' inner lives," and goes on to propose a thematic approach. Nonetheless, his reading continues to focus only on two isolated agents, Lindsay and Gilnockie, reading them as purely moral, ahistorical types. He sees the play as "the exploration of the value, in human and practical terms, of the two conflicting qualities—temperance and intemperance" (Dodd 1977, 323–39). He then defines the two qualities in Aristotle's abstract terms and reconstructs the play as almost a moral allegory. The consequence is that he ignores all the historical particularity so explicitly and diligently sketched in by Arden, which determines not only the kind of responses, behaviors, and events in the play but also its overall structure of relationships.

9. In a 1966 interview, Arden recalled how, during the initial stages of writing, he got "a bit tangled in a confusion of baronial and episcopal minutiae, until Margaretta D'Arcy had the idea that I should use the Papal Legate—until then a very minor character—to pull the whole play together and set it in a framework of medieval theology and cosmology" (Marowitz and Trussler 1967, 52).

10. Arden is here on the strictly solid ground of the most recent historiographic research, as summarized in the monograph of Wilfred Warren (1961), which he obviously used while writing the play.

Chapter Four

1. Another commonly used English term was *pageant,* which in one of its senses denoted, as Kolve has observed, "trick, deceit, or merry-game" (1966, 14). See also Chambers (1925, 2:104); Baskerville (1920, 8); and Wickham (1974, 2–5). Kolve also points out that, in contrast to the vernacular, Latin drama preferred terms like *imitatio, similitudo, exemplum,* and *representatio,* which emphasized, to a relatively greater degree, the mimetic and didactic aspect of drama. He finds it striking that

> the vernacular cycle drama, which came into existence in the last quarter of the fourteenth century, in naming itself rarely used an English translation of any of these words. Instead, it employed English equivalents of a much rarer term, ludus, which seems to have been used only in late Latin plays. (p. 12)

This ceases to be surprising, however, when we consider it in the context of the popular, nonecclesiastical tradition with which the vernacular drama—both religious and secular—interacted in more than one way. (For these connections, see Axton 1974.) It is also interesting to note that, of Kolve's four examples of late Latin texts using the term *ludus,* the first two come from *Carmina Burana,* a composition usually attributed to the wandering students of the thirteenth century whose connections with the life and culture of the "vulgar" masses caused them much trouble from the religious orthodoxy of the time.

About the variety of things (from gladiator games to proper dramatic performances) to which the term *ludus* was applied in Roman antiquity, Glynne Wickham writes:

> There is, nevertheless, a common factor linking all uses of the word *ludus* . . . an underlying sense of energy released in action. It is this imperative quality of something done, of doing, of activity that links the athlete to the actor . . . however, the game or recreational element is paramount. . . . Both are limitations "in game" and not "in earnest." (Wickham 1974, 3)

2. For example, in the Middle Ages, the Corpus Christi play depicted the grim subject of Christ's Passion by means of games and jests. (For an illuminating discussion of the dramatic representation of the Passion and Resurrection in the Mystery plays, see Kolve 1966, 175–205.) An early moral allegory like *Mankind* could also be composed so as to become, despite its expressly didactic preoccupation, one of the bawdiest and rowdiest comedies in English. About *Mankind,* Richard Axton argues, interestingly, that the play

> may be seen . . . as belonging in the tradition of early pre-cycle plays in England, a tradition propagated by worldly clerks and friars of preaching orders, whose method was the conversion of popular "game" by joining it to sermons. . . . This drama flourished side by side with the community drama of the cycle plays, which shares some of its motives and its sense that drama consisted of a mixture of pious exposition and vigorous, often pantomimic, conflict between actors and audience. (1974, 203)

A similar approach is found in Brown 1952.

3. Auerbach also points out that in the scene between Falstaff and Prince Hal in *Henry IV, Part 2* (II.ii), Shakespeare actually ridicules the scholarly separation of styles (1974, 312ff.). A similar mockery of the neoclassical position may be detected in Shakespeare's comical treatment of Polonius, for whom "Seneca cannot be too heavy, nor Plautus too light" (*Hamlet,* II.ii, 391).

4. Bethel also argues that "Shakespeare, or any play in the popular tradition, can be enjoyed while it is realized as 'only a play', [while] such consciousness of the play as play would ruin the effect of naturalistic dialogue and production" (1944, 21).

5. A case in point here is a famous speech from Shakespeare's *Antony and Cleopatra.*

> Antony
> Shall be brought drunken forth, and I shall see
> Some squeaking Cleopatra boy my greatness
> I'th' presence of a whore.
>
> (V.ii, 218–21)

In the Elizabethan context, these lines clearly suggest a playful approach to the art of theater and the nature of artistic illusion. An Elizabethan boy-actor pretending to be an ancient Egyptian queen refers, futuristically, to his own inadequacies as an Elizabethan boy-actor. Involved here is a theatrically exciting interplay not only of the actor and his role but also of two historically distinct and remote times and places. Shakespeare's delight—which he seems to share with his public—in deliberately breaking open the artistic illusion and exposing its fragile and precarious basis also compels us to regard the play-world and the empirical world (namely, ancient Egypt and Elizabethan England) simultaneously, encompassing them both within a single playful vision.

6. About the early Soviet theater, Daniel Gerould writes:

Throughout the first decade of its existence, Soviet theatre sought inspiration and new directions in the popular arts. In the period after the Revolution, the most innovative Russian directors and writers, by turning to the clowning and novelty acts of circus and music-hall attempted a complete break with the traditions of bourgeois drama—its plotting, psychology, and domestic themes—in order to create a vital, broad appeal to the masses. (1974, 71)

Gerould also quotes Eisenstein's editor, Sergei Yutkevitch: "The whole young generation of Soviet artists had turned towards minor genres, the kind of popular art which the aristocracy and bourgeoisie had scorned . . . the music hall, the circus, and the cinema" (p. 71).

During this period, similar developments were taking place in the German theater. Working in conscious opposition to the established forms of the bourgeois theater, many young and talented artists—like Max Reinhardt, Erwin Piscator, and Bertolt Brecht—were turning toward the popular forms of the cabaret,, the clown show, the popular ballad, and the Chaplinesque comedy in search of new and radical forms of theater. They often worked in close collaboration with popular entertainers. For example, the famous Munich comedian Karl Valentin's influence on Brecht is well known (see Calandra 1974, 86–98; and Brecht 1965, 69–70).

7. About the same time as his urgent appeal for an emphasis on "sport" in the theater, Brecht was also declaring that "the theatre's future is philosophical" (1964, 24). He saw no incompatibility between the ludic and philosophical emphases but regarded them as essential aspects of any meaningful theater activity. At another time he said: "A theatre in which you're not supposed to laugh is a theatre about which you have to laugh" (quoted in McGowan 1982, 63).

8. About the make up of the audiences that the new drama was attracting in London during the mid-1950s, Alan Sinfield says that they

were likely to have been from predominantly grammar school and redbrick backgrounds. . . . But though they were less privileged they were probably upwardly mobile and shared some of the aspirations of the public school and Oxbridge people. . . . Such an audience felt its exclusion from power, but its educational attainment promised dividends without radical change. (Sinfield 1983, 180)

9. Throughout the late fifties, many English playwrights and directors were engaged in an energetic debate about how to revitalize the English stage. Although all were agreed that the contemporary English theater was moribund and needed to be revitalized, there was a good deal of confusion about how this was to be achieved, and even about what constituted vital theater. Some said that the stage needed more plays, like *Look Back in Anger,* on political subjects, on commitment, and about working-class life. Others, like Wesker with his Centre-42, wanted to take certain examples of the existing theater to working-class areas and factories. Lindsay Anderson recognized that what was really needed was "a new conception of the relationship between art and audience, a total change of cultural atmosphere," and he even mentioned Brecht's name, though he failed to elaborate on it. Significantly, throughout the debate there was little reference to popular forms of theater. For some of the views in this debate, see Marowitz et al. (1965, 40–51).

10. This is evident, for example, in the imagery of food and carnal pleasure that he often uses to describe theater and theatrical experience. In the above quotation, written in 1959, he likened good theater to a well-cooked Christmas dinner. In 1961 he wrote:

A play that is a sermon and no more will be in danger of preaching only to the converted. But if the sermon is expressed in terms of a poetic statement . . . and given to the audience to hold, as it might be a ripe apple, so that they could look at it all round and decide for themselves whether it is sound or not—then one may have some hope of affecting a change in somebody's heart. (1961b, 194–95)

Two years later, he declared in his preface to *The Business of Good Government:*

The performance of plays is an activity that should come as naturally as preparing a meal, eating it, singing, dancing, kissing or football. It should not be associated with snobbishness, superior accents, and an enviable knowledge of "what they do in London."

11. Sidney Homan argues that "at certain moments the theatre abandons the metaphors . . . available to other media and turns to itself, to metaphors taking their source not directly from life but from art" (1976, 408). Lionel Abel's term *self-reference* (Abel 1963) means many more things than what we have here described as the device of autoreferentiality.

12. As Raymond Williams observes,

In the case of soliloquy there has been some unnecessary confusion because of an unnoticed assimilation, in the modern period, of the conventions of "naturalist" drama. Here the relations between actors and audience are negatively defined. The audience is of course present, and the actors are conscious of it, but the controlling convention is that the actors do not dramatically notice the audience; instead they play out their action before it, in a space defined by the raising or lowering of curtains or lights. It usually follows from this that the actors are understood as invariably *talking to each other*. When only one actor is on the stage, he has then, within the convention, *nobody to speak to but himself*. Then since "talking to oneself" carries certain habitual social and psychological implications, what had once been the *soliloquy* is felt to be "unnatural." This is generally known, but what is less often noticed is the common (retroactive) conclusion that when an actor is alone on the stage and speaks he is "talking to himself," as in the dominant sense of *soliloquy*. For who else, within the "naturalist" convention, could he be talking to? That he might be talking *to* rather than in the unnoticed presence of, an audience has been conventionally ruled out. (Williams 1981b, 44)

See also Bradbrook (1960b, Themes 111–12).

13. As M. C. Bradbrook has observed, "Silent movement is always doubly significant on the stage" (Bradbrook 1960b, 44).

14. The text of the trilogy was finalized soon after Arden and D'Arcy's prolonged visit to India in 1969–70. During their year-long stay, they witnessed a number of folk-theater performances. Many of these traditional forms are famous for their varied entertainment structure and martial grandeur. They specialize, like similar forms in other parts of the country, in staging mythological and folkloric narratives in complex epic forms, using emblems, songs, masks, music, dances, mimes, and rituals. The experience had a profound influence on Arden and D'Arcy's political consciousness as well as on their artistic practice. They revised the early drafts of *The Island of the Mighty* drastically in light of their Indian experience, weaving into the dramaturgic fabric of the trilogy many elements and conventions derived from traditional Indian theaters. The "structures of the scenes" themselves, D'Arcy points out in her preface, "were devised to suit a style of staging like that which we had seen in India."

The Chhau form is found in three distinct variations in three neighboring districts of Purulia (West Bengal), Saraikella (Bihar), and Mayurbhanj (Orrissa). Of these, the Purulia Chhau is particularly remarkable for its theatrical vigor. It was this version of the Chhau that Arden and D'Arcy witnessed in India. Practiced almost exclusively by the socioeconomically depressed classes, it is tribal in origin and festive and communal in form. It usually dramatizes tales from the epics, the *Mahabharata* and the *Ramayana,* and does so in a highly stylized form. Its style is martial and its dance movements include not only walking in rhythmic steps but spectacular leaps and jumps. A special feature of this drama, for example, is the actor taking a very long jump or a very high leap and landing on his knees with perfect ease and suppleness. The spectacular quality of this dance form is further, and substantially, enhanced by the use of grotesque masks with bold colors (yellow for the gods and heroes, black and red for the demons, white for the sages, and so on) as well as highly accentuated eyes, mouths, teeth, and hair.

The Purulia Chhau is performed to the accompaniment of vocal and instrumental music that has a strong martial flavor and rhythm, consisting mainly of percussion from two kinds of drums, the *dhol* and the *dhensa*.

15. The marriage between Arthur and Gwenhwyvar has to do with politics rather than matters of the heart. Goddodin, a small native Christian prince who is seeking to strengthen his dilapidated kingdom with the support of Arthur's Roman army, offers to repudiate his contract with the English invaders on the condition that Medraut, the General's nephew and putative heir, marry Gwenhwyvar. Gwenhwyvar has the reputation of a dangerous woman who killed her previous husband. However, the politics of this proposal are complicated when Arthur sees in it a challenge to his role as the reigning "champion" of Britain.

> If this lady is as dangerous
> As you report her to be
> If this lady is as dangerous
> as she reports herself to be—
> It is a feat for a champion
> to master her body and soul.

He declares that he is still the undisputed champion of Britain and that "the sword of Maximus Emperor" shall not pass out of his hand yet. He also boasts about his physical strength and sexual prowess, adding, "Medraut shall *not* supplant me." This rhetoric reflects his male chauvinist bias. However, it is a bias that goes beyond the realm of gender relationships and becomes part of a larger conflict between the forces of freedom and those of repression.

16. Arden and D'Arcy successfully experimented with such fairground performance conditions in 1975 in their Dublin performance of *The Non-Stop Connolly Show*. The performance of this six-part historical play took place in Liberty Hall, the headquarters of the Irish Transport and General Workers' Union, with a cast of about fifty people, and lasted more than twenty-four hours. During the intervals there were films and other short plays by guest groups. Several groups of musicians and singers also performed. There were food stalls where the audience as well as the performers could eat during the intervals. For a detailed description of this event, see Arden (1977, 92–180).

Chapter Five

1. In their preface to *The Hero Rises Up,* Arden and D'Arcy write the following about Nelson.

This play is about a man who was, by accident of birth and rearing, committed to a career governed by the old Roman "rectilinear" principles. He himself was one of asymmetrical "curvilinear" temperament to an unusually passionate degree. But the English [who have inherited the Roman mantle] soon discovered how to handle him. He was *done properly:* wasted his extraordinary energy, courage, and humanity upon having men killed (in the end himself killed).

2. This section draws mainly upon the separate prefaces by Arden and D'Arcy to *The Island of the Mighty*. Unless indicated, all quotations without reference come from these texts.

3. The play's first production, by the Royal Shakespeare Company under David Jones's direction, was the subject of a serious controversy and has been disowned by the playwrights.

4. The term *folkloric* is not to be taken as representing an exotic historical pageant or a marginalized eccentricity. On the contrary, it is to be taken in a positive or "strong" sense in which folklore approaches ethnology and anthropology, or even a social history of the nonruling classes.

A checklist of Plays by John Arden and Margaretta D'Arcy, in order of their first public appearance.

Arden

The Waters of Babylon (1957). In *Three Plays*. Harmondsworth: Penguin, 1964.
Live Like Pigs (1958). In *Three Plays*. Harmondsworth: Penguin, 1964.
When Is a Door Not a Door (1958). In *Soldier, Soldier and Other Plays*. London: Methuen, 1967.
Serjeant Musgrave's Dance (1959). London: Methuen, 1960.
The Business of Good Government (1960). London: Methuen, 1963.
Soldier, Soldier (1960). In *Soldier, Soldier and Other Plays*. London: Methuen, 1967.
Wet Fish (1961). In *Soldier, Soldier and Other Plays*. London: Methuen, 1967.
The Workhouse Donkey (1962). London: Methuen, 1964.
Ironhand (1963). London: Methuen, 1965.
Armstrong's Last Goodnight (1964). London: Methuen, 1965.
Left-Handed Liberty (1965). London: Methuen, 1965.
The True History of Squire Jonathan and His Unfortunate Treasure (1968). In *Two Autobiographical Plays*. London: Methuen, 1971.
The Bagman or the Impromptu of Muswell-Hill (1970). In *Two Autobiographical Plays*. London: Methuen, 1971.
Pearl (1978). London: Methuen, 1979.
The Adventures of the Ingenious Gentleman Don Quixote de la Mancha (1980). Unpublished.
Garland for a Hoar Head (1982). Unpublished.
The Old Man Sleeps Alone (1982). In *Best Radio Plays of 1982*. London: Methuen, 1983.

Arden and D'Arcy

The Happy Haven (1962). In *Three Plays*. Harmondsworth: Penguin, 1964.
"*Ars Longa, Vita Brevis*" (1964). *Encore* (March–April 1964): 13–20.

Friday's Hiding (1966). In *Soldier, Soldier and Other Plays*. London: Methuen, 1967.

The Royal Pardon (1966). London: Methuen, 1967.

Harold Muggins is a Martyr (1968). Unpublished.

The Hero Rises Up (1968). London: Methuen, 1969.

The Ballygombeen Bequest (1972). *Scripts* 9 (September 1972): 4–50.

The Island of the Mighty (1972). London: Methuen, 1974.

The Non-Stop Connolly Show (1975). 5 vols. London: Pluto, 1977.

The Little Gray Home in the West (1978). London: Pluto, 1982.

Vandaleur's Folly (1978). London: Methuen, 1981.

The Manchester Enthusiasts (1984). Unpublished.

Whose Is the Kingdom? (1988). London: Methuen, 1988.

Works Cited

Abel, Lionel. 1963. *Metatheater: A new vision of dramatic form.* New York: Hill and Wang.

Arden, John. 1959. Correspondence. *Encore* 20 (May-June): 41–43.

———. 1960. A thoroughly romantic view. *London Magazine* 7:11–15.

———. 1961a. Delusion of grandeur. *Twentieth Century* 169 (February): 200–206.

———. 1961b. Some thoughts upon left-wing drama. In *International theatre annual–V,* ed. Harold Hobson, 187–96. London: John Calder.

———. 1963. Arden of Chichester. *Plays and Players* 10:16–18.

———. 1964a. Building the play. In *The new British drama,* ed. Henry Popkin, 581–606. New York: Grove.

———. 1964b. Poetry and theatre. *Times Literary Supplement* August 6: 705.

———. 1964c. Theatre and leisure. *Socialist Commentary* (August): 29–30.

———. 1965a. On comedy. *Encore* 57 (September-October): 13–19.

———. 1965b. Questions of expediency. *Plays and Players* 12:14–15.

———. 1965c. Telling a true tale. In *The Encore reader,* ed. Charles Marowitz et al., 125–29. London: Methuen.

———. 1966. Who's for a revolution? *Tulane Drama Review* 34 (Winter): 41–53.

———. 1967. Interview. In *Theatre at work,* ed. Charles Marowitz and Simon Trussler, 36–57. London: Methuen.

———. 1977. *To present the pretence: Essays on the theatre and its public.* London: Eyre Methuen.

Arden, John, and Margaretta D'Arcy. 1988. *Awkward corners.* London: Methuen.

Aristotle. 1970. *The poetics of Aristotle,* trans. Preston H. Epps. Chapel Hill: University of North Carolina Press.

Auerbach, Erich. 1974. *Mimesis,* trans. Willard R. Trask. Princeton: Princeton University Press.

Axton, Marie, and Raymond Williams, eds. 1977. *English drama: Forms and development.* Cambridge: Cambridge University Press.

Axton, Richard. 1974. *European drama of the early Middle Ages.* London: Hutchinson.

Bakhtin, Mikhail. 1968. *Rabelais and his world,* trans. Helene Iswolsky. Cambridge, Mass.: MIT Press.

———. 1981. *The dialogic imagination,* ed. Michael Holquist, trans. Caryl Emerson and Michael Holquist. Austin: University of Texas Press.

Barthes, Roland. 1972. *Critical essays.* Evanston: Northwestern University Press.

———. 1973. *Image, music, text,* trans. Stephen Heath. Glasgow: Fontana.

———. 1975. An introduction to the structural analysis of narrative. *New Literary History* 6:237–72.

Bartram, Graham, and Anthony Waine, eds. 1982. *Brecht in perspective.* London: Longman.

Baskerville, Charles. 1920. Dramatic aspects of medieval folk festivals in England. *Studies in Philology* 17:19–87.

Beckerman, Bernard. 1969. Shakespeare's technique. In *The Pelican Shakespeare,* ed. Alfred Harbage. Baltimore: Penguin.

———. 1970. *Dynamics of drama.* New York: Knopf.

Benjamin, Walter. 1969. *Illuminations,* ed. Hannah Arendt, trans. Harry Zohn. New York: Schocken.

———. 1977. *Understanding Brecht,* trans. Anna Bostock. London: New Left.

Bentley, Eric. 1964. *The life of drama.* New York: Atheneum.

———, ed. 1968. *The theory of the modern stage.* Harmondsworth: Penguin.

Bethel, S. L. 1944. *Shakespeare and the popular dramatic tradition.* London: P. S. King and Staples.

Bloch, Ernst. 1972. Entfremdung, verfremdung: Alienation, estrangement, trans. Anne Halley and Darko Suvin. In *Brecht,* ed. Erika Munk, 3–11. New York: Bantam.

———. 1973. "The meaning of utopia." In *Marxism and art,* ed. Maynard Solomon, 578–82. New York: Knopf.

Bluestone, Max. 1974. *From story to stage.* The Hague and Paris: Mouton.

Bradbrook, M. C. 1955. *Growth and structure of Elizabethan comedy.* London: Chatto and Windus.

———. 1960a. *Elizabethan stage conditions.* Cambridge: Cambridge University Press.

———. 1960b. *Themes and conventions of Elizabethan tragedy.* Cambridge: Cambridge University Press.

Braudel, Fernand. 1980. *On history,* trans. Sarah Mathews. Chicago: University of Chicago Press.

Brecht, Bertolt. 1964. *Brecht on theatre,* trans. John Willet. New York: Hill and Wang.

———. 1965. *The Messingkauf dialogues,* trans. John Willet. London: Methuen.

Bristol, Michael D. 1983. Carnival and the institutions of Theater in Elizabethan England. *ELH* 50:637–54.

Brody, Alan. 1970. *The English mummers and their plays.* Philadelphia: University of Pennsylvania Press.

Brook, Peter. 1977. *The empty space.* Harmondsworth: Penguin.

Brown, Arthur. 1952. Folklore element in medieval drama. *Folklore* 63:65–78.

Brown, John Russel. 1966. Laughter in the last plays. In *Later Shakespeare: Stratford-upon-Avon studies–8,* ed. John Russel Brown. London: Arnold.

———. 1968. Introduction. In *Modern British dramatists,* ed. John Russell Brown, 1–14. Englewood Cliffs, N.J.: Prentice Hall.

————. 1972. *Theatre language: A study of Arden, Osborne, Pinter and Wesker*. London: Penguin.

Calandra, Denis. 1974. Karl Valentin and Bertolt Brecht. *Drama Review* 18, (Fall):86–98.

Cawte, E. C., Alex Helm, and N. Peacock. 1967. *English ritual drama: a geographical index*. London: The Folk-Lore Society.

Chambers, E. K. 1925. *The medieval stage*. 2 vols. London: Oxford University Press.

————. 1966. *The English folk-play*. New York: Haskell House.

Chatman, Seymour. 1978. *Story and discourse*. Ithaca: Cornell University Press.

Child, F. J. 1965. *The English and Scottish popular ballads*. 5 vols. New York: Dover.

Clinton, Craig. 1978. John Arden: The promise unfulfilled. *Modern Drama* 21:47–57.

Davies, Alistair, and Peter Saunders. 1983. Literature, politics and society. In *Society and literature, 1945–1970*, ed. Alan Sinfield, 13–50. London: Methuen.

Dodd, P. 1977. A thematic approach to John Arden's *Armstrong's Last Goodnight*. *Revues des langues vivantes* 43:323–29.

Doran, Madeleine. 1954. *The endeavours of art*. Madison: University of Wisconsin Press.

Dryden, John. 1912. Of heroic plays. In his *Essays*, 87–94. London: Dent, and New York: Dutton.

Eagleton, Terry. 1981. *Walter Benjamin*. London: Verso.

Elam, Keir. 1980. *The semiotics of theatre and drama*. London and New York: Methuen.

Eliot, T. S. 1960. *Selected essays*. New York: Harcourt.

————. 1967. *Elizabethan dramatists*. London: Faber and Faber.

Erven, Eugene Van. 1988. *Radical people's theatre*. Bloomington: Indiana University Press.

Esslin, Martin. 1969. Brecht and the English theatre. In *Reflections*, 75–86. Garden City, N.Y.: Doubleday.

Fergusson, Francis. 1955. *The idea of a theatre: The art of drama in changing perspective*. Garden City, N.Y.: Doubleday.

Findlater, Richard. 1952. *The unholy trade*. London: Gollancz.

Forsas-Scott, Helena. 1983. Life and Love and Serjeant Musgrave. *Modern Drama* 26 (March): 1–11.

Fry, Christopher. 1977. Untitled. In *Essays and Studies*, 86. London: John Murray.

Gerould, Daniel. 1974. Eisenstein's Wisemen. *Drama Review* 18, (Fall):71–76.

Gilman, Richard. 1966. Arden's unsteady ground. *Tulane Drama Review* 11 (Winter):54–62.

Goormay, Howard. 1981. *The theatre workshop story*. London: Methuen.

Gurvitch, G. 1964. *The spectrum of social time*, trans. Myrtle Korenbaum. Dordrecht, Holland: Riedel.

Happe, P. 1964. The vice and the folk drama. *Folklore* 75:161–93.

Harvey, David. 1989. *The condition of postmodernity*. Oxford: Blackwell.

Hauser, Arnold. 1951. *The social history of art,* trans. Stanley Goodmann. 4 vols. New York: Vintage.

Hayman, Ronald. 1988. The conversion of John Arden. Radio talk, BBC-3, 25 August.

Hewison, Robert. 1981. *In anger: Culture in the Cold War, 1945–60.* Oxford: Oxford University Press.

Hirsh, James E. 1981. *The structure of Shakespeare's scenes.* New Haven: Yale University Press.

Homan, Sidney. 1976. When the theatre turns to itself. *New Literary History* 8:405–17.

Hunt, Albert. 1974. *Arden: A study of his plays.* London: Methuen.

Itzin, Catherine. 1980. *Stages in the revolution.* London: Methuen.

Jameson, Fredric. 1971. *Marxism and form.* Princeton: Princeton University Press.

———. 1981. *The political unconscious.* London: Methuen.

Jones, Geraint. 1964. *The art and truth of the parables.* London: S.P.C.K.

Kantrowitz, Joanne Spencer. 1975. *Dramatic allegory: Lindsay's "Ane satyre of the thrie estaitis."* Lincoln: University of Nebraska Press.

Kennedy, Andrew D. 1975. *Six dramatists in search of a language: Studies in dramatic language.* London: Cambridge University Press.

Kershaw, Baz. 1992. *The politics of performance.* London and New York: Rutledge.

Kiernan, A. G. 1964. Human relationships in Shakespeare. In *Shakespeare in a Changing World,* ed. Arnold Kettle, 43–64. London: Lawrence and Wishart.

Kolve, V. A. 1966. *The play called Corpus Christi.* London: Arnold.

Lattimore, Richmond A. 1964. *Story patterns in Greek tragedy.* Ann Arbor: University of Michigan Press.

Lotman, Juri. 1977. *The Structure of the artistic text,* trans. Gail Lenhoff and Ronald Vroom. Ann Arbor: University of Michigan Press.

Lukács, Georg. 1968. The sociology of modern drama. In *The theory of the modern stage,* ed. Eric Bentley, 425–50. Harmondsworth: Penguin.

———. 1971. Narrate or describe? In *Writer and critic, and other essays,* ed. and trans. Arthur D. Kahn, 110–48. London: Merlin.

Marowitz, Charles, Tom Milne, and Owen Halle, eds. 1965. *The encore reader.* London: Methuen.

Marowitz, Charles, and Simon Trussler, eds. 1967. *Theatre at work.* London: Methuen.

Mayer, Hans. 1971. Bertolt Brecht and the tradition. In *Steppenwolf and Everyman,* trans. Jack D. Zipes. New York: Crowell.

McGowan, Moray. 1982. Comedy and volksstuck. In *Brecht in Perspective,* ed. Graham Bartram and Anthony Waine, 63–79. London: Longman.

McGrath, John. 1981. *A goodnight out.* London: Methuen.

———. 1990. *The bone won't break.* London: Methuen.

McNamara, Brooks. 1974. Scenography of popular entertainment. *Drama Review* 18, Fall:16–24.

Munk, Erika, ed. 1972. *Brecht.* New York: Bantam.

O'Connell, Mary. 1971. Ritual elements in John Arden's *Serjeant Musgrave's Dance. Modern Drama* 13:356–59.

Owen, Robert. 1817. *A new view of society*. 3d ed. London: Longman.

Percy, Thomas. 1966. *Reliques of ancient English poetry*, ed. Henry B. Wheatley. 3 vols. New York: Dover.

Piscator, Erwin. 1978. *The political theatre*, trans. Hugh Morrison. New York: Avon.

Postlewait, Thomas. 1988. The criteria for periodization in theatre history. *Theatre Journal* 40, no. 3:299–318.

Rosenberg, Marvin. 1958. A metaphor for dramatic form. *Journal of Aesthetics and Art Criticism* 17:174–80.

Schechter, Joel. 1985. *Durov's pig: Clowns, politics and theatre*. New York: Theatre Communications Group.

Sinfield, Alan, ed. 1983. *Society and literature, 1945–1970*. London: Methuen.

Skloot, Robert. 1975. Spreading the word. *Educational Theatre Journal* 27:208–19.

Solomon, Maynard, ed. 1973. *Marxism and art*. New York: Knopf.

Strindberg, August. 1965. Preface to *Miss Julie*, trans. Elizabeth Sprigge. New York: Avon.

Suvin, Darko. N.d. On metaphoricity and narrativity in fiction: The chronotope as the *differentia generica*. Typescript.

———. 1976. "Utopian" and "scientific": Two attributes for socialism from Engels. *Minnesota Review* 6:59–70.

———. 1984. *To Brecht and beyond: Soundings in modern dramaturgy*. Brighton: Harvester, 1984.

———. 1988. Can people be (re)presented in fiction? In *Marxism and the interpretation of culture*, ed. Cary Nelson and Lawrence Grossberg, 663–96. Urbana and Chicago: University of Illinois Press.

Szondi, Peter. 1987. *Theory of the modern drama*. Minneapolis: University of Minnesota Press.

Taylor, John Russell. 1963. *Anger and after: A guide to the new British drama*, 72–92. Rev. ed. Harmondsworth: Penguin.

Todorov, Tzvetan. 1977. *The poetics of prose*, trans. Richard Howard. Ithaca: Cornell University Press.

Trussler, Simon. 1968. British neo-naturalism. *Drama Review* 13 (Winter):130–36.

———. 1969. Political progress of a paralysed liberal. *Drama Review* 13 (Summer):181–91.

Tynan, Kenneth. 1976. *A view of the English stage*. St. Albans: Paladin.

Udall, J. S. 1880. Christmas mummers in Dorsetshire. *Folklore Record* 3, no. 1:87–111.

Via, Dan O. *The parables*. 1967. Philadelphia: Fortress.

Warren, Wilfred L. 1961. *King John*. London: Eyre and Spottiswoode.

Weimann, Robert. 1978. *Shakespeare and the popular tradition in the theatre*. Baltimore: Johns Hopkins University Press.

Wellek, Rene, and Austin Warren. 1977. *Theory of literature*. New York: Harcourt.

Wickham, Glynne. 1974. *The medieval theatre*. London: Weidefeld and Nicolson.

———, ed. 1976. *English moral interludes*. London: Dent.

Willet, John. *The theatre of Bertolt Brecht: A study from eight aspects.* London: Methuen.

Williams, Raymond. 1961. *The long revolution.* London: Chatto and Windus.

———. 1966. *Modern tragedy.* London: Chatto and Windus.

———. 1976a. *Drama from Ibsen to Brecht.* Harmondsworth: Penguin.

———. 1976b. *Key-words: A vocabulary of culture and society.* Glasgow: Fontana.

———. 1977. Social environment and theatrical environment. In *English drama,* ed. Marie Axton and Raymond Williams, 203–23. Cambridge: Cambridge University Press.

———. 1981a. *Culture.* Glasgow: Fontana.

———. 1981b. *Writing in society.* London: Verso.

Zola, Emile. 1968. Naturalism in the theatre. In *The theory of the modern stage,* ed. Eric Bentley, 351–72. Harmondsworth: Penguin.

Index

Abel, Lionel, 193n
Absurd drama, 33, 48, 88, 188n
Anderson, Lindsay, 193n
Aristophanes, 21, 114
Aristotle, 68, 188n, 190
Armstrong's Last Goodnight, 51, 56–
  58, 60, 66, 75, 77, 80, 93–95, 97,
  115, 118, 126–27, 128, 130, 141,
  142, 149, 188n, 190n
Auden, W. H., 12
Auerbach, Erich, 104, 191
Axton, Richard, 190n, 191n

*Bagman, or the Impromptu of Muswell
  Hill, The*, 147–48, 174
Bakhtin, Mikhail, 7, 31, 121
Ballad, 15, 37, 51, 77, 93, 192n
Barthes, Roland, 41, 72, 101, 102,
  188n
Baskerville, Charles, 190n
Beck, Julian, 34
Beckerman, Bernard, 42, 44, 47,
  49, 52–53, 187n, 188n
Beckett, Samuel, 29, 50
Behan, Brendan, 107
Benjamin, Walter, 9
Bentley, Eric, 188n
Berliner Ensemble, 11, 185n
Bethel, S. L., 47, 104, 191n
Bloch, Ernst, 159, 182, 186n
Bluestone, Max, 187n
Boal, Augusto, 1
Bradbrook, M. C., 46, 187n, 188n,
  194n
Brecht, Bertolt, 5, 7, 12, 15, 18, 21,
  24, 33, 35–41, 47, 51, 64, 69, 71–
  73, 75, 77, 93, 105, 108, 109,

111, 112, 114, 115, 125, 130, 143,
  144, 146, 149, 181, 185n, 186n,
  188n, 189n, 192n, 193n
The Caucasian Chalk Circle, 39, 53,
  185n
Mother Courage and Her Children,
  39, 185
Breughel, Pieter, 82, 189
Bristol, Michael D., 133
Brody, Alan, 131
Brook, Peter, 36
Brown, John Russell, 21–22, 103–4,
  191n
Business of Good Government, The,
  135–36, 193n

Calandra, Denis, 192n
Carmina Burana, 190n
Cartoon Archetypal Slogan Theatre,
  The, 146
Cawte, E. C., 187n
Chambers, E. K., 187n, 190n
Chaplin, Charles, 105
Character-based dramaturgy, 42–
  43, 47–49, 51, 64, 74
Chatman, Seymour, 45, 187n, 188n
Chaucer, Geoffrey, 15, 187n
Chekhov, Anton, 186n
Chhau dance, the, 131–32, 194–95n
Commitment, 17–19, 21, 139–43,
  149
Corpus Christi cycles, The, 44, 49,
  191n

D'Arcy, Margaretta, 1–6, 15, 22,
  40, 63, 65, 69, 113, 130–33, 135–
  37, 139, 141, 143–50, 154, 164,